Nazirites in Late Second Temple Judaism

Ancient Judaism
and
Early Christianity

Arbeiten zur Geschichte des antiken
Judentums und des Urchristentums

Edited by

Martin Hengel (Tübingen),
Pieter W. van der Horst (Utrecht),
Martin Goodman (Oxford),
Daniel R. Schwartz (Jerusalem),
Cilliers Breytenbach (Berlin),
Friedrich Avemarie (Marburg),
Seth Schwartz (New York)

VOLUME 60

Nazirites in Late Second Temple Judaism

A Survey of Ancient Jewish Writings, the New Testament, Archaeological Evidence, and Other Writings from Late Antiquity

by

Stuart Chepey

BRILL

LEIDEN • BOSTON

2005

This book is printed on acid-free paper.

Library of Congress Cataloging-in-Publication Data

Chepey, Stuart Douglas, 1970-
　　Nazirites in late Second Temple Judaism : a survey of ancient Jewish writings, the New Testament, archaeological evidence, and other writings from late antiquity / by Stuart Chepey.
　　　p. cm. — (Ancient Judaism and early Christianity, ISSN 0169-734X ; v. 60 = Arbeiten zur Geschichte des antiken Judentums und des Urchristentums)
　　Revision of the author's thesis (doctoral)—University of Oxford, 2002.
　　Includes bibliographical references (p.) and index.
　　ISBN 90-04-14465-X (alk. paper)
　　1. Nazarite (Judaism) 2. Judaism—History—Post-exilic period, 586 B.C.–210 A.D. 3. Vows in rabbinical literature. 4. Rabbinical literature—History and criticism. 5. Vows in the Bible. 6. Bible. N.T.—Criticism, interpretation, etc. I. Title. II. Arbeiten zur Geschichte des antiken Judentums und des Urchristentums ; Bd. 60.

BM720.N3C44 2005
296.4'9—dc22

　　　　　　　　　　　　　　　　　　　　　　　　　　　　　　　　2005046965

ISSN 0169-734X
ISBN 90 04 14465 X

CONTENTS

ABBREVIATIONS

ANTC	Abingdon New Testament Commentaries
AbrNSup	Abr-Nahrain: Supplemental Series
AB	Anchor Bible
ABD	*Anchor Bible Dictionary*. Edited by D. N. Freedman. 6 vols., New York, 1992
ArBib	The Aramaic Bible
BWANT	Beiträge zur Wissenschaft vom Alten und Neuen Testament
BJS	Brown Judaic Studies
BASOR	*Bulletin of the American School of Oriental Research*
BIOSCS	*Bulletin of the International Organization for Septuagint and Cognate Studies*
CBQ	*Catholic Biblical Quarterly*
CSJH	Chicago Studies in the History of Judaism
EHAT	Exegetisches Handbuch zum Alten Testament
ExpTim	*Expository Times*
HSM	Harvard Semitic Monographs
HJPAJC	*History of the Jewish People in the Age of Jesus Christ*
ICC	International Critical Commentary
IEJ	*Israel Exploration Journal*
JSNTSup	Journal for the Study of the New Testament: Supplemental Series
JSOTSup	Journal for the Study of the Old Testament: Supplemental Series
JSPSup	Journal for the Study of the Pseudepigrapha: Supplemental Series
JBL	*Journal of Biblical Literature*
JJS	*Journal of Jewish Studies*
JTS	*Journal of Theological Studies*
LCL	Loeb Classical Library
NAS	New American Standard
NEB	New English Bible
NJB	New Jerusalem Bible
NRSV	New Revised Standard Version
NovT	*Novum Testamentum*
OBO	Orbis biblicus et orientalis

SNTSMS   Society for New Testament Studies Monograph Series
SBLSCS   Society of Biblical Literature Septuagint and Cognate
            Studies
SJ   Studia judaica
StPB   Studia post-biblica
SJLA   Studies in Judaism in Late Antiquity
NovTSup   Supplements to Novum Testamentum
VTSup   Supplements to Vetus Testamentum
TZ   *Theologische Zeitschrift*
THAT   *Theologisches Handwörterbuch zum Alten Testament*. Edited by
            E. Jenni, with assistance from C. Westermann. 2 vols.,
            Stuttgart, 1971–6
ThWAT   *Theologisches Wörterbuch zum Alten Testament*. Edited by G. J.
            Botterweck and H. Ringgren. Stuttgart, 1970–
TNTC   Tyndale New Testament Commentaries
WBC   Word Biblical Commentaries
ZNW   *Zeitschrift für die neutestamentliche Wissenschaft und die Kunde
            der älteren Kirche*

ACKNOWLEDGEMENTS

The following comprises a revised edition of my doctoral dissertation submitted to the Faculty of Oriental Studies, University of Oxford, in September 2002. I would like to thank the many people whose generous support helped make this project a reality.

First, I would like to express my gratitude to my Oxford colleagues whose continued support proved immeasurable: Jeremy Boccabello, Kevin Sullivan, and Jill Middlemas. I would especially like to thank Kevin Sullivan for his considerable advice in the publishing process and for allowing me the many post-Degree Day late night phone calls during the summer of 2004 in which I muttered something merely to the effect of, "It's over."

Thanks are also due to my adviser and instructor at Oxford from 1998–2003, Professor Martin Goodman. Though the faults of this work are none but my own, his attention and encouragement beyond my status as a doctoral student were especially appreciated. I must also express my gratitude to Professors Christopher Rowland (University of Oxford) and Philip Alexander (University of Manchester) for their many helpful suggestions.

Finally, I wish to thank my family whose general support was immense; my colleagues at The Parish Episcopal School in Dallas, Texas for putting up with my manic ways (especially Diane Webber and Becky Crawford) and for helping me with the manuscript (Kim Raschke); my religion students at Richland College, Dallas, Texas for their continued inspiration; U2 for putting out a great new album; and Sony Corporation for producing a pair of long lasting, high quality headphones that were able to take a significant amount of abuse during the completion of this work.

INTRODUCTION

Nazirites, those who made a special vow to abstain from certain behavior such as drinking wine, cutting their hair, or having contact with a corpse, appear on a number of occasions in sources of the late Second Temple period. According to the historian Josephus, for instance, a group of Nazirites appeared in Jerusalem on the occasion of Agrippa I's reinstatement to the throne of Judaea in ca. AD 41,[1] and Bernice, the sister of Agrippa II, is said to have visited Jerusalem to discharge a vow during the tumult under Florus in AD 66.[2] Even the apostle Paul, according to the author Luke,[3] is said to have observed a temple ritual involving four men under a vow, an event which led to his arrest and eventual deportation to Rome where later, according to tradition, he met his fate.

Despite an association with key personalities and tendency to appear at peculiar junctures, little is known about Nazirites in this period, in particular, what role they held within the social lives of Jews. Nominally, the name in Greek (Ναζιραῖος, pl. Ναζιραῖοι) resembles the nomenclature of known socio-religious groups of the period, such as the Pharisees (Φαρισαῖοι), Sadducees (Σαδδυκαῖοι), and Essenes (Ἐσσαῖοι, or Ἐσσηνοι), and some have speculated whether Nazirites comprised such a group, perhaps one akin to the sect of the *Nazarenes* mentioned in the book of Acts and in the writings of the early church fathers.[4] Although similar in name to these groups, however, pertinent sources never describe Nazirites as constituents of any voluntary association. Rather, they are described merely as partakers of a private, albeit very popular, form of religious activity, namely that of making a special kind of vow.

---

[1] Josephus, *A. J.* 19.294.
[2] Josephus, *B. J.* 2.313–4.
[3] Acts 21.23–7ff.
[4] See n. 16, p. 152.

Nazirite Origins in the Hebrew Bible

The Hebrew Bible makes relatively few attestations to Nazirites, and consequently little is known about them prior to the close of the biblical period. Samson, the hero in the book of Judges, who clad in flowing locks slew the Philistine armies with the jawbone of an ass and tore down the gates of Gaza with his bare hands, is the only person actually named a Nazirite. Samuel, the prophet of YHWH during the formative years of Israel's monarchy is described in terms closely resembling one, if, like Samson, his prescribed lifelong abstinence from the use of a razor is taken as a mark denoting a Nazirite (I Sam. 1.11).[5] Nazirites are referred to, arguably, on only two other occasions in the Bible: once in the prophetic book of Amos (2.11–2) as those who were "forced to drink wine" by contemptuous Israel; and once as the implied subjects of a vow, called the "vow of the Nazirite," legislated for in the book of Numbers (6.1–21).[6]

The term "Nazirite" (alternatively spelled Nazarite) is a transliteration into English of the Hebrew nominative *nazir* (נזיר), based on the Latin *nazareus*.[7] נזיר, a derivative of the root *nzr* (נזר), which means in its verbal sense "to separate,"[8] and in other syntactical forms "separation," "consecration," or even "crown," "headpiece," or "anointing oil" (such as worn of a king or the High Priest),[9] carries the meaning of someone or something separated or consecrated for a special purpose. In Gen. 49.26 and Deut. 33.16, for example, the term is used in reference to Joseph as one who was "set apart (RSV)" or "distinguished (NAS)" from his brethren,[10] and in Lev. 25.5,11

---

[5] There is a strong tradition in later Jewish literature that Samuel was a Nazirite (I Sam. 1.11 LXX, 4QSam.ª, and Ben Sira 46.13 [Heb.]). Evidence that some thought that Samuel was not a Nazirite, however, may be found in *m. Naz.* 9.5 and *Tg. J.* to I Sam. 1.11.

[6] Lamentations 4.7 also makes reference to נזיריה, "her Nazirites," or "her anointed ones"? However, no description of abstinence is stated such as in Amos 2.11–2. נזרים in this context likely refers to a more generic group of "consecrated ones (NAS)," perhaps a reference to some form of officialdom.

[7] For useful word studies on נזיר, see *THAT*, vol. 2, s. v. "נזיר," by J. Kühlewein; and *ThWAT*, vol. 5, s. v. "נזר," by G. Mayer; see also A. Salvesen, "נזר," in *Semantics of Ancient Hebrew* (ed. T. Muraoka; AbrNSup 6; Louvain-la-Nueve: Peeters, 1998).

[8] Cf. Lev. 15.31, 22.2.

[9] Cf. Lev. 8.9, 21.12; 2 Ki. 11.12.

[10] In later rabbinic literature, Joseph is thought to have been a Nazirite in the likeness of Num. 6.1–21, et al.; cf. *Midrash Rabbah Gen.* 98.20 where although the "crown" (Aramaic כליל for MT נזיר) of his brethren, Joseph was nonetheless a

to vines left un-pruned during the special agricultural sabbatical year. In the passages cited previously, נזיר is used in both a negative and positive sense to refer to a person: (a) separated *from* certain behavioral norms, such as cutting the hair of the head, drinking wine, or having contact with a corpse; and (b) separated *to* God. Samson, for instance, was a "Nazirite *to* God" from his mother's womb (Judg. 13.5,7; 16.17) and similarly Samuel, by the vow of his mother Hannah, was dedicated "*to* the Lord all the days of his life" (I Sam. 1.11). Likewise, according to the legislation of Num. 6.2ff., one who made a Nazirite vow promised to separate himself/herself "*to* the Lord" until the entire period of the vow was complete. In the religious technical sense then, a נזיר, or "Nazirite," refers to a person dedicated or consecrated to God (*Göttgeweihter*) via certain behavioral proscriptions.[11]

Beyond the semantics of Hebrew terminology, formulating any general characterization of the Nazirite in the biblical period is difficult. This is due not only to the scarcity of and lack of detail provided in available sources, but also to the very disparate nature of what those sources convey. For when the legislation for the Nazirite vow in Num. is compared with the actual portrayal of Nazirites in biblical literature, contrary to the ideals prescribed in the Law, a variety of Nazirite behavior is revealed.

According to the law of Num. 6.1–21, for example, a Nazirite was an individual man or woman who vowed, or verbally promised,[12] to be a Nazirite for a self-designated period of time. The stipulations were that s/he avoid all grape produce; the cutting of the hair of the head; and all contact with a human corpse, even if a member of the immediate family (Num. 6.1–8). At the end of the avowed

---

Nazirite who abstained from wine during his twenty-two years in Egypt. I hold to the modern consensus that נזיר here refers simply to Joseph's distinction over his brethren.

[11] H. Salmanowitsch, "Das Naziraät nach Bibel und Talmud" (Ph. D. diss., Gießen, 1931), 1.

[12] I take this partial definition of "vow" from T. Cartledge, *Vows in the Hebrew Bible and the Ancient Near East* (JSOTSup 147; Sheffield, Eng.: Sheffield Academic Press, 1992), 12ff.; I leave aside for the moment the argument as to whether the Nazirite vow was a conditional or unconditional promise. Cartledge argues at length in the work cited above, and also in his article, "Were Nazirite Vows Unconditional?" *CBQ* 51 (1989): 409–22, that Nazirite vows, like all other known forms of vows in the Hebrew Bible and the ancient Near East, were conditional arrangements. Cartledge argues against the view that Nazirite vows were unconditional promises of piety typified by de Vaux in *Ancient Israel: Its Life and Institutions* (trans. John McHugh; London: Darton, Longman & Todd, 1961), 465–6.

period, the votary was to appear at the central place of worship and offer a significant number of sacrifices (a male lamb a year old for a whole-burnt-offering, a ewe lamb a year old for a sin-offering, and a ram for a peace-offering, together with accompanying cereal offerings and libations) in addition to whatever else s/he could afford. The uncut hair of the head, designated as "holy to the Lord," was then to be shaved and placed on the fire cooking the peace-offering.[13] After such rites, the votary could once again drink wine (6.13–21). If while under the vow a corpse was accidentally contacted, the hair on the head was to be shaved following a seven-day purification rite; on the eighth day, appropriate sacrifices were to be made (two turtle doves or pigeons, one for a whole-burnt-offering, the other for a sin-offering, and a male lamb a year old for a guilt-offering) and the period of the vow started afresh (6.9–12).

When the Num. legislation is compared with the descriptions of Samson, Samuel, and the Nazirites in Amos, all fail to meet them. In none of these cases do Nazirites make temporary vows, nor do they appear to observe the same forms of behavior. Samson, for example, was appointed a Nazirite prior to his birth by the pronouncement of an angel, and was declared a Nazirite "from the womb to the day of his death" (Judg. 13.7). Similarly, although the aspect of a vow was present in the plight of his barren mother Hannah, Samuel too was likely a Nazirite from birth and for life. Even in Amos, Nazirites appear to be those "raised up" by the hand of God, rather than those who made vows:

> "Then I raised up some of your sons to be prophets
> And some of your young men to be Nazirites.
> Is this not so, O sons of Israel?" declares the Lord.
> But you made the Nazirites drink wine,
> And you commanded the prophets saying, "You shall
> not prophesy!"[14]

---

[13] Uncomfortable with the English rendering, "peace offering," W. R. Smith interprets שלמים as more of a "payment offering" in accordance with the verb *shillem*, "to pay," and the association of the offering with the fulfillment of vows, see Smith, *Religion of the Semites; the Fundamental Institutions* (New York: Meridian Books, 1956), 237; Similarly, E. P. Sanders has recently argued for the NEB translation, "shared sacrifice," or "shared offering," of which votive offering are said to have formed a sub-division, *Judaism: Practice and Belief, 63 BCE–66 CE* (London: SCM, 1992), 110–2.

[14] Amos 2.11–2 (NAS).

Again, although in the prophecy of Amos abstinence from wine is described as a characteristic of Nazirite behavior, in the cases of Samson and Samuel only abstinence from the use of a razor is mentioned. Samson's mother was forbidden wine, strong drink, and unclean food (Judg. 13.4,7); some scholars have reasoned that these stipulations applied to Samson as well,[15] but there is no evidence supporting this notion. Furthermore, both individuals certainly violated the regulation for corpse purity: Samson by his slaying of thousands and Samuel by his slaughter of Agag (I Sam. 15.33).[16] Finally, in no cases are Nazirites described participating in the temple rites prescribed in either Num. 6.9–12 or Num. 6.13–21.

The precise relationship between these rather disparate pieces of evidence has been the subject of much discussion among biblical scholars. A majority see in these passages glimpses of the Nazirite custom as it developed over a thousand year period or more: the final stage of the development being marked not by the text in Amos, but by the Numbers legislation.[17] As part of the so-called Priestly Code[18] in the Pentateuch, the law for the temporary Nazirite vow, so the theory suggests, originated sometime prior to the establishment of the Second Temple during the period of return and religious reformation under the hereditary priesthood.[19] Nazirites, in other words, were not always individuals who made vows of consecration.[20] Based on the early Hebrew narrative in Judges, Nazirites first appeared as God-ordained charismatics who, in the period of the conquest, functioned primarily as longhaired warriors for the cause of YHWH.[21] Up until the eight-century BC,[22] the custom

---

[15] See for example J. Pedersen, *Israel: Its Life and Culture* (vols. 3–4; London: Geoffrey Cumberlege, 1949), esp. p. 264; and J. Milgrom, *Numbers = [Ba-midbar]: The Traditional Hebrew Text with the New JPS Translation* (The JPS Torah Commentary; Philadelphia: Jewish Publication Society, 1990), 356.

[16] Milgrom, 357.

[17] G. B. Gray, "The Nazirite," *JTS* 1 (1900): 201–11; cf. n. 22 below.

[18] See E. W. Nicholson, *The Pentateuch in the Twentieth Century: The Legacy of Julius Wellhausen* (New York: Oxford University Press, 1998).

[19] Gray, for instance, dates the origin of the law to ca. 500 BCE, p. 202. W. Eichrodt, however, would date the priestly alterations to the older form of Naziriteship to the monarchial period, *Theology of the Old Testament* (trans. J. A. Baker; vol. 1; Old Testament Library; London: SCM, 1961), 303–4.

[20] de Vaux, 467.

[21] Eichrodt, 303–4; de Vaux, 467.

[22] Gray, *A Critical and Exegetical Commentary on Numbers* (ICC; Edinburgh: T & T Clark, 1903), 57.

retained its charismatic element as evidenced in the figures of Samuel and those described in the text of Amos; however, already in the case of Samuel an association with a *vow* began to be present.[23] By the time of the return from Babylonian exile, the priesthood then brought the already existing custom under its control by: (1) creating the institution of the temporary Nazirate, into which *anyone* could enter by means of a vow; (2) adding stipulations that formed the Nazirite into a priest-like ascetic;[24] and (3) adding sacrificial requirements as part of the vow for the purpose of drawing in for the priests a substantial income.[25]

Nazirites in the Late Second Temple Period

Irrespective of whether one agrees with the history of the custom as elucidated by the majority of biblical scholars, seeking comparative evidence from the late Second Temple period has been the approach of many.[26] Such an approach is justifiable in that sources for this period are more plentiful and more detailed. Scholarly assessments of the evidence, however, and what it says respecting the role of the

---

[23] de Vaux, 467.

[24] Milgrom sees the additions as priestly *limitations* on asceticism, 358.

[25] M. Jastrow, "The 'Nazir' Legislation," *JBL* 33 (1914): 269, 278.

[26] Gray, 203; The theory is intriguing, not in the least because it attempts to identify the possible roles the Nazirite held in the developmental stages of Israelite/Judaic religious history, including the Second Temple period. However, the theory is at best speculative and not entirely supported by the meager biblical evidence. Rather than earlier stages of the custom, it might be argued that the descriptions of Nazirites in the Bible represent special, or exceptional, cases of a custom normally observed in accordance with the Law in Num. (taking in other words, a more traditional date for Num. 6.1–21). The narrative in Judges presupposes an already existing institution in the same manner as does Num. 6.1–21, and the story seems to draw out the very exceptional nature of Samson's calling. *He*, in other words, was a Nazirite from the womb until death, whereas Nazirites normally were not. Likewise, Samuel, due to the exceptional circumstance of his mother's barrenness, may have been vowed into lifelong Naziriteship as a form of extreme petition. Little is said of the Nazirites in Amos, yet simply because there it is stated that Nazirites were "raised up" by the hand of God in the likeness of the prophets does not necessitate that as a general principle Nazirites, at that time, were handpicked by the divine. It may have been the case that the charismatic role of these figures was the cause, rather than the consequence, of their appointment to lifelong Naziriteship; cf. G. von Rad, *Old Testament Theology* (trans. D. M. G. Stalker; vol. 1; Edinburgh: Oliver & Boyd, 1963), 62–3; von Rad handles the disparities by suggesting that although lifelong Nazirites took vows of dedication, ". . . probably every Nazirite was a special case, particularly every lifelong Nazirite," 63.

Nazirite in late Second Temple times, much like their biblical precedent, are both speculative and multifarious. Secondary studies in general, furthermore, have addressed the topic with only partial interest; for where scholars have examined the sources of the late Second Temple period, it has been typically for the purpose of examining the Nazirite custom only as it relates to either biblical or more general Judaic religious history, its supposed appearance in the New Testament canon, or in forming brief introductions to commentaries on rabbinic literature pertaining to the Nazirite vow. Be that as it may, some of the more detailed studies have offered insights on many of the peculiar characteristics of Nazirites in this period, and it seems beneficial to review those works here.

Previous Studies

W. R. Smith

One of the more influential studies discussing Nazirites as they appear in late Second Temple sources is that of the late nineteenth-century British Orientalist, William Robertson Smith. Smith addresses the topic in his series of lectures entitled, *Religion of the Semites*, delivered in Aberdeen, Scotland between 1888–1891. He discusses the Nazirite vow briefly in his ninth lecture entitled, "The Sacramental Efficacy of Animal Sacrifice, and Cognate Acts of Ritual—the Blood Covenant—Blood and Hair Offerings," and again in a brief supplemental note added prior to the *editio princeps* of his first lecture series entitled, "The Taboos Incident to Pilgrimages and Vows."[27] In keeping with his general comparative religions theme, in lecture nine Smith compares the Nazirite vow as evidenced in Num. 6.1–21[28]

---

[27] The second and third series of Smith's lectures, which were never published originally due to Smith's untimely death, were recently discovered in the Robertson Smith Archive in the Cambridge University Library and edited and published by J. Day, *Lectures on the Religion of the Semites: Second and Third Series* (JSOTSup 183; Sheffield, Eng.: Sheffield Academic Press, 1995). Smith, however, makes no reference to Nazirites or the practice of hair offerings within these series.

[28] Smith, based on the works of contemporaries Wellhausen and Kuenen, dates Num. 6.1–21 to the late Second Temple period, 215; cf. Smith's preface to the *editio princeps*, p. vii; cf. "Nineteenth-century Views of Religious Development," in G. M. Bediako, *Primal Religion and the Bible: William Robertson Smith and His Heritage* (JSOTSup 246; Sheffield, Eng.: Sheffield Academic Press, 1997); see also J. W. Rogerson, *The Bible and Criticism in Victorian Britain: Profiles of F. D. Maurice and William Robertson Smith* (JSOTSup 201; Sheffield, Eng.: Sheffield Academic Press, 1995), 95ff.

and Josephus' account of the vow of Bernice in *B. J.* 2.313–4 with
other similar "hair-offerings" practiced among the ancient Greeks
and Semites. In the additional note he compares the Nazirite specifically
with the Arabic votive pilgrim known from the Arabic rite of *Ihram*.

In general, Smith posits that the shaving and offering of one's hair
was a practice common in rituals of mourning and individual worship; the principle behind the two being closely related. In the shaving of the hair in mourning, a person deposited with the departed
something of attached and living significance, much like a lover when
leaving a lock of hair during a time of perceived prolonged absence.
In the instance of worship, the offering of the hair was to "knit more
closely" the bond between the worshipper and his/her deity when
felt estranged.[29]

Smith specifically assesses that there were two particular occasions
for hair-offerings among the ancient Semites and Greeks: (1) the
offering of the hair as a rite of passage or act of social maturation,
and (2) the offering of the hair in a vow, taken in times of personal
distress (especially common among Greeks) or when making pilgrimage to some sacred shrine (evidenced among the Arabs).[30] Among
the Hebrews, taking Josephus' account of the vow of Bernice into
consideration (a vow taken while in some form of distress), such hair-
offerings were, ". . . exactly parallel to the ordinary Greek vow to
offer the hair on deliverance from urgent danger."[31] Unlike the Arabic
pilgrim, however, among the Hebrews, ". . . at least in later times
when stated pilgrimages to Jerusalem were among the ordinary and
imperative exercises of every man's religion, the pilgrimage did not
involve a hair offering, . . ."[32] Furthermore, regarding the consecrated
state of the Nazirite and the abstinence from certain behavior associated with such a state (i.e., from drinking wine, cutting the hair,
and contacting a corpse), the votary's state of consecration was in,
and only in, direct relation to his/her promised hair.[33] The vow was
thus, ". . . a promise for the performance of which one at once begins

---

[29] Smith, 325ff.
[30] Ibid., 326ff.
[31] Ibid., 332.
[32] Ibid.
[33] Ibid., 482–3; Although Smith recognizes that נזיר refers to "a consecrated person," nonetheless it is the hair that is the object of the vow, and the Hebrew
Nazirite is consecrated only in respect to the promised hair.

to make active preparation, so that the life of the votary from the time when he assumes the engagement is taken out of the ordinary sphere of secular existence, and becomes one continuous act or religion."[34] Like the Greek votary Achilles, the hair was the visible sign of the Nazirite's state of consecration, inviolate until the very moment for discharging the vow had arrived.[35]

G. B. Gray

Whereas Smith approaches the subject from the perspective of comparative religion, G. B. Gray in his 1899 article, "The Nazirite," approaches it from a history of religions point of view.[36] Gray is interested primarily in the Nazirite of the biblical period, and the article appears to articulate his historical-critical view of Num. 6.1–21 found in his latter commentary on Numbers (1903).[37] Gray's purpose is to trace signs of development in the institution of Naziriteship as it spanned the millennium or so between the story of Samson in the ca. tenth-century BC to the first-century AD.[38] Gray examines six particular topics: (1) the vow, (2) term of Naziriteship, (3) treatment of the Nazirite's hair, (4) avoidance of pollution by a dead body, (5) abstinence from all products of the vine and from all intoxicants, and (6) the offerings. Much of Gray's position has already been presented, as it typifies the historical-critical argument for the late date of Num. 6.1–21 previously discussed. There is no need to represent it again here, suffice to mention that for Nazirites in the late Second Temple period Gray holds to the opinion that those of a lifelong duration in the likeness of Samson and Samuel failed to exist in the post-exilic period until the period of the Mishnah, where they are again discussed by the later rabbis (although even in the rabbinic period, their actual existence, as opposed to mere legalistic speculation, is suspect).[39] He rejects the idea that either John the Baptist in the Gospel tradition or James the brother of Jesus (whose lifestyle is described by the early church father Hegesippus) was a lifelong Nazirite. Instead, these figures were simply "permanent

---

[34] Ibid., 332–3.
[35] Ibid., 333.
[36] For bibliographic information see n. 17.
[37] Gray, *Numbers*, 57ff.
[38] Gray, "The Nazirite," 201.
[39] Ibid., 203–4.

ascetics" of whom Nazirite behavior formed only a part of their social existence.[40] Between the post-exilic and rabbinic periods, Nazirites made only temporary vows in the likeness of the legislation of Num. 6.1–21 (as evidenced in I Macc. and Acts), and these vows lasted typically for only thirty days (as described in Josephus' *B. J.* 2.313–4 and the Mishnah).[41] With regard to the treatment of the hair, Gray also notes that for the temporary Nazirite, the hair would not have acquired sufficient length in only a thirty-day period. Consequently, like Smith's assessment, the hair became a "hair-offering," and the sacrifices in sum became the primary significance of the vow rather than the consecrated state of the individual.[42]

Hillel Salmanowitsch

In his 1931 Ph. D. dissertation, "Das Nasiräat nach Bibel und Talmud," Hillel Salmanowitsch compares the institution of the Nazirite vow as it appears in the Bible with the Nazirate as represented in Talmudic literature. The thesis specifically concerns the period under present investigation in his brief section entitled "Nasiräer in der nachexilischen und talmudischen Zeit."[43] There, as an introduction and background to his primary subject, Salmanowitsch provides an historical overview of how the Nazirite vow was observed within the aforesaid period. In a rather terse manner, he highlights some of the more obvious features of the custom as found within various late Second Temple sources, and concludes that the Nazirate in this period was basically a form of popular asceticism.

Regarding some of his specific observations, Salmanowitsch notes rather ubiquitously that Nazirites were popular, and that the practice of the vow was a widespread phenomenon. This is evidenced by their large numbers and by the fact that they appear in the sources from within all layers of society: aristocrats, common folk, rabbis, and even the Christians as evidenced in such figures as John the Baptist and the four individuals under a vow associated with the apostle Paul in the book of Acts. Why the practice was so popular, for Salmanowitsch, was due in part to a widespread interest in asceti-

---

[40] Ibid.
[41] Ibid., 203.
[42] Ibid., 204, 210.
[43] Salmanowitsch, 18–26.

cism during the period, as indicated by the presence of such ascetic-oriented groups as the Therapeutae and Ebionites.[44] For those interested in such a lifestyle, the various forms of abstention maintained by the Nazirite would have been an attractive manner of life, even if only for a temporary period of time.

Salmanowitsch also explains that it was considered a pious deed to pay for the sacrificial costs of a Nazirite's offerings, and that it was common for a king, or other patron such as Paul in the book of Acts, to do so.[45] Regarding the length of time for the Nazirite vow, it was mostly for thirty days, although lifelong Naziriteships in the likeness of Samson and Samuel, contrary to the view of Gray, were practiced.[46]

Why the vow was taken was for a variety of reasons: childlessness, as a request for safekeeping on a journey or in a time of war, sickness, remorse over sin, or even rashly out of excitement while gambling.[47] The popularity of the custom, according to Salmanowitsch, declined after the destruction of the temple in AD 70 due to the incapacity to offer the required sacrificial offerings.[48]

Markus Bockmuehl

One of the more recent treatments on the topic is that of Markus Bockmuehl in an article dealing with one of the so-called "hard sayings" of Jesus in Matthew 8.22 and parallels.[49] Although many have seen in the saying "Let the dead bury their dead" evidence for Jesus' attitude toward and departure from conventional Jewish Torah piety with respect to one's duty to bury the deceased, especially one's own relatives (the saying is directed to a disciple claiming that he could no longer follow Jesus due to the need to bury his departed parents), Bockmuehl rehashes an argument proposed by Tertullian in the second-century AD[50] and proposes the possibility that rather than Jesus asserting an attack on the Law, he was simply drawing on

---

[44] Ibid., 23–4.
[45] Ibid., 24–5.
[46] Ibid., 18.
[47] Ibid., 18–21.
[48] Ibid., 23.
[49] M. Bockmuehl, " 'Let the Dead Bury their Dead' (Matt. 8.22/Luke 9.60): Jesus and the Halakhah," *JTS* 49/2 (1998): 553–81.
[50] Tertullian, *Marc.* 4.23.

Nazirite motifs as a means of creating an analogy for his teaching on radical discipleship. Bockmuehl's primary objective is thus two-fold. First, it is to demonstrate that Nazirites were such a common feature of late Second Temple Palestinian Jewish society that Jesus could have made a recognizable analogy to them; and second, to demonstrate that in Jewish thought of the period Nazirite vows were regarded as a "significant manifestation of Jewish piety."[51]

For support of his theory, Bockmuehl refers to the works of Philo and the early rabbinic corpus where discussions of Nazirite behav-ior lead to comparisons between Nazirites and priests, especially the High Priest.[52] Furthermore, reference is made to a recent discovery in Palestine of a first-century AD Nazirite's tomb of substantial archi-tectural design, which, for Bockmuehl, indicates the Nazirite might have been held in high esteem.[53] In light of such evidence, Bockmuehl suggests that Nazirites were regarded as "uniquely dedicated to God, and temporarily comparable in status to priests."[54] For their popu-larity, he refers to their large numbers when appearing in Jerusalem to fulfill their sacrificial obligations, as found in sources such as I Macc., Josephus, and the Jerusalem Talmud.[55] Additionally for Bockmuehl, the very fact that the Mishnah and Tosefta contain entire tractates devoted to the subject of Nazirites, and that these tractates are placed in the order dealing with the topic of women, attest not only to the custom's general popularity but also to its popularity among the female gender.[56]

A difficulty is encountered, however, when Bockmuehl examines the evidence for Nazirite motifs within the New Testament and early Christian tradition. Within Luke/Acts, the suspected allusion to Naziriteship in the birth narrative of John the Baptist, unlike the explanation offered by Salmanowitsch, simply remains unclear to Bockmuehl (though parallels with the narrative of Samson in Judges are noted).[57] Paul was possibly a Nazirite while under a vow in Acts 18.18 and 21.23–6 (sic), though, likewise for Bockmuehl, the evi-

---

[51] Bockmuehl, 569.
[52] Ibid., 568–9.
[53] Ibid., 569.
[54] Ibid., see also p. 567
[55] Ibid., 568–9.
[56] Ibid.
[57] Ibid., 570.

dence remains inconclusive.[58] With regard to Jesus himself, Matthew's infancy narrative referring to Jesus as a "Nazarene" (ναζωραῖος) in Mt. 2.23 is asserted as a possible reflection of "Nazirite" (ναζιραῖος), as evidenced in equations between the two Greek terms found within later patristic sources. According to Bockmuehl, however, there is little indication within the Gospel tradition that Jesus or his earliest followers observed the lifestyle of Nazirites. Only one other possible allusion to a Nazirite vow in respect to Jesus appears in the Gospel tradition for Bockmuehl, namely in the saying of Jesus at the final Passover meal, "I shall not drink of the fruit of the vine until that day when I drink it anew in the kingdom of God." Bockmuehl sees there "unmistakable Nazirite connotations" when viewed in its first-century setting.[59] Lastly, Bockmuehl considers the description of James the brother of Jesus in the testimony of Hegesippus, like Gray, to be highly legendary.[60]

Bart J. Koet

Lastly, Bart J. Koet addresses the text of Acts 18.18 in his 1998 article entitled, "Why did Paul Shave His Hair (Acts 18.18)? Nazirate and Temple in the book of Acts."[61] His basic purpose is to determine whether or not Luke means to portray Paul as under a Nazirite vow, and if so, for what purpose. He approaches the issues by providing a brief survey of late Second Temple evidence on the Nazirite vow, and concludes that Luke did portray Paul as a Nazirite for the purposes of demonstrating Paul's allegiance to the Jewish Law.[62] For Koet, Nazirites were those who took upon themselves voluntary commandments and because of the expenses required in the sacrificial obligations of their vows, participated in a common practice where one could "show off" his/her law abidingness (sic).[63]

To substantiate his thesis, Koet briefly examines the law of Num. 6.1–21 and other evidence in the writings of Philo, Josephus, I Macc.,

---

[58] Ibid., 572–3.
[59] Ibid., 571.
[60] Ibid., 574.
[61] B. J. Koet, "Why Did Paul Shave His Hair (Acts 18.18)? Nazirate and Temple in the Book of Acts," in *The Centrality of Jerusalem: Historical Perspectives* (eds. M. Poorthuis and Ch. Safrai; Kampen: KoK Pharos, 1996), 128–42.
[62] Ibid., 130.
[63] Ibid., see also p. 136.

and the Mishnah. Koet sees in Philo's exegesis of Num. 6.1–21 in *Spec.* 1 as evidence that Philo likened the Nazirite to a temporary priest.[64] Similarly, in I Macc. 3.49, Nazirites were gathered at Mizpah along with sacerdotal objects prior to the battle of Emmaus, and thus they were associated with the priesthood and the Temple.[65] References in Josephus and the Mishnah are cited to highlight the popularity of Nazirites in this period and to show that the Nazirite vow was an integral part of common Jewish religious practice.[66] Taking these features into consideration, Luke's description of Paul as under a vow in Acts 18.18 is thus seen by Koet as an effort by Luke to align Paul with a custom associated with a prevalent form of piety commonly considered above and beyond what was religiously required of the average Jew.

Other Works

Other works that have addressed the topic have done so primarily out of an interest in Nazirites as they appear in the Hebrew Bible, the New Testament, or in early rabbinic literature. Like those just cited, these works typically have made recourse to the sources of the late Second Temple period for possible illumination on perceived difficulties within, or for the purpose of writing introductions to, these respective literary corpora. Tony Cartledge, for example, argues that Nazirite vows in the Hebrew Bible were "more likely than not" conditional promises rather than a form of expressing unconditional personal piety.[67] To help substantiate his argument, he cites several sources from the period of the late Second Temple where conditional motivation in assuming the Nazirite vow is described. Similarly, many critics of Luke, such as Ernst Haenchen[68] and Hans Conzelmann,[69] among others, have argued extensively that the portrayal of Paul's behavior while under a vow in Acts 18.18 and 21.23–7 contradicts known rules for the Nazirate in the period (as described by Josephus

---

[64] Ibid., 134.
[65] Ibid., 132–3.
[66] Ibid., 133–5.
[67] Cartledge, "Were Nazirite Vows Unconditional?" 422.
[68] See testimony 2.4 following.
[69] Ibid.

and the Mishnah). Rather than discuss the views of these scholars
here, I will examine their assertions where relevant to the detailed
examination of sources to follow.

The Need for Further Study

Secondary studies have thus revealed several of the general characteristics of Nazirites within the late Second Temple period, but there
is inconsistency among these works with respect to many of the
details. Moreover, the precise role of the Nazirite remains unclear.
The lack of consistency and clarity is due primarily to the very nature
of previous studies, for as was discussed, secondary works have typically culled from relevant sources only what is beneficial to partially
related concerns.

The purpose of this study is to provide a general survey of the
available evidence for Nazirites in the late Second Temple period.
It is also to assess what that evidence reveals regarding the possible
role they held within the social lives of Jews. My objective, it must
be stated, is thus a narrow one. It is narrow in that what this study
is *not* attempting to do is to write a complete history of the Nazirite
or the institution of the Nazirite vow in this era. For to do so would
entail a much broader survey of other comparative evidence within
Judaism and in the Mediterranean world at large, as well as perhaps, the incorporation of broader anthropological perspectives. I
intend, rather, merely to layout for the reader the available evidence
for Nazirites, examine each source on its own merits and in context, and assess the informative value of that evidence for the aforementioned purposes alone. I believe this approach, though a marginal
one by comparison, is nonetheless a needed one. For in order to
accomplish an historical work of greater magnitude a groundbreak-
ing initiative on this topic must be taken, and it is the goal of the
present study to provide this course of action.

SOURCES AND METHODOLOGY

With respect to the sources for Nazirites in the late Second Temple period, one is immediately faced with a peculiar problem; namely, what sources are relevant is not entirely clear. Among a significant number of literary works, for example, particularly those of the Greek narrative genre, Nazirite imagery is often used when describing individual behavior *sans* the respective technical nomenclature. Establishing the relevance of these sources, therefore, as noted with respect to previous studies on Nazirites, involves a certain degree of conjecture. Rather than taking an exclusive approach, whereby I might excise such works from examination, because I believe in their possible relevance, I will simply include them and treat them separately and secondarily under a section entitled, "Possible and Tangential Evidence for Nazirites." All other sources I will treat initially under the rubric, "Direct Evidence for Nazirites."

In each of the aforementioned sections, I will examine the available sources in roughly chronological order. Moreover, I will introduce them and address such critical concerns as date, genre, and general relevance where appropriate to each. Additionally, since the process of examining pertinent evidence will involve textual citations, some of which are lengthy, where appropriate I will supply an English translation with key foreign terms provided in brackets. For testimonies involving a significant amount of comparison between texts in ancient languages, such as translation material, where relevant, I will supply a complete version of each ancient text together with an English translation. Lastly, because of the number and length of textual data being examined, following the examination of each testimony, I will provide a brief recapitulation of possible evidence in a sub-section entitled, "Summary of Evidence."[1]

---

[1] Editions of primary sources used are listed in the Bibliography, pp. 201–2.

CHAPTER ONE

DIRECT EVIDENCE FOR NAZIRITES

Texts inherited, composed, and being circulated by Jews in the late
Second Temple period are vast in number. Of the many surviving,
those pertaining directly to the discussion of Nazirites consist of a
variety of genres, most of which date in composition or final redaction roughly between the mid-third century BC and the eighth century AD. Inherited texts include those found within the sources of
the Hebrew Bible. Various passages in the Bible referring to Nazirites
have been mentioned and discussed already in the Introduction (Num.
6.1–21; Judg. 13–16; I Sam. 1.11; Amos 2.11–2); however, the matter of textual variants of these texts surviving in Hebrew and dated
to this period, as well as versions of them being composed in other
known languages spoken by Jews, draws attention to a second series
of literary sources of relevance, namely textual variants and translations of the Hebrew Bible. Specific sources of these genres include
one scroll fragment discovered in the Judaean desert near Khirbet
Qumran containing a portion of the book of I Sam. in Hebrew
(4QSam^a), the Greek version of the Bible known as the Septuagint
(LXX), and translations of the Bible into Aramaic which were preserved and transmitted by the rabbis of the first to eighth centuries
AD. Another surviving and relevant textual source of the period
includes the Hebrew wisdom text Ben Sira (a work translated into
Greek in the late second century BC and transmitted along with the
Septuagint under the name of Sirach). Other sources of direct relevance to the discussion of Nazirites include various philosophical
treatises written by the first-century AD Jewish philosopher, Philo
Judaeus of Alexandria; the works of the Jewish historian, Flavius
Josephus, also of the first century AD; and the legal material and
works of Bible interpretation composed and redacted by the rabbis
of the third to sixth centuries AD. One, yet highly significant, piece
of non-literary evidence for Nazirites also exists in this period; namely,
that of a first-century AD tomb thought by archaeologists to belong
to a Nazirite and his family.

1.1 4QSam^a

Among the scrolls and fragments of literature discovered in the caves along the Dead Sea near Khirbet Qumran between 1948 and 1956, only one is of direct relevance to the topic at hand, namely the Hebrew manuscript 4QSam^a. The date of the 4QSam^a MS is reckoned to be between 50–25 BC,[1] though the reading contained in the fragment is certainly much older (as will be discussed). 4QSam^a concerns the present study because of its representation of the figure Samuel. In I Sam. 1.22 of 4QSam^a, Samuel is explicitly named a "Nazirite forever," a specification unparalleled in other surviving versions of the Samuel story.

4QSam^a I Samuel 1.11, 22

v. 11 . . . of men and I will give him before you as a Nazirite until the day of his death. And he will drink no wine or strong drink and a razor will not pass over his head

v. 22 . . . and I will give him as a Nazirite forever

v. 11 [ר יזנ : ךי נ פ]ל והיתתנו   מ[ו י ש נ א   ]

[ה ת ש י   א ל ד ר כ ש ו   ןי י   ו ת ו מ   ם ו י   ד ע]

[ו ש א ר ד ל]ע   ר ו ב ע י   א ל   ה ר ו מ   ן]

v. 22]²[ת נ ו]   ם ל ו ע   ד ע   ר י ז נ   ו הי ת

I provide here the reading of the 4QSam^a fragments in reconstructed form. The bracketed words in Hebrew represent words and/or portions of terms reconstructed by scholars but absent in the original 4Q fragments due to textual lacunae. According to the story of I Sam. in the Hebrew Bible, in chapter one v. 22 Hannah states her intention to keep her boy Samuel at her side until he is weaned, and only then will she fulfill her promise to bring the child to Shiloh "that he may appear before the Lord and remain there forever." 4QSam^a at this point contains a phrase absent in all extant MSS of the Hebrew Bible (Masoretic Text [MT]) and the Septuagint (LXX):

---

[1] E. D. Herbert, "4QSam^a and its Relationship to the LXX: An Exploration in Stemmatological Analysis," in *IX Congress of the International Organization for Septuagint and Cognate Studies* (ed. B. A. Taylor; SBLSCS 45; Atlanta, Ga.: Scholars Press, 1997), 38; Ulrich states that the paleographical evidence suggests a date for the first half of the first century BC, see *The Qumran Text of Samuel and Josephus* (HSM 19; Missoula, Mont.: Published by Scholars Press for Harvard Semitic Museum, 1978), 10.

[2] Ulrich, 39, 165.

"and I will give him as a Nazirite forever" (ונת[חיהו נזיר עד עולם]).[3] McCarter holds the reading of 4QSam^a to be original with the phrase later dropping out of LXX and MT due to "an ordinary haplography caused by *homoioteleuton*,"[4] the *homoioteleuton* being the repetition of עד עולם when the two phrases are conjoined (e.g., עד עולם [ונת[חיהו נזיר עד עולם).[5] Pisano, on the other hand, suggests that 4QSam^a represents the latter of the three readings, the additional phrase being a later expansion.[6] It is more likely, given the widespread agreement between LXX I Sam. and 4QSam^a, that 4QSam^a represents the general Vorlage of LXX, a position argued by Cross an Ulrich.[7] McCarter's argument, therefore, seems the most plausible.

The presence of the term נזיר in v. 11 is also a possibility, though it is purely hypothetical due to a lacuna in the extant 4Q fragment. The reconstruction by Cross (supported by Ulrich and McCarter) is reasonable due to the number and length of Hebrew words needed to fill in the space between the extant portions of text. However, McCarter admits that the term is secondary due to its presence in v. 22.[8] The absence of any clear equivalent for נזיר in LXX I Sam. 1.11 further hinders the reconstruction from having any certainty (see 1.2.3 following).

I find it interesting that the reference to Samuel as a נזיר occurs in v. 22. Hannah's declaration to dedicate Samuel as a Nazirite appears to be in conjunction with her promise to dedicate him to the temple at Shilo, the latter perhaps being intended in the 4QSam^a narrative as the simultaneous initiation of the former.

Summary of Evidence

Regardless of the lack of clarity concerning the presence of the term נזיר in v. 11, unlike LXX or MT (which will be discussed in more detail following), 4QSam^a I Sam. 1.22 does make an explicit reference to Samuel as a "Nazirite forever." For those familiar with the

---

[3] Ibid., 165.

[4] P. K. McCarter, *I Samuel: A New Translation* (AB 8; New York: Doubleday, 1980), 54.

[5] Ibid.

[6] S. Pisano, *Additions or Omissions in the Book of Samuel: The Significant Pluses and Minuses in the Massoretic, LXX and Qumran Texts* (OBO 57; Gottingen: Vandenhoeck und Ruprecht, 1984), 21–2.

[7] See n. 29, p. 36.

[8] McCarter, 54.

reading in this period, therefore, the status of Samuel as a perpetual Nazirite was indubitable.[9]

1.2 *The Septuagint*

There are five passages in the Greek version of the Bible that are of interest to the discussion of Nazirites. These include the legislation for the Nazirite vow in the book of Numbers (6.1–21), the representations of Samson and Samuel in the Greek versions of Judges (13.5,7; 16.17) and I Samuel (1.11, 21) respectively, as well as references to Nazirites found in the books of Amos (2.11–2) and Lamentations (4.7–8). The reason for the relevance of these passages is due to their peculiar content; for they contain interesting differences from parallels found in the Hebrew Bible.

The origins of the LXX are somewhat uncertain;[10] albeit evidence suggests that by the end of the second century BC, the Jewish community of Alexandria, Egypt possessed a copy of all, or nearly all, of the Hebrew biblical books in Greek.[11] Furthermore, by the first century AD, the use of the Greek Bible was extensive among Jews both in Egypt,[12] as well as in Palestine.[13] In terms of approaching

---

[9] Likely based on MT, there appears in the Mishnah (*m. Naz.* 9.5) a debate regarding the Nazirite status of Samuel, see the discussion of testimony 1.8.22 following.

[10] Detailed discussions on the origins of the Septuagint may be found in H. B. Swete, *An Introduction to the Old Testament in Greek* (2nd ed.; Cambridge, Eng.: Cambridge University Press, 1914), 12–4; and S. Jellicoe, *The Septuagint and Modern Study* (Oxford: The Clarendon Press, 1968), 38–47; see also N. F. Marcos, *The Septuagint in Context: Introduction to the Greek Version of the Bible* (Leiden: Brill, 2000), 44–50; and M. Müller, *The First Bible of the Church: A Plea for the Septuagint* (JSOTSup 206; Sheffield, Eng.: Sheffield Academic Press, 1996), 61–78.

[11] Sweet, 23–5; A suggested chronology for the translations of the Prophets, the Writings, and Apocryphal books is given by G. Dorival, *La Bible graecque des Septante: du Judaïsme Hellénistique au Christianisme Ancien* (Initiations au Christianisme Ancien; Paris: Éditions du CERF, 1988), 111.

[12] For evidence of literary dependence on the LXX among Egyptian Jews writing in Greek, see C. R. Holladay, *Fragments from Hellenistic Jewish Authors* (vol. 1; Texts and Translations 20; Chico, Calif.: Scholars Press, 1983), 51–2, 189–90, 262; There is also evidence suggesting the LXX was used liturgically in Egyptian synagogues, see Swete, 19–20, who notes that the style of Greek in the Pentateuch is far from literary, and Marcos who states that the translation was made "basically for liturgical and didactic, but not expressly literary, reasons, as can be gathered from a simple comparison of the Pentateuch with the style of Josephus, [and] Philo . . .," 40; Writing in the first century AD, Philo mentions that the Jews in Alexandria commemorated the translation in an annual festival held on the island of Pharos, *Mos.* 2.26–44.

[13] Use of the version among Greek-speaking Jews in Palestine is well attested.

the LXX for the purposes of the present study, therefore, as a translation it becomes particularly informative where it contains expressions of meaning or other data that explain its original Hebrew
source text. Where a translation becomes Bible interpretation, it will
naturally reflect the translator's own understanding of his Vorlage,
and furthermore, may reflect wider and more commonly held perceptions prevalent within the author's broader social context. Perceptions, in other words, that may have borne an influence on the
translator's choice of rendering. Conversely, because of its principal
purpose, as a translation it will have made an impact on the way
its readers understood a biblical text. Taking these few factors into
consideration alone, the use of the LXX as a source of information
on how a great number of Jews in this period understood certain
customs, such as the Nazirite vow, or regarded certain biblical per-
sona thought to be Nazirites, such as Samson and Samuel, is invaluable. One problem facing the historian that should be mentioned is
whether or not what is represented in available Greek and Hebrew
MSS represents either the true reading of the original translator or
his Vorlage. I shall deal with this problem where relevant to the
examination of texts to follow.

1.2.1 *Numbers 6.1–21*

[1]And the Lord spoke to Moses, saying, [2]"Speak to the sons of Israel, and
say to them, 'If a man or woman specially vows a vow to purify himself
as one of purity to the Lord, [3]he shall purify himself from wine and
strong drink; he shall drink no vinegar of wine or vinegar of strong
drink; and whatever is made of the grape he shall not drink; neither
shall he eat fresh grapes or raisins. [4]All the days of his vow he shall
eat nothing that is produced from the vine, wine from the grape-seeds
to the skin. [5]All the days of the vow of purity a razor shall not come
upon his head; until the days are fulfilled which he has vowed to the
Lord he shall be holy, allowing the hair of his head to grow long. [6]All
the days of his vow to the Lord he shall not go near a dead body;
[7]either to his father or his mother, or to his brother or his sister. He
shall not defile himself for them when they have died because the vow
of his God is upon his head. [8]All the days of his vow he shall be holy
to the Lord.

Literary dependence is evidenced most apparently in the works of the historian
Josephus and the New Testament. Common knowledge of the LXX among Palestinian
Jews might also be attested by the frequent efforts to revise the work during the
first to second centuries AD under the auspices of the rabbinate (e.g., Aquilla and
Theodotion).

⁹And if any one should die suddenly beside him, immediately the head of his vow shall be defiled; and he shall shave his head on whatever day he shall be purified; on the seventh day he shall be shaved. ¹⁰And on the eighth day he shall bring two turtledoves, or two young pigeons, to the priest, to the doors of the tabernacle of witness, ¹¹and the priest shall offer one for a sin offering; and the other for a whole burnt offering; and the priest shall make atonement for him concerning the sin respecting the dead body, and he shall sanctify his head on that day, ¹²the day on which the days of the vow were sanctified to the Lord, and he shall bring a lamb of a year old for a guilt offering, and the former days shall be void, because the head of his vow was defiled.

¹³And this is the law of the one who has vowed: on whatever day the days of his vow are fulfilled, he himself shall bring the offering to the doors of the tabernacle of witness. ¹⁴And he shall bring his gift to the Lord, one he-lamb a year old without blemish for a whole burnt offering, and one ewe-lamb a year old without blemish for a sin offering, and one ram without blemish for a peace offering; ¹⁵and a basket of unleavened bread of fine flour, even loaves kneaded with oil, and unleavened cakes anointed with oil, and their grain offerings and their libations. ¹⁶And the priest shall bring them before the Lord and shall offer his sin offering and his whole burnt offering, ¹⁷and he shall offer the ram as a peace offering to the Lord with the basket of unleavened bread; and the priest shall offer its grain offerings and libations. ¹⁸And the one who vowed shall shave the head of his vow at the doors of the tabernacle of witness, and shall place the hair on the fire that is under the peace offering. ¹⁹And the priest shall take the boiled shoulder of the ram, and one unleavened loaf from the basket, and one unleavened cake, and shall put them on the hands of the one who has vowed after he has shaved his vow. ²⁰And the priest shall present them as an offering before the Lord, they shall be holy to the priest together with the breast of heave offering and the shoulder of wave offering; and after these things the one who has vowed may drink wine. ²¹This is the law of the one who has vowed, concerning the vow in which he has vowed to the Lord his gift, in addition to whatever else he may be able to afford according to the power of his vow, which he vowed according to the law of purity."

The only passage in the Bible that lays out the rules of behavior for one wishing to become a Nazirite, a process taken for granted as being initiated by the making of a vow, is Num. 6.1–21. The law for the Nazirite vow in LXX Num. 6.1–21 contains some interesting differences from the law as found in MT.

For the most part, LXX does closely follows MT. It consists of the same basic outline detailing the legislation for the vow: vv. 1–8 deal with general regulations, vv. 9–12 with procedures following a votary's accidental contamination by a corpse, and vv. 13–21 with instructions following the successful completion of the vow. While much of the translation may be described as somewhat wooden, there are portions of the Greek version that move significantly beyond what is made explicit in the Hebrew. In general, LXX Num. 6.1–21 translates *the vow of the Nazirite* as it is known technically in Hebrew into Greek as a non-technical *special purity vow*.

LXX Numbers 6.1–21	MT Numbers 6.1–21

¹καὶ ἐλάλησεν κύριος πρὸς Μωυσῆν λέγων ²λάλησον τοῖς υἱοῖς Ισραηλ καὶ ἐρεῖς πρὸς αὐτούς ἀνὴρ ἢ γυνή ὃς ἐὰν **μεγάλως εὔξηται εὐχὴν ἀφαγνίσασθαι ἁγνείαν** κυρίῳ ³ἀπὸ οἴνου καὶ σικερα **ἁγνισθήσεται** ἀπὸ οἴνου καὶ ὄξος ἐξ οἴνου καὶ ὄξος ἐκ σικερα οὐ πίεται καὶ ὅσα κατεργάζεται ἐκ σταφυλῆς οὐ πίεται καὶ σταφυλὴν πρόσφατον καὶ σταφίδα οὐ φάγεται ⁴πάσας τὰς ἡμέρας **τῆς εὐχῆς αὐτοῦ** ἀπὸ πάντων ὅσα γίνεται ἐξ ἀμπέλου οἶνον ἀπὸ στεμφύλων ἕως γιγάρτου οὐ φάγεται ⁵πάσας τὰς ἡμέρας **τῆς εὐχῆς τοῦ ἁγνισμοῦ** ξυρὸν οὐκ ἐπελεύσεται ἐπὶ τὴν κεφαλὴν αὐτοῦ ἕως ἂν πληρωθῶσιν αἱ ἡμέραι ὅσας **ηὔξατο** κυρίῳ ἅγιος ἔσται τρέφων κόμην τρίχα κεφαλῆς ⁶πάσας τὰς ἡμέρας **τῆς εὐχῆς** κυρίῳ ἐπὶ πάσῃ ψυχῇ τετελευτηκυίᾳ οὐκ εἰσελεύσεται ⁷ἐπὶ πατρὶ καὶ ἐπὶ μητρὶ καὶ ἐπ᾽ ἀδελφῷ καὶ ἐπ᾽ ἀδελφῇ οὐ μιανθήσεται ἐπ᾽ αὐτοῖς ἀποθανόντων αὐτῶν ὅτι **εὐχὴ** θεοῦ αὐτοῦ ἐπ᾽ αὐτῷ ἐπὶ κεφαλῆς αὐτοῦ ⁸πάσας τὰς ἡμέρας **τῆς εὐχῆς αὐτοῦ** ἅγιος ἔσται κυρίῳ

⁹ἐὰν δέ τις ἀποθάνῃ ἐξάπινα ἐπ᾽ αὐτῷ παραχρῆμα μιανθήσεται **ἡ κεφαλὴ εὐχῆς αὐτοῦ** καὶ ξυρήσεται τὴν κεφαλὴν αὐτοῦ ᾗ ἂν ἡμέρᾳ καθαρισθῇ τῇ ἡμέρᾳ τῇ ἑβδόμῃ ξυρηθήσεται ¹⁰καὶ τῇ ἡμέρᾳ τῇ ὀγδόῃ οἴσει δύο τρυγόνας ἢ δύο

¹וַיְדַבֵּר יְהוָה אֶל־מֹשֶׁה לֵּאמֹר: ²דַּבֵּר אֶל־בְּנֵי יִשְׂרָאֵל וְאָמַרְתָּ אֲלֵהֶם אִישׁ אֽוֹ־אִשָּׁה כִּי יַפְלִא לִנְדֹּר נֶדֶר **נָזִיר לְהַזִּיר** לַֽיהוָה: ³מִיַּיִן **וְשֵׁכָר יַזִּיר** חֹמֶץ יַיִן וְחֹמֶץ שֵׁכָר לֹא יִשְׁתֶּה וְכָל־מִשְׁרַת עֲנָבִים לֹא יִשְׁתֶּה וַעֲנָבִים לַחִים וִיבֵשִׁים לֹא יֹאכֵל: ⁴כֹּל יְמֵי **נִזְרוֹ** מִכֹּל אֲשֶׁר יֵעָשֶׂה מִגֶּפֶן הַיַּיִן מֵחַרְצַנִּים וְעַד־זָג לֹא יֹאכֵל: ⁵כָּל־יְמֵי **נֶדֶר נִזְרוֹ** תַּעַר לֹא־יַעֲבֹר עַל־רֹאשׁוֹ עַד־מְלֹאת הַיָּמִם אֲשֶׁר־**יַזִּיר** לַֽיהוָה קָדֹשׁ יִהְיֶה גַּדֵּל פֶּרַע שְׂעַר רֹאשׁוֹ: ⁶כָּל־יְמֵי **הַזִּירוֹ** לַֽיהוָה עַל־נֶפֶשׁ מֵת לֹא יָבֹא: ⁷לְאָבִיו וּלְאִמּוֹ לְאָחִיו וּלְאַחֹתוֹ לֹא־יִטַּמָּא לָהֶם בְּמֹתָם כִּי **נֵזֶר אֱלֹהָיו עַל־רֹאשׁוֹ**: ⁸כֹּל יְמֵי **נִזְרוֹ** קָדֹשׁ הוּא לַֽיהוָה:

⁹וְכִֽי־יָמוּת מֵת עָלָיו בְּפֶתַע פִּתְאֹם וְטִמֵּא **רֹאשׁ נִזְרוֹ** וְגִלַּח רֹאשׁוֹ בְּיוֹם טָהֳרָתוֹ בַּיּוֹם הַשְּׁבִיעִי יְגַלְּחֶנּוּ: ¹⁰וּבַיּוֹם הַשְּׁמִינִי יָבִא שְׁתֵּי תֹרִים אוֹ שְׁנֵי בְּנֵי יוֹנָה אֶל־הַכֹּהֵן אֶל־פֶּתַח אֹהֶל מוֹעֵד: ¹¹וְעָשָׂה הַכֹּהֵן אֶחָד לְחַטָּאת וְאֶחָד לְעֹלָה וְכִפֶּר עָלָיו מֵאֲשֶׁר חָטָא עַל־הַנָּפֶשׁ

νεοσσοὺς περιστερῶν πρὸς τὸν
ἱερέα ἐπὶ τὰς θύρας τῆς σκηνῆς
τοῦ μαρτυρίου ¹¹καὶ ποιήσει ὁ
ἱερεὺς μίαν περὶ ἁμαρτίας καὶ
μίαν εἰς ὁλοκαύτωμα καὶ ἐξιλάσε-
ται περὶ αὐτοῦ ὁ ἱερεὺς περὶ ὧν
ἥμαρτεν περὶ τῆς ψυχῆς καὶ ἁγιάσει τὴν κεφαλὴν αὐτοῦ ἐν ἐκείνῃ
τῇ ἡμέρᾳ ¹²ᾗ ἡγιάσθη κυρίῳ τὰς
ἡμέρας τῆς εὐχῆς καὶ προσάξει
ἀμνὸν ἐνιαύσιον εἰς πλημμέλειαν
καὶ αἱ ἡμέραι αἱ πρότεραι ἄλογοι
ἔσονται ὅτι ἐμιάνθη κεφαλὴ εὐχῆς
αὐτοῦ

¹³καὶ οὗτος ὁ νόμος τοῦ
εὐξαμένου ᾗ ἂν ἡμέρᾳ πληρώσῃ
ἡμέρας εὐχῆς αὐτοῦ προσοίσει
αὐτὸς παρὰ τὰς θύρας τῆς σκηνῆς
τοῦ μαρτυρίου ¹⁴καὶ προσάξει τὸ
δῶρον αὐτοῦ κυρίῳ ἀμνὸν
ἐνιαύσιον ἄμωμον ἕνα εἰς ὁλοκαύ-
τωσιν καὶ ἀμνάδα ἐνιαυσίαν ἄμωμον μίαν εἰς ἁμαρτίαν καὶ κριὸν
ἕνα ἄμωμον εἰς σωτήριον ¹⁵καὶ
κανοῦν ἀζύμων σεμιδάλεως
ἄρτους ἀναπεποιημένους ἐν ἐλαίῳ
καὶ λάγανα ἄζυμα κεχρισμένα ἐν
ἐλαίῳ καὶ θυσία αὐτῶν καὶ
σπονδὴ αὐτῶν ¹⁶καὶ προσοίσει ὁ
ἱερεὺς ἔναντι κυρίου καὶ ποιήσει
τὸ περὶ ἁμαρτίας αὐτοῦ καὶ τὸ
ὁλοκαύτωμα αὐτοῦ ¹⁷καὶ τὸν κριὸν
ποιήσει θυσίαν σωτηρίου κυρίῳ
ἐπὶ τῷ κανῷ τῶν ἀζύμων καὶ
ποιήσει ὁ ἱερεὺς τὴν θυσίαν αὐτοῦ
καὶ τὴν σπονδὴν αὐτοῦ ¹⁸καὶ
ξυρήσεται ὁ ηὐγμένος παρὰ τὰς
θύρας τῆς σκηνῆς τοῦ μαρτυρίου
τὴν κεφαλὴν τῆς εὐχῆς αὐτοῦ καὶ
ἐπιθήσει τὰς τρίχας ἐπὶ τὸ πῦρ ὅ
ἐστιν ὑπὸ τὴν θυσίαν τοῦ σωτηρίου
¹⁹καὶ λήμψεται ὁ ἱερεὺς τὸν
βραχίονα ἐφθὸν ἀπὸ τοῦ κριοῦ καὶ
ἄρτον ἕνα ἄζυμον ἀπὸ τοῦ κανοῦ
καὶ λάγανον ἄζυμον ἓν καὶ
ἐπιθήσει ἐπὶ τὰς χεῖρας τοῦ
ηὐγμένου μετὰ τὸ ξυρήσασθαι

וְקִדַּשׁ אֶת־רֹאשׁוֹ בַּיּוֹם הַהוּא׃
¹²וְהִזִּיר לַיהֹוָה אֶת־יְמֵי נִזְרוֹ וְהֵבִיא כֶּבֶשׂ
בֶּן־שְׁנָתוֹ לְאָשָׁם וְהַיָּמִים
הָרִאשֹׁנִים יִפְּלוּ כִּי טָמֵא נִזְרוֹ׃

¹³וְזֹאת תּוֹרַת הַנָּזִיר בְּיוֹם מְלֹאת יְמֵי נִזְרוֹ
יָבִיא אֹתוֹ אֶל־פֶּתַח אֹהֶל
מוֹעֵד׃ ¹⁴וְהִקְרִיב אֶת־קָרְבָּנוֹ לַיהֹוָה כֶּבֶשׂ
בֶּן־שְׁנָתוֹ תָמִים אֶחָד לְעֹלָה
וְכַבְשָׂה אַחַת בַּת־שְׁנָתָהּ תְּמִימָה לְחַטָּאת
וְאַיִל־אֶחָד תָּמִים לִשְׁלָמִים׃
¹⁵וְסַל מַצּוֹת סֹלֶת חַלֹּת בְּלוּלֹת בַּשֶּׁמֶן
וּרְקִיקֵי מַצּוֹת מְשֻׁחִים
בַשָּׁמֶן וּמִנְחָתָם וְנִסְכֵּיהֶם׃ ¹⁶וְהִקְרִיב הַכֹּהֵן
לִפְנֵי יְהֹוָה וְעָשָׂה אֶת־חַטָּאתוֹ
וְאֶת־עֹלָתוֹ׃ ¹⁷וְאֶת־הָאַיִל יַעֲשֶׂה זֶבַח שְׁלָמִים
לַיהֹוָה עַל סַל הַמַּצּוֹת
וְעָשָׂה הַכֹּהֵן אֶת־מִנְחָתוֹ וְאֶת־נִסְכּוֹ׃ ¹⁸וְגִלַּח
הַנָּזִיר פֶּתַח אֹהֶל מוֹעֵד
אֶת־רֹאשׁ נִזְרוֹ וְלָקַח אֶת־שְׂעַר רֹאשׁ נִזְרוֹ
וְנָתַן עַל־הָאֵשׁ אֲשֶׁר־תַּחַת זֶבַח
הַשְּׁלָמִים׃ ¹⁹וְלָקַח הַכֹּהֵן אֶת־הַזְּרֹעַ בְּשֵׁלָה
מִן־הָאַיִל וְחַלַּת מַצָּה אַחַת
מִן־הַסַּל וּרְקִיק מַצָּה אֶחָד וְנָתַן עַל־כַּפֵּי
הַנָּזִיר אַחַר הִתְגַּלְּחוֹ אֶת־נִזְרוֹ׃
²⁰וְהֵנִיף אוֹתָם הַכֹּהֵן תְּנוּפָה לִפְנֵי יְהֹוָה
קֹדֶשׁ הוּא לַכֹּהֵן עַל חֲזֵה
הַתְּנוּפָה וְעַל שׁוֹק הַתְּרוּמָה וְאַחַר יִשְׁתֶּה
הַנָּזִיר יָיִן׃ ²¹זֹאת תּוֹרַת הַנָּזִיר
אֲשֶׁר יִדֹּר קָרְבָּנוֹ לַיהֹוָה עַל־נִזְרוֹ מִלְּבַד
אֲשֶׁר־תַּשִּׂיג יָדוֹ כְּפִי נִדְרוֹ
אֲשֶׁר יִדֹּר כֵּן יַעֲשֶׂה עַל תּוֹרַת נִזְרוֹ׃

αὐτὸν **τὴν εὐχὴν αὐτοῦ** [20]**καὶ**
προσοίσει αὐτὰ ὁ ἱερεὺς ἐπίθεμα
ἔναντι κυρίου ἅγιον ἔσται τῷ ἱερεῖ
ἐπὶ τοῦ στηθυνίου τοῦ ἐπιθέματος
καὶ ἐπὶ τοῦ βραχίονος τοῦ
ἀφαιρέματος καὶ μετὰ ταῦτα
πίεται ὁ **ηὐγμένος** οἶνον [21]οὗτος
ὁ νόμος **τοῦ εὐξαμένου** ὃς ἂν
εὔξηται κυρίῳ δῶρον αὐτοῦ κυρίῳ
περὶ **τῆς εὐχῆς** χωρὶς ὧν ἂν εὕρῃ
ἡ χεὶρ αὐτοῦ κατὰ δύναμιν **τῆς
εὐχῆς αὐτοῦ** ἣν ἂν **εὔξηται κατὰ
νόμον ἁγνείας**

There are four locations in the translation where this transformation
of the Nazirite vow into a *special purity* vow is most apparent, namely
vv. 2, 3, 5, and 21. In v. 2, the translator describes the making, or
uttering, of the vow as a "special" act[14] using the Greek adverb
μεγάλως to render the Hebrew hiphil imperfect of פלא, a term meaning in other contexts either "to fulfill" or "to make explicit."[15] In
v. 2, the translator furthermore appears to construe the Hebrew word
נזיר with the Greek ἁγνείαν, a choice that renders the Hebrew phrase
meaning "to vow a vow of a *Nazirite* to separate himself" (לנדר נדר
נזיר להזיר) as "to vow a vow to separate himself as one of *purity*"[16]
(εὔξηται εὐχὴν ἀφαγνίσασθαι ἁγνείαν). Vowing to become a Nazirite
thus appears to be interpreted in v. 2 as an action bringing the
votary into some state of purification. Verses 3, 5, and 21 develop
this notion further. In v. 3 of MT, the law reads that the Nazirite
is merely to separate himself from wine and strong drink (מיין ושכר
יזיר), while the translator of LXX renders the imperfect form of נזר
with ἁγνισθήσεται, producing a version that reads more specifically,

---

[14] J. W. Wevers, *Notes on the Greek Text of Numbers* (SBLSCS 46; Atlanta, Ga.:
Scholars Press, 1998), 94. Wevers states that the translator's use of μεγάλως here
is "unique and unexpected." This may be an overstatement. The meaning of the
Hebrew פלא is debated among scholars (see n. 15 following).

[15] J. Berlinerblau, *The Vow and the "Popular Religious Groups" of Ancient Israel* (JSOTSup
210; Sheffield, Eng.: Sheffield Academic Press, 1996), 177–8. Berlinerblau lists three
major theories regarding the meaning of פלא נדר: (1) to fulfill a vow, (2) to specifically
utter a vow, or (3) פלא is used to describe a vow as being special or set apart. He
opts for meaning (3) in two passages: Lev. 27 and Num. 6.2.

[16] Wevers, 94.

"he shall *purify* himself from wine and strong drink." Likewise in v. 5, where MT states that the Nazirite is forbidden to allow a razor to pass over his head all the days "of the vow of his separation" (נדר נזרו), the translator of LXX renders the phrase impersonally and as an act to be performed all the days "of the vow of *purification*" (τῆς εὐχῆς τοῦ ἁγνισμοῦ). Similarly, once again in v. 21, the law in MT describes the votary's verbal contract as "the law of his separation" (תורת נזרו), and LXX again renders the phrase impersonally, and the vow is described specifically as that which must be performed "according to the law of *purity*" (κατὰ νόμον ἁγνείας).

In addition to the translator's use of ἁγν-, where MT reads נזר in the previous cases, another prominent feature of LXX Num. 6.1–21 which reveals the translator's peculiar interpretation of the vow is the frequent use of forms of εὐχή, "vow," for forms of both the Hebrew נדר, "vow," and נזר, "separation." Three contemporary scholars who have commented on this particular facet of the Num. translation are G. Dorival, J. W. Wevers, and A. Salvesen. Dorival believes that, in light of the frequency of the translator's usage of εὐχή for the rendering of both נדר and נזר, a version of the Hebrew text differing from MT must have been used.[17] This opinion is based on little support, however, and is correctly rejected by both Wevers and Salvesen.[18] Wevers, on the other hand, suggests an alternative, yet equally extreme notion, stating that the Greek version simply exhibits "inadequacies and incompetence" on the part of the translator.[19] The usage of εὐχή for both Hebrew terms is ultimately linguistic oversight in which the translator fails to distinguish the variance in meaning of the words. Salvesen, however, represents a more medial position, stating that the translator's frequent use of εὐχή was neither due to the use of another Hebrew Vorlage nor the result of incompetence on the part of the translator, but rather to the translator's probably thinking that εὐχή was simply a good "catch-all" term for the semantics of נזר used throughout the passage.[20] In my opinion Salvesen is correct for the following reasons.

---

[17] G. Dorival, "Remarques sur L'Originalite du Livré Grec des Nombres," In *VIII Congress of the International Organization for Septuagint and Cognate Studies, Paris 1992* (eds. L. Greenspoon and O. Munnich; SBLSCS 41; Atlanta, Ga.: Scholars Press, 1995), 93.
[18] Wevers, 94, n. 2; see also Salvesen, 94.
[19] Wevers, p. xiii.
[20] Salvesen, 94.

The translator of LXX Num. 6.1–21 ubiquitously renders the Hebrew root נזר with the Greek term εὐχή. In the twenty-four occurrences of forms of נזר in MT, the author of LXX renders the root with a variety of syntactical forms of εὐχή seventeen times. There are places in which נזר is also rendered by other words, most often a form of the root ἁγν- (as discussed previously), yet in such a case as v. 19 where the Hebrew version instructs that following the provision of sacrifices the votary must shave נזרו, "his hair," or "the hair of his consecration," the LXX again renders נזר with εὐχή, translating a peculiarity in the Hebrew with an even greater oddity in Greek: he shall shave τὴν εὐχὴν αὐτοῦ, "his vow." Such a consistent choice in translation, even at the cost of clarity, can only suggest one of two possibilities: (a) either the translator of the Numbers passage was *wholly* ignorant of the meaning of נזר, following Wevers' opinion, or (b) the translator's usage of εὐχή consistently for נזר was quite deliberate, despite their different meanings.

In support of the latter, it may have been the case that the translator assumed ignorance on the part of his readership regarding the religious technical term נזיר.[21] As a result, the translator frequently rendered forms of נזר with forms of the Greek word εὐχή in an effort to consistently translate what was probably unknown to his readers. The specific "vow of the Nazirite" represented in the Hebrew text was thus translated into a "vow of purity." Any ambiguities in the meaning of the Hebrew נזר, "Naziriteship, to separate or consecrate, etc." was smoothed over by a consistent rendering using forms of εὐχή. In addition to the frequency of substituting εὐχή for נזר, two additional features in the translation that support this suggestion are (1) the usage of the word ἁγνεία, "purity," as it appears in vv. 2, 3, 5, 21 (as discussed above), and (2) the absence of the Greek transliteration ναζιρ/ναζιραῖος for the term נזיר. Found in other LXX translations (Judg. 13.5 [Codex B], 7; 16.17 [Codex A]; Lam. 4.7) and other Greek texts of Jewish authorship (I Macc. 3.49; Josephus, *A. J.* 19.294), the transliteration of נזיר into ναζιρ/ναζιραῖος is completely absent in LXX Num. 6.1–21. The translator it seems, based on the Hebrew in MT, had multiple opportunities to utilize such a transliteration given the five occurrences of the Hebrew noun in MT.

---

[21] E. Tov, "Loan-Words, Homophony, and Transliterations in the Septuagint," *Biblica* 60 (1979): 231. I follow Tov in labeling נזיר a "religious technical term."

For the most part, however, he opted instead to translate the term
using the participial form of εὐχή (εὐξάμενος and ηὐγμένος) as simply "one who vows" or "one who has vowed."

On a point-by-point comparative basis, the translation of the LXX
may seem the result of incompetence and confusion on the part of
the translator. Read as a whole, however, and taking the above features into consideration, the translation appears consistent and coherent.

Summary of Evidence

With these features taken into consideration, I suggest what may be
gathered from the LXX translation of Num. 6.1–21 for the purposes
of identifying both the translator's conception of the custom and
readership knowledge (or lack thereof) regarding the rite is as follows: (1) From the translator's perspective, the Nazirite vow was
thought to be a special kind of a vow in comparison with other
vows. (2) The Nazirite vow was also thought to be a vow of purity.
The votary's pledged separation from contact with a corpse, as well
his/her promised abstinence from the consumption of grape produce
and the cutting of the hair, was considered an act bringing one into
a greater state of personal purification. (3) From the perspective of
the LXX readership, on the basis of LXX Num. 6.1–21, Greek-
speaking Jews would have certainly understood the vow in this same
way and may have *only* known the vow in Num. 6.1–21 as the *special purity vow* and not by its designated name in Hebrew, "the vow
of the Nazirite."

1.2.2 *Judges 13.5, 7 (4–7); 16.17 Codex Vaticanus*

> [13.4]"And now be very careful, and drink no wine nor strong drink, nor
> eat anything unclean; [5]for behold, you are with child and you will
> bring forth a son; and a razor shall not pass over his head because
> the child will be a Nazirite of God from the womb; and he will begin
> to deliver Israel out of the hand of the Philistines." [6]And the woman
> went in and spoke to her husband, saying, "A man of God came to
> me, and his appearance was like an angel of God, very fearful; and
> I did not ask him where he was from, and he did not announce to
> me his name. [7]And he said to me, 'Behold, you are with child and
> you will bring forth a son; now drink no wine nor strong drink, nor
> eat anything unclean, because the child will be a holy one of God
> from the womb until the day of his death.' "

[16.17]Then he announced to her everything in his heart, and said to her, "A razor has never crossed over my head, because I am a holy one of God from my mother's womb; if then I should be shaved, my strength will leave me, and I will become weak, and I will be like all other men."

The depiction of Samson in LXX Judges also shows interesting differences from MT. LXX Judg. represents one of the many books, or portions of books, in the Greek Bible that have been transmitted in double literary editions. Reasons for the origin and transmission of duplicate editions are probably varied, but in general they tend to represent either preserved revisions of one version by another or separate revisions of a common Greek text now lost, rather than separate competing translations.[22] In the case of LXX Judg., the two primary MS families representing two very distinct readings have survived: the fifth-century codex Alexandrinus (LXX[A]) and the fourth-century codex Vaticanus (LXX[B]), both of which are printed in parallel fashion in Rahlfs' modern critical edition. Scholars differ in their dating of the two readings. Most recently, Bodine has substantiated Barthélemy's theory that LXX[B] Judg. represents part of an early recension of LXX dating back to the turn of the era, popularly referred to as the καίγε-recension. LXX[A], on the other hand, represents a much later version similar in character to Origen's Hexaplaric recension of the third century AD.[23]

LXX[B] Judges 13.4–7; 16.17	MT Judges 13.4–7; 16.17
[4]καὶ νῦν φύλαξαι δὴ καὶ μὴ πίῃς οἶνον καὶ μέθυσμα καὶ μὴ φάγῃς πᾶν ἀκάθαρτον [5]ὅτι ἰδοὺ σὺ ἐν γαστρὶ ἔχεις καὶ τέξῃ υἱὸν καὶ σίδηρος οὐκ ἀναβήσεται ἐπὶ τὴν	[4]וְעַתָּה הִשָּׁמְרִי נָא וְאַל־תִּשְׁתִּי יַיִן וְשֵׁכָר וְאַל־תֹּאכְלִי כָּל־טָמֵא: [5]כִּי הִנָּךְ הָרָה וְיֹלַדְתְּ בֵּן וּמוֹרָה לֹא־יַעֲלֶה עַל־רֹאשׁוֹ כִּי־נְזִיר אֱלֹהִים יִהְיֶה

---

[22] Marcos, 102–3.

[23] Ibid., 94–6; and W. R. Bodine, *The Greek Text of Judges: Recensional Developments* (HSM 23; Chico, Calif.: Scholars Press, 1980). See his conclusions regarding Barthélemy's theory of the Vaticanus Greek text of Judges and the καιγε-recension, 185–6; see also Bodine, "*Kaige* and Other Recensional Developments in the Greek Text of Judges," *BIOSCS* 13 (1980), 45–57; With respect to the specific reading at hand, 13.7 and 16.17, its early date is evidenced by its use in the Synoptic Gospels (see 2.1–3 following). That LXX[A] represents a later revision of the reading in LXX[B] may be witnessed by the following: (1) its consistent use of the Greek transliteration ναζιραῖος where MT reads נזיר, and (2) its unparalleled use of ἅγιος in 13.5, "the boy will be sanctified a Nazirite (ἡγιασμένον ναζιραῖον) to God."

κεφαλὴν αὐτοῦ ὅτι **ναζιρ** θεοῦ ἔσται
τὸ παιδάριον ἀπὸ τῆς κοιλίας καὶ
αὐτὸς ἄρξεται τοῦ σῶσαι τὸν Ισραηλ
ἐκ χειρὸς Φυλιστιιμ ⁶καὶ εἰσῆλθεν
ἡ γυνὴ καὶ εἶπεν τῷ ἀνδρὶ αὐτῆς
λέγουσα ἄνθρωπος θεοῦ ἦλθεν πρός
με καὶ εἶδος αὐτοῦ ὡς εἶδος ἀγγέλου
θεοῦ φοβερὸν σφόδρα καὶ οὐκ
ἠρώτησα αὐτὸν πόθεν ἐστίν καὶ τὸ
ὄνομα αὐτοῦ οὐκ ἀπήγγειλέν μοι
⁷καὶ εἶπέν μοι ἰδοὺ σὺ ἐν γαστρὶ
ἔχεις καὶ τέξῃ υἱόν καὶ νῦν μὴ πίῃς
οἶνον καὶ μέθυσμα καὶ μὴ φάγῃς πᾶν
ἀκάθαρτον ὅτι **ἅγιον** θεοῦ ἔσται τὸ
παιδάριον ἀπὸ γαστρὸς ἕως ἡμέρας
θανάτου αὐτοῦ

¹⁶·¹⁷καὶ ἀνήγγειλεν αὐτῇ τὴν πᾶσαν
καρδίαν αὐτοῦ καὶ εἶπεν αὐτῇ
σίδηρος οὐκ ἀνέβη ἐπὶ τὴν κεφαλήν
μου ὅτι **ἅγιος** θεοῦ ἐγώ εἰμι ἀπὸ
κοιλίας μητρός μου ἐὰν οὖν
ξυρήσωμαι ἀποστήσεται ἀπ᾽ ἐμοῦ ἡ
ἰσχύς μου καὶ ἀσθενήσω καὶ ἔσομαι
ὡς πάντες οἱ ἄνθρωποι

הַנַּעַר מִן־הַבָּטֶן וְהוּא יָחֵל לְהוֹשִׁיעַ
אֶת־יִשְׂרָאֵל מִיַּד
פְּלִשְׁתִּים׃ ⁶וַתָּבֹא הָאִשָּׁה וַתֹּאמֶר לְאִישָׁהּ
לֵאמֹר אִישׁ
הָאֱלֹהִים בָּא אֵלַי וּמַרְאֵהוּ כְּמַרְאֵה
מַלְאַךְ הָאֱלֹהִים
נוֹרָא מְאֹד וְלֹא שְׁאִלְתִּיהוּ אֵי־מִזֶּה הוּא
וְאֶת־שְׁמוֹ
לֹא־הִגִּיד לִי׃ ⁷וַיֹּאמֶר לִי הִנָּךְ הָרָה
וְיֹלַדְתְּ בֵּן וְעַתָּה
אַל־תִּשְׁתִּי יַיִן וְשֵׁכָר וְאַל־תֹּאכְלִי
כָּל־טֻמְאָה כִּי־**נְזִיר**
אֱלֹהִים יִהְיֶה הַנַּעַר מִן־הַבֶּטֶן עַד־יוֹם
מוֹתוֹ׃

¹⁶·¹⁷וַיַּגֶּד־לָהּ אֶת־כָּל־לִבּוֹ וַיֹּאמֶר לָהּ
מוֹרָה
לֹא־עָלָה עַל־רֹאשִׁי כִּי־**נְזִיר** אֱלֹהִים אֲנִי
מִבֶּטֶן אִמִּי
אִם־גֻּלַּחְתִּי וְסָר מִמֶּנִּי כֹחִי וְחָלִיתִי
וְהָיִיתִי כְּכָל־הָאָדָם׃

LXXᴬ Judges 13.4–7; 16.17

⁴καὶ νῦν φύλαξαι δὴ καὶ μὴ πίῃς οἶνον καὶ σικερα καὶ μὴ φάγῃς πᾶν ἀκάθαρτον ⁵ὅτι ἰδοὺ σὺ ἐν γαστρὶ ἔχεις καὶ τέξῃ υἱόν καὶ οὐκ ἀναβήσεται σίδηρος
ἐπὶ τὴν κεφαλὴν αὐτοῦ ὅτι **ἡγιασμένον ναζιραῖον** ἔσται τωῷ θεῷ τὸ παιδάριον
ἐκ τῆς γαστρός καὶ αὐτὸς ἄρξεται τοῦ σῷζειν τὸν Ισραηλ ἐκ χειρὸς ἀλλοφύλων
⁶καὶ ἦλθεν ἡ γυνὴ καὶ εἶπεν τῷ ἀνδρὶ αὐτῆς λέγουσα ὅτι Ἄνθρωπος τοῦ θεοῦ
ἦλθεν πρός με καὶ ἡ ὅρασις αὐτοῦ ὡς ὅρασις ἀγγέλου τοῦ θεοῦ ἐπιφανὴς
σφόδρα καὶ ἠρώτων πόθεν ἐστίν καὶ τὸ ὄνομα αὐτοῦ οὐκ ἀπήγγειλέν μοι ⁷καὶ
εἶπέν μοι ἰδοὺ σὺ ἐν γαστρὶ ἕξεις καὶ τέξῃ υἱόν καὶ νῦν μὴ πίῃς οἶνον καὶ
σικερα καὶ μὴ φάγῃς φάγῃς ἀκαθαρσίαν ὅτι **ναζιραῖον** θεοῦ ἔσται τὸ παιδάριον
ἀπὸ τῆς γαστρὸς ἕως ἡμέρας θανάτου αὐτοῦ

¹⁶·¹⁷καὶ ἀπήγγειλεν αὐτῇ πάντα τὰ ἀπο καρδίας αὐτοῦ καὶ εἶπεν αὐτῇ Συρὸν
οὐκ ἀναβήσεται ἐπὶ τὴν κεφαλήν μου ὅτι **ναζιραῖος** θεοῦ ἐγώ εἰμι ἐκ κοιλίας
μητρός μου καὶ ἐὰν ξυρήσωμαι ἀποστήσεται ἀπ᾽ ἐμοῦ ἡ ἰσχύς μου καὶ
ἀσθενήσω καὶ ἔσομαι κατὰ πάντας τοὺς ἀνθρώπους

Of the two literary editions, LXXᴮ concerns the study at hand where
it differs from both MT and LXXᴬ in one, albeit highly significant,
respect. Whereas LXXᴬ parallels MT by referring to the figure
Samson as a "Nazirite" in 13.5, 7 and 16.17 using the Greek translit-

eration ναζιραῖος (in correspondence with the Hebrew term נזיר in MT), LXX[B] utilizes a form of the transliteration in 13.5 (ναζιρ), while substituting ἅγιος for נזיר in 13.7 and 16.17. In this manner LXX[B] not only depicts Samson as a Nazirite, but also appears to define what a Nazirite like Samson is—ἅγιος, a "holy person."

Why the version contains these disparities[24] is most likely due to an influence of Num. 6.5, 8, "all the days of his separation he shall be holy."[25] First, the probability that an alternative Hebrew Vorlage other than MT was used is slim, due to the lack of any known Hebrew MS or other version agreeing with the reading of LXX[B] here (although alternative Hebrew versions otherwise unattested are quite possible). Some other factor probably accounts for the uniqueness of the text. Secondly, the only proscription mentioned for Samson in the narrative is the use of a razor. In Num. 6.5, the Nazirite is first described as being "holy to the Lord" in relation to his abstinence from the use of the razor: "All the days of his vow of separation no razor shall come upon his head; until the days are fulfilled which he has sep-arated himself to the Lord he shall be holy (ἅγιος ἔσται—LXX; קדש יהיה —MT), allowing the hair of his head to grow long." Similarly, in v. 8 where the command for the Nazirite to be holy occurs for the second and final time, it is in context of the proscription against contacting a corpse. Verses 9–12 following, however, indicate that the basis of the Nazirite's holiness and reason for abstaining from a corpse is the sanctity of his/her hair; for if a corpse is accidentally contacted it is the hair that must be shaved and consecrated anew

---

[24] I have discussed this issue in slightly more detail in "Samson the 'Holy One': A Suggestion Regarding the Reviser's Use of ἅγιος in Judg. 13,7; 16,17 LXX Vaticanus," appearing in *Biblica* 83 (2002): 97–9.

[25] I should mention here the theories of O. Pretzl and E. Zuckschwerdt regard-ing the reason behind this oddity in translation. Pretzl holds that the disparity is due to the reviser thinking ναζιρ was unintelligible to his audience. In "doublet" fashion, the term is replaced by the well known ἅγιος. Zuckschwerdt, who argues with Pretzl, sees an influence on the reviser of the practice of *Kethib-Qere*, wherein what was written remained written in 13.5 (ναζιρ), but what was normally read out was written down in 13.7 and 16.17 (ἅγιος). Pretzl's hypothesis is the more likely of the two. It is doubtful that the practice of the Masoretes was active at the time this version was composed. Further, if there was such a *Kethib-Qere* rendering for נזיר it certainly fell out of use, for there is no trace of it where one might expect to find it, namely in either the Mesorah or the rabbinic Targumim. See Pretzl, "Septuagintaprobleme im Buch der Richter," *Biblica* 7 (1926): 374–5; and E. Zuckschwerdt, "Nazoraios in Matth. 2,23," *TZ* 31 (1975): 71–7.

(ἁγιάσει—LXX; קדשׁ—MT) along with the avowed number of days. These passages seem too contextually similar with the texts at hand to be coincidental, and, in my opinion, give reason for the translator's equating the two terms: קדשׁ in Num. 6.5, 8 and נזיר in Judg. 13.5, 7; 16.17. The translator simply followed the association between the two terms already present in Num. 6.5, 8 and used them interchangeably in his Greek version (ναζιρ in Judg. 13.5 and ἅγιος in Judg. 13.7 and 16.17), probably as a means of introducing the technical, and for his readers likely non-intelligible, term.[26]

Interestingly, such an association between ναζιρ and ἅγιος in the case of Samson is certainly mitigated by the general narrative context of Judg. 13–16. Samson is far from holy in the priest-like sense. He partakes in a drinking bout (14.10), has questionable relationships with women (14.2; 16.1), eats honey taken from the carcass of a lion (14.8–9), slays over a thousand men (14.19; 15.15), and ultimately discloses the secret source of his power to a Philistine harlot resulting in his downfall (16.4–31). Such disparities, however, important as they are to the modern source critic in precluding any formal association between the original Judg. 13–16 and the Nazirite vow in the Priestly source of Num. 6.1–21, seem to have been relatively inconsequential to our translator, who as demonstrated previously, seems to have a textual conflation of the two sources in mind.

Summary of Evidence

For the purposes of the present study, a single, though significant, piece of evidence regarding Nazirites may be drawn from LXX[B] Judg. Based on the association between the terms "Nazirite" and "holy one" in the LXX narrative, the translator of the passage, and certainly those familiar with his Greek version of the story, would have regarded Nazirites primarily as holy individuals.

---

[26] I believe there is further evidence that the reviser worked with LXX Num. 6.1–21 before him. Although lexically, in reference to Samson's abstinence from a razor, our translator uses σίδηρος (razor) and ἀναβήσεται (pass over) in 13.5; 16.17 rather than ξυρός (razor) and ἐπελεύσεται (pass over) as in LXX Num. 6.5, and although he uses μέθυσμα rather than the more familiar σικερα for "strong drink" in 13.4, 7, via doublet he does introduce σικερα in 13.14 by the odd rendering σικερα μέθυσμα; see Pretzl, 374.

1.2.3 *I Samuel 1.11, 21*

[11]And she vowed a vow to the Lord, saying, "Adonai, Lord God of Hosts, if you will indeed look upon the humiliation of your maidservant and remember me and give to your maidservant a male child, then I will dedicate him to you as a gift before you until the day of his death; and he shall drink no wine nor strong drink, and no razor shall come upon his head."

[21]And the man Helkana went up with his entire household to offer the yearly sacrifice in Salem along with his vows and all the tithes of his land.

LXX I Samuel 1.11, 21

[11]καὶ ηὔξατο εὐχὴν κυρίῳ λέγουσα Αδωναι κύριε ελωαι σαβαωθ ἐὰν ἐπιβλέπων ἐπιβλέψῃς ἐπὶ τὴν ταπείνωσιν τῆς δούλης σου καὶ μνησθῇς μου καὶ δῷς τῇ δούλῃ σου σπέρμα ἀνδρῶν καὶ δώσω αὐτὸν ἐνώπιόν σου **δοτὸν** ἕως ἡμέρας θανάτου αὐτοῦ καὶ **οἶνον καὶ μέθυσμα οὐ πίεται** καὶ σίδηρος οὐκ ἀναβήσεται ἐπὶ τὴν κεφαλὴν αὐτοῦ

[21]καὶ ἀνέβη ο ἄνθρωπος Ελκανα καὶ πᾶς ὁ οἶκος αὐτοῦ θῦσαι ἐν Σηλωμ τὴν θυσίαν τῶν ἡμερῶν καὶ τὰς εὐχὰς αὐτοῦ **καὶ πάσας τὰς δεκάτας τῆς γῆς αὐτου**

MT I Samuel 1.11, 21

[11]וַתִּדֹּר נֶדֶר וַתֹּאמַר יְהוָה צְבָאוֹת אִם־רָאֹה תִרְאֶה בָּעֳנִי אֲמָתֶךָ וּזְכַרְתַּנִי וְלֹא־תִשְׁכַּח אֶת־אֲמָתֶךָ וְנָתַתָּה לַאֲמָתְךָ זֶרַע אֲנָשִׁים וּנְתַתִּיו לַיהוָה כָּל־יְמֵי חַיָּיו וּמוֹרָה לֹא־יַעֲלֶה עַל־רֹאשׁוֹ׃

[21]וַיַּעַל הָאִישׁ אֶלְקָנָה וְכָל־בֵּיתוֹ לִזְבֹּחַ לַיהוָה אֶת־זֶבַח הַיָּמִים וְאֶת־נִדְרוֹ׃

In the LXX version of the birth and dedication of Samuel, the vow of Hannah in I Sam. 1.11 is more reminiscent of a Nazirite vow than it is in MT. In addition, v. 21 appears to associate Elkanah's annual pilgrimage to Shilo with the annual giving of first-fruits, an association not entirely clear in MT.

LXX I Sam. 1.11 contains a phrase altogether absent in MT, namely the promise by Hannah that her male child, if she is granted one by the Lord, will abstain from wine and strong drink (οἶνον καὶ μέθυσμα οὐ πίεται). Together with the avowed proscription on the child's use of a razor, paralleled in MT, Hannah's vow undoubtedly reflects the regulations for the Nazirite as given in Num. 6.2–5. There appears to be no direct dependence upon LXX Num., however, for the translator uses μέθυσμα rather than σικερα, and σίδηρος οὐκ ἀναβήσεται rather than ξυρὸν οὐκ ἐπελεύσεται in similar fashion as LXX[B] Judg. 13.4–5, 7. In terms of linguistic influence, the portrayal of Samson in LXX[B] Judg. may be the more influential of the two texts here, but that Num. 6.1–21 lay before our translator is plausible.

Though less ambiguous than MT in its portrayal of Samuel as a Nazirite, like MT, the passage is marked by the absence of the religious technical term *nazir* (ναζιρ/ναζιραῖος). Moreover, such a term is never used of Samuel in the LXX. It is possible, as suggested by Ulrich, that "one given" (δοτος), a hapax in LXX, is a translation of נזיר based perhaps on the Vorlage of 4QSam[a], but this is speculative (see 1.1, discussed previously).[27] If our translator was familiar with LXX[B] Judg., as suggested above, it is doubtful that the transliteration ναζιρ (present in 13.5) would have been overlooked, and therefore, why the translator opted to either ignore the transliteration on the one hand, or translate the Hebrew term (if his Vorlage contained it) using δοτος on the other hand, is unclear.

The variants between LXX and MT again raise the question of Vorlage. Pisano holds that MT lies behind LXX I Sam. 1.11 and that LXX represents part of the gradual "naziritization" of Samuel, as evident in other texts within this period.[28] McCarter, as with Ulrich and Cross, on the other hand, sees 4QSam[a] as the reading behind LXX rather than MT.[29] It must be conceded that it is more difficult to see the primary variant discussed here as a case of omission on the part of MT than it is an addition for clarification's sake on the part of LXX and 4QSam[a]. However, the evidence for a dependence on 4QSam[a] by LXX I Sam. is strong and, as suggested by Tsevat, the variant reading in MT is likely due to MT's dependence on a reading prevalent among an alternate Hebrew MS family than it is the reflection of a scribal error or purposeful omission.[30]

In LXX I Sam. 1.21, again in contradistinction to MT, Elkanah's

---

[27] Ulrich, 165. Ulrich does note, however, that the use of δοτος here is "ambiguous."

[28] Pisano, 21–2.

[29] McCarter, 53–4; Cross's original thesis that 4QSam[a] is the Vorlage of LXX, presented in "A New Qumran Biblical Fragment Related to the Original Hebrew Underlying the Septuagint," *BASOR* 132 (1953): 15–26, is substantiated by the work of Ulrich in *The Qumran Text of Samuel and Josephus*.

[30] M. Tsevat, "Was Samuel a Nazirite?" in *Sha'arei Talmon: Studies in the Bible, Qumran, and the Ancient Near East Presented to Shemaryahu Talmon* (eds. M. Fishbane and E. Tov; Winona Lake, Ind.: Eisenbrauns, 1992), 201–2.

offering in Shilo includes not only the "sacrifice of days" (זבח הימים—MT; θυσίας τῶν ἡμερῶν—LXX) and the payment of his vows, but also the offering of "all the tenths of his land" (πάσας τὰς δεκάτας τῆς γῆς αὐτοῦ),[31] an offering omitted in MT, but present in Josephus' version of the story (see 1.6.3, to follow). The tenths of the land may be an allusion to the annual giving of first-fruits, and LXX may be identifying Elkanah's annual pilgrim trek with the yearly festival in which produce of the land was given in support of the priest-hood. If this is the case, then the birth narrative of I Sam. as we have it in the LXX associates Hannah's dedication of Samuel (a dedication which takes place during the annual pilgrimage to Shilo in vv. 24–8) with the giving of yearly first-fruits, Samuel perhaps symbolically being Hannah's own first-fruit offering.

Summary of Evidence

Based on the similarities in lexicography between the text at hand and LXX[B] Judg. 13.7, together with the similarity in proscriptive behavior as that required of a Nazirite in Num. 6.2–5, I believe what can be gained from LXX I Sam. 1.11 is evidence that (1) the translator clearly thought of Samuel as a Nazirite in the likeness of Samson. (2) Moreover, because of the proscription on wine and strong drink in Hannah's vow, the translator and those familiar with his version would have associated the proscriptions for the Nazirite vow (or *the special purity vow*) in Num. 6.1–21 with Samuel, an association altogether ambiguous in MT. (3) Lastly, it is possible that LXX I Sam. 1.21 identifies Elkanah's annual pilgrimage with the annual giving of first-fruits. If so, then those familiar with this rendition of the story may have associated Samuel's dedication with the annual pilgrim dedication of first-fruits, Samuel, perhaps, being understood symbolically as Hannah's own first-fruit offering.

1.2.4 *Amos 2.11–2*

[11]"And I took some of your sons for prophets and some of your young men for a consecration. Are these things not so, oh sons of Israel," says the Lord. [12]"But you made those who were consecrated drink wine, and you commanded the prophets saying, 'Do not prophesy!' "

---

[31] MSS pr and x read γενηματων, "of the fruits of the earth."

LXX Amos 2.11–2

¹¹καὶ ἔλαβον ἐκ τῶν υἱῶν ὑμῶν εἰς προφήτας καὶ ἐκ τῶν νεανίσκων ὑμῶν **εἰς ἁγιασμόν** μὴ οὐκ ἔστιν ταῦτα υἱοὶ Ισραηλ λέγει κύριος ¹²καὶ ἐποτίζετε **τοὺς ἡγιασμένους** οἶνον καὶ τοῖς προφήταις ἐνετέλλεσθε λέγοντες οὐ μὴ προφητεύσητε

MT Amos 2.11–2

¹¹וָאָקִים מִבְּנֵיכֶם לִנְבִיאִים וּמִבַּחוּרֵיכֶם לִנְזִרִים הַאַף אֵין־זֹאת בְּנֵי יִשְׂרָאֵל נְאֻם־יְהוָה׃ ¹²וַתַּשְׁקוּ **אֶת־הַנְּזִרִים** יַיִן וְעַל־הַנְּבִיאִים צִוִּיתֶם לֵאמֹר לֹא תִּנָּבְאוּ׃

In LXX Amos 2.11–2 "Nazirites" (נזרים—MT), those whom God selected from among Israel's young men in the likeness of the prophets, and whom Israel in its contempt of Yahweh forced to drink wine, are represented as "those who were consecrated" (ἡγιασμένοι). Like LXX Num. 6.1–21 and LXX^B Judg. 13.7; 16.17, נזיר is translated rather than transliterated, and the choice of rendering is similar to LXX^B Judg. (where נזיר is introduced initially as ναζιρ, but then subsequently translated ἅγιος, "holy one"). It is interesting that, as in Judg. 13.5, 7, the religious technical term occurs twice in close succession, yet unlike LXX^B Judg., the translator has chosen not to introduce a transliteration. Rather, נזיר is consistently rendered using forms of the Greek ἁγιασμός.

In v. 11 εἰς ἁγιασμον, "for a consecration," is used for the Hebrew לנזרים, "to be Nazirites." The very literal choice of εἰς for ל is offset by the odd use of the accusative singular ἁγιασμόν for the plural נזרים (cf. the use of the accusative plural προφήτας for נביאים in the preceding clause). Verse 12 follows by rendering נזרים a second time with the accusative perfect passive participle, ἡγιασμένους, "those who were consecrated."

Summary of Evidence

LXX Amos 2.11–2 provides additional evidence that Nazirites (נזרים) were perceived principally as those who were holy, the use of ἁγιασμός being a slight nuance of the holiness theme witnessed in LXX^B Judg. 13.7; 16.17. Here, at least the translator may have understood Nazirites as individuals who sanctify, consecrate, or religiously dedicate themselves, a primary aspect of which included abstaining from wine as a manner of lifestyle.

1.2.5 Lamentations 4.7–8

⁷Her Nazirites were made purer than snow, they were whiter than milk, they were purified as with fire, their polishing was superior to

sapphire stone. [8]Their countenance became blacker than soot; they became unknown in the streets; their skin has cleaved to their bones; they became withered, they became as wood.

LXX Lamentations 4.7–8

[7]ἐκαθαριώθησαν **ναζιραῖοι** αὐτῆς ὑπὲρ χιόνα ἔλαμθαν ὑπὲρ γάλα ἐπυρρώθησαν ὑπὲρ λίθους σαπφείρου τὸ ἀπόσπασμα αὐτῶν [8]ἐσκότασεν ὑπὲρ ἀσβόλην τὸ εἶδος αὐτῶν οὐκ ἐπεγνώσθησαν ἐν ταῖς ἐξόδοις ἐπάγη δέρμα αὐτῶν ἐπὶ τὰ ὀστέα αὐτῶν ἐξηράνθησαν ἐγενήθησαν ὥσπερ ξύλον

MT Lamentations 4.7–8

[7]זַכּוּ נְזִירֶיהָ מִשֶּׁלֶג צַחוּ מֵחָלָב אָדְמוּ עֶצֶם מִפְּנִינִים סַפִּיר גִּזְרָתָם: ס [8]חָשַׁךְ מִשְּׁחוֹר תָּאֳרָם לֹא נִכְּרוּ בַּחוּצוֹת צָפַד עוֹרָם עַל־עַצְמָם יָבֵשׁ הָיָה כָעֵץ: ס

Set within the context of a poetic lamentation over the destruction of Jerusalem by Nebuchadnezzar's army (ca. 586 BC), the author of Lamentations (traditionally identified as the prophet Jeremiah), in synonymous parallel fashion, describes the slaughter of the city's anointed ones (נזיריה—MT) by contrasting the state of their physical appearance before and after the tumultuous event. Whereas the precise meaning of נזיריה in Lam. 4.7 (MT) is unclear (her anointed ones/her Nazirites?), LXX translates the Hebrew construct using the transliteration ναζιραῖοι plus αὐτης. For the translator of LXX Lam. then, the text undoubtedly refers to Nazirites.

In general v. 7, "purer than snow" (זכו משלג—MT; Ἐκαθαριώθησαν ὑπὲρ χιόνα—LXX) and "whiter then milk" (צחו חלב—MT; ἔλαμψαν ὑπὲρ γάλα—LXX), tend to convey notions of purity. The following depictions of the Nazirites in v. 7, together with the contrasting descriptions in v. 8, tend to follow suit. Such an emphasis on purity of physicality seems to convey in poetic fashion the author's perceptions of the inner qualities of the persons (as a contradistinction to their corporeal demise).

Summary of Evidence

Given that the translator understood his Hebrew Vorlage as a reference to Nazirites, LXX Lam. 4.7–8 seems to suggest that others familiar with this reading (as with LXX Num. 6.1–21) may have regarded Nazirites as being concerned with maintaining some manner of personal purification.

1.3 *Ben Sira*

In the Hebrew version of Ben Sira, Samuel is directly referred to as a נזיר and this appears to support the notion, much like 4QSam[a] and LXX I Sam. 1.11, that Samuel was regarded as a Nazirite in this period. Unfortunately, the Hebrew phraseology in the context in which the term is found makes this less clear than some suggest.[32]

Between 1896 and the 1960's, scholars discovered what might possibly be fragments of the original Hebrew version of Sirach, or Ben Sira as it is known in Hebrew. Four Hebrew manuscripts discovered in a Cairo Genizah in 1896 (A–D) were augmented by the discovery of an additional manuscript in 1931 (E), and further fragments in the 1960's found among the Dead Sea Scrolls (2Q18 and 11QPs[a]) and at Masada (26 leather fragments). A sixth manuscript from the genizah in Cairo (F) was published in 1982.[33] In total, the manuscripts comprise roughly 68 percent of the complete text and represent, in some instances, the oldest manuscripts of the book available.[34]

Scholarly assessments of the Hebrew manuscripts vary. Some have proposed that they represent retro-versions, or re-translations of a Greek or possibly Syriac version back into Hebrew; however, this view lacks support among most scholars.[35] Some, on the other hand, have suggested that the Hebrew manuscripts, though containing variances and a variety of Hebrew forms, represent in part the original reading translated by Ben Sira's grandson in 132 BC.[36]

Ben Sira 46.13

Beloved by the people and pleasing to his Creator was he who was dedicated from his mother's womb [ה מ ש ו א ל מ ב ט ן א מ ו], a nazirite [sic] of Yahweh in the prophetic function [נ ז י ר י י כ ב ו א ה], Samuel judge and priest; by the word of Yahweh he instituted the kingdom.[37]

---

[32] See n. 39, p. 41.

[33] R. J. Coggins, *Sirach* (Guides to Apocrypha and Pseudepigrapha; Sheffield, Eng.: Sheffield Academic Press, 1998), 34–5; and P. C. Beentjes, *The Book of Ben Sira in Hebrew: A Text Edition of All Extant Hebrew Manuscripts and a Synopsis of All Parallel Hebrew Ben Sira Texts* (VTSup 68; Leiden: Brill, 1997), 1–6.

[34] Coggins, 35.

[35] L. Hartman, "Sirach in Hebrew and in Greek," *CBQ* 23 (1961): 445.

[36] For a succinct treatment on the debates regarding the value of the Hebrew manuscript finds see E. Schürer, *HJPAJC* (rev. ed.; eds. F. Millar et al.; vol. 3.1; Edinburgh: T&T Clark, 1986), 203–5.

[37] NJB.

Although the text of Ben Sira 46.13 describes Samuel as נזיר יי (נזיר is present in the Syriac, יי is absent),[38] it is not entirely clear whether נזיר is intended in the religious technical sense, i.e. Nazirite, or the more generic "one consecrated," viz. Samuel's role as prophet. In light of the subsequent prepositional phrase בנבואה, "in/with prophecy," the latter may be the intended meaning. However, the technical, rather than more generic use of the term seems more tenable.[39]

First, there are a number of features that do make the generic use of the term at least plausible. Regarding the reference's wider context, 46.13 lies within a panegyric on biblical heroes (44–50) of whom many are said to be prophets (cf. 46.1 where the same phrase בנבואה is used of Joshua). In keeping with Ben Sira's general interest, therefore, rather than portraying Samuel as a Nazirite, Samuel may be delineated simply as one consecrated via the prophetic office, "Der Jahwe Geweihte im Prophetenamt."[40] Moreover, the earliest external witness supporting the generic reading of נזיר is the text's earliest known interpreter, Ben Sira's grandson. Among the best available Greek MSS of Sirach, none refer to Samuel as a Nazirite, but only a prophet of the Lord (προφήτης κυρίου).

In support of the religious technical rendering, however, within the preceding clause, Samuel is referred to as "he who was dedicated from his mother's womb" (המשואל מבטן אמו), and this is doubtless a reference to Hannah's vow in I Sam. 1.11. This may be an indirect reference to Samuel's Nazirite status; however, as suggested in discussion of testimony 1.2.3, Naziriteship expressed in Hannah's vow is less clear in some biblical MSS than in others, and a definitive MS affiliation with the text at hand is beyond certainty (could it be 4QSamᵃ?). Furthermore, the use of המשואל might possibly represent a play-on-words (שמואל—משואל) reflecting Hannah's repetitive use of

---

[38] Tsevat, 200; see also D. Barthélemy and D. Rickenbacher, *Konkordanz zum hebräischen Sirach: mit syrisch-hebräischem Index* (Göttingen: Vanderhoeck & Ruprecht, 1973), 257.

[39] Pisano holds that this represents the only biblical text that refers to Samuel as a Nazirite (נזיר), 21; Skehan also believes this is a reference to Samuel as a Nazirite proper, *The Wisdom of Ben Sira: A New Translation with Notes* (AB 39; Garden City, N.Y.: Doubleday, 1987), 518 (see also his translation omitting the term, however, on p. 516); see also N. Peters who holds that the term is inspired by I Sam. 1.11, *Das Buch Jesus Sirach oder Ecclesiasticus* (EHAT 25; Münster in Westf: Aschendorff Verlagsbuchhandlung, 1913), 398; cf. Tsevat, 199–200, and Barthélemy and Rickenbacher, "נבואה," 248, on the other hand, who maintain that the reference is unclear.

[40] Peters, 396.

שָׁאַל in I Sam. 1.28 (e.g., הוּא שָׁאוּל לַיהוה, "he is one dedicated to
the Lord"—MT). A more certain appeal may be made to the passage's wider context. Though other figures are described as prophets,
including Joshua with whom, as stated previously, the very phrase
בנבואה is used, only in reference to Samuel does the term נזיר appear.
This hapax seems to indicate more than a mere accentuation of the
sanctifying function of the prophetic office. Furthermore, it was shown
in discussion of testimonies 1.1 and 1.2.3 that Samuel was regarded
as a Nazirite by two other sources in this period. Taking these factors
into consideration, there is good reason to believe that Ben Sira is
indeed portraying Samuel as a Nazirite proper *in addition* to his role
as prophet. In response to the witness of the Greek translation, it
may have been the case that Ben Sira's grandson either misunderstood
the Hebrew phraseology, or perhaps even disagreed with his grand-
father's depiction of the biblical figure. Disagreement over the Nazirite
status of Samuel is evidenced in the Mishnah.[41]

Summary of Evidence

Taking the above points into consideration, I believe Ben Sira's reference to Samuel as a נזיר is more likely a reference to Samuel's
status as a Nazirite proper than it is a generic reference to his "consecration" via the prophetic office. For Jewish thought on the Nazirite
status of Samuel in this period then, Ben Sira provides further evidence that some regarded Samuel as a Nazirite of the Lord.

1.4   *I Maccabees*

One significant reference appears in the historical narrative of I
Maccabees. I Maccabees was copied and transmitted in Greek by
Christians along with the Septuagint, although an original Hebrew
or Aramaic version was known possibly as late as the third century
AD.[42] The original work is likely dated to the last quarter of the

---

[41] *m. Naz.* 9.5.
[42] Eusebius cites the name of the Semitic version known to Origen (ca. AD
185–232) as Σαρβὴθ Σαβαναιέλ in *Hist. eccl.* 6.25.2; Jerome also states that the work
was originally written in Hebrew, *Prol. galeatus* 28. Col. 593ff.; Scholars have debated
the precise meaning of the name and whether or not it signifies that the work was
originally composed in Hebrew or Aramaic. Based on internal linguistic grounds,

second century BC[43] and covers the history of the Maccabaean revolt against the Seleucids of Syria from 165–135/4 BC.

I Maccabees 3.49 (46–53)

[46]Then they gathered together and went to Mizpah, opposite Jerusalem, because Israel formerly had a place of prayer in Mizpah. [47]They fasted that day, put on sackcloth and sprinkled ashes on their heads, and tore their clothes. [48]And they opened the book of the law to inquire into those matters about which the Gentiles consulted the likeness of their gods. [49]They also brought the vestments of the priesthood and the first fruits and the tithes, and they stirred up the nazirites [sic] who had completed their days [ἤγειραν τοὺς ναζιραίους, οἳ ἐπλήρωσαν τὰς ἡμέρας]; [50]and they cried aloud to Heaven, saying, "What shall we do with these? Where shall we take them? [51]Your sanctuary is trampled down and profaned, and your priests mourn in humiliation. [52]Here the gentiles are assembled against us to destroy us; you know what they plot against us. [53]How will we be able to withstand them, if you do not help us?"[44]

The reference to Nazirites in I Maccabees 3.49 appears in a context in which the author is describing the preparatory activities of Jewish revolutionaries soon to face the forces of Antiochus IV at the battle of Emmaus in 165 BC. Seeking to liberate the Jerusalem temple from Gentile occupation, the author records that a group of zealots, led by Judas Hasmonaeus (Maccabee), assembled a collection of sacred items connected with the temple. Among those items were supposedly a number of "Nazirites who had completed their days." The author's primary interest is in the offerings of these Nazirites, as it is the offerings in this context that formed the primary significance of the vows. Based on his tacit assumptions about these figures, however, at least two additional features may be evidenced from his

---

however, no one denies that the Greek text of I Macc. represents at least a translation of either an Aramaic or Hebrew version.

[43] The date cannot be later than the beginning of the Roman period (63 BC) since the author only knows the Romans as allies and friends. The narrative concludes with a reference to a source containing a narrative of the reign of John Hyrcanus (I Macc. 16.23–4), and so the work may have originated toward the end of Hyrcanus' reign (ca. 104 BC); cf. Schürer who dates it to as late as the first decades of the first century BC, p. 181; cf. also S. Schwartz, who dates it to as early as the 130's BC in "Israel and the Nations Roundabout: I Maccabees and the Hasmonean Expansion," *JJS* 42 (1995): 16–38.

[44] NRSV.

narrative; namely, those whom he describes as Nazirites have taken only temporary vows in the likeness of the vow legislated for in Num. 6.1–21; and secondly, making the Nazirite vow was a known activity at the time I Macc. was composed.

First, in terms of the details of the author's description, it is implicit he is describing Nazirites who made temporary vows, like the vow of Num. 6.1–21. This is evidenced by the relative clause, "who had completed their days" (οἳ ἐπλήρωσαν τὰς ἡμέρας).[45] Based on the information in the passage and the legislation of Num. 6.1–21, "completed their days" can only refer to the end of an avowed period.[46] Consequently, this phrase is also an indirect reference, again when compared to the Num. 6.1–21 legislation, to the point at which sacrificial dues were required.[47] Examined from within the passage's context, it was the intended offering of these sacrifices that contributed to the sacred collection at Mizpah.

The narrative also seems to convey the notion that for the author it was the intended sacrifices, at least in this peculiar context, which formed the most important aspect of the temporary Nazirite vow, rather than the consecrated state of the individuals.[48] Like the vestments of the priesthood, the first-fruits, and tithes, the sacrifices of Nazirites were the elements powerfully catalytic in eliciting God's attention and intervention in a time of distress. This appears to be the overall function of the Nazirites within the narrative as evidenced by the idea that they were "stirred up" (ἤγειραν) by the leaders in an effort to add their offerings to the collected goods.[49] Indicated by the prayer of supplication in lines 50–3, the sacerdotal objects collectively formed

---

[45] Gray, "The Nazirite," 203.

[46] Num. 6.13–21.

[47] Ibid.; J. N. Epstein, "נזירות ללשון" in *Magnes Anniversary Book* (eds. F. I. Baer et al.; Jerusalem: Hebrew University Press, 1938), 15–6. Epstein makes a reference to Cod. 55 of I Macc., which in v. 49 has ἔκειραν, "shaved," in place of ἤγειραν, "stirred up." He states that the verb is a translation of the Hebrew לנלה, an idiom found in later rabbinic sources that refers to the sacrificial offerings of a Nazirite (cf. my discussions of testimony 1.6.5 and 1.8.4 following).

[48] Cf. Gray, 208.

[49] Rather than portraying a state of accidental helplessness, I believe the calamity described in the narrative is less accidental and more manufactured on the part of the Hasmonaeans, as indicated partially by the verb ἤγειραν, "stirred up," in reference to the Nazirites; cf. J. A. Goldstein, *I Maccabees: A New Translation, with Introduction and Commentary* (AB 41; Garden City, N.Y.: Doubleday, 1976), 262.

a means of barter to elicit God's succor, and the Nazirites, with their multiplicity of sacrificial goods to offer, formed an integral part of that collection. For unless God aided them in the ensuing battle and delivered the temple into Jewish hands, the Nazirite sacrifices would have no place to be offered and God, as a result, would lose what was rightfully his.

The notion that the sacrifices formed the primary focus of the author is also supported by the very narrative upon which I Macc. 3.46ff. is modeled. In I Macc. 3.46 the author states that Judas and followers gathered at Mizpah because "Israel formerly had a place of prayer in Mizpah." This is a literary allusion to I Sam. 7.5–14, a narrative recalling the deliverance of Israel from the hands of the Philistines: a deliverance that began when the prophet Samuel gathered Israel together at Mizpah for prayer and supplication. According to the author of I Sam., the Israelites drew water, poured it out before the Lord, fasted and prayed (I Sam. 7.6), and then Samuel offered up a sacrifice to the Lord (I Sam. 7–9) to which God responded with a great thunder that confused the Philistine army. At the sign of their stumbling enemies, Israel then pursued them, striking them down on the battlefield (I Sam. 7.10–1). The details of the narrative are amazingly similar to the events described in I Macc. 3.46ff., even to the extent that the Judaean rebels blow trumpets and bellow a loud shout (I Macc. 3.54) in the likeness of God's thunder in I Sam. 7.10. Just as sacrifice gained God's attention in I Sam., so it seems the sacrifices of Nazirites, in addition to the other items mentioned, were efficacious to secure God's help in delivering Israel from the advance of their oppressors.

If one compares this conception of the role of Nazirites in I Macc. 3.49 to their role as (possibly) revealed in the book of Judg. in the Hebrew Bible, I Macc. provides an ironic twist to the history of Nazirite behavior, particularly in relation to the field of battle. Whereas the consecrated state of the warrior Samson was directly relevant to his ability to inflict God-inspired casualties on the enemies of Israel, here in I Macc. it is the sacrifices offered by Nazirites that attain divine succor. Like Samson, Nazirites in the Maccabaean era aided Israel in battle, however, in an entirely different manner: not with their *selves* but with their various gifts.

In addition to describing Nazirites of the temporary type, a second implicit feature about Nazirites revealed in I Macc. is that the

author assumes they were a recognizable phenomenon at the time
I Macc. was composed.[50] The very fact that Nazirites are mentioned
in the plural, together with the author reckoning they were able to
form a significant contribution to the gathering of holy items, indicates that Nazirite vow-making may have been common. By his tacit
assumptions, the author reveals that Nazirites were common at least
to the degree that they *could* have appeared in large numbers and
on a singular occasion.

Summary of Evidence

I Maccabees 3.49 reveals at least three things about Nazirites. First,
for the author and in this particular context, it was the sacrifices
offered at the end of an avowed period that formed the most significant
feature of the Nazirite vow, as they, rather than the consecrated
state of the individual, were the elements able to attract God's attention in a time of national distress. Secondly, because of this emphasis on sacrificial goods, I Macc. 3.49 is evidence for the existence of
Nazirites in the likeness of Num. 6.1–21. Thirdly, the narrative suggests that making the Nazirite vow was a known, and perhaps common, practice in the Maccabaean period.

1.5   *Philo*

There are four passages in the works of Philo of direct relevance to
the topic at hand. Philo, writing in Alexandria, Egypt in the early
first century AD,[51] is generally interested in the vow of the Nazirite,
called by him "the Great Vow," and has a peculiar preoccupation
with the biblical law of Num. 6.9; namely, the legislation introducing procedures for a Nazirite who has accidentally become impure
because of nearness to a corpse. Due to its largely irrelevant philo-
sophic jargon, much of Philo's commentary on the Great Vow is of
little interest to the present study. I treat here only those references
that I believe are most beneficial to the discussion at hand.

---

[50] Salmanowitsch, "Die Stelle lehrt, dass das Naziräats damals im Volke verbrei-
tet war," 18.
[51] For the biographical details on Philo of Alexandria see E. R. Goodenough, *An
Introduction to Philo Judaeus* (2nd ed.; Oxford: Basil Blackwell, 1962), 2–3; and J. Morris,
"The Jewish Philosopher Philo," in Schürer, vol. 3.2, p. 815, n. 14; see also the
"General Introduction" by F. H. Colson and G. A. Whitaker in *Philo*, vol. 1, p. ix.

It is Philo's commentaries on biblical law and a few of his various philosophical treatises that are of particular interest. Critically, Philo's interest in biblical legislation is bookish, and his preoccupation with extracting Platonic and Stoic philosophical meaning out of the biblical text is evidence in itself that much of his opinion reflects personal contemplation rather than the sphere of thoughts and beliefs commonly held among Jews. On occasion, however, Philo does appear to make recourse to actual known facts about Nazirites, as well as to the general practice of making vows. For information, therefore, regarding the Nazirate, and how those who took part in it may have behaved in this period, Philo's commentary should be taken seriously.

1.5.1 *De specialibus legibus 1.247–54*

[247]After laying down these ordinances about each particular kind of sacrifice, whole-burnt-offering [ὁλοκαύτου], preservation-offering [σωτηρίου] and sin-offering [ἁμαρτίας], he institutes rules for another which partakes of the three, to shew [sic] the friendship [φίλας] and kinship [συγγενεῖς] which exists between them. This connecting link between them is called the Great Vow [εὐχὴ μεγάλη]. [248]I must explain why it has acquired this name. When people have paid first-fruits of every part of their property, in wheat, barley, oil, wine and their finest orchard-fruits and also in the first-born males of their livestock, consecrated in the case of the clean species and valued at an adequate compensation in the case of the unclean, as they have no more material resources with which to give a pledge of their piety [εὐσέβειαν], they dedicate and consecrate themselves [αὐτοὺς ἀνατιθέασι καὶ καθιεροῦσιν], thus shewing [sic] an amazing sanctification [ἄλεκτον ὁσιότητα] and a surpassing devotion to God [ὑπερβολήν τινα γνώμης φιλοθέου]. And therefore it is fitly called the Great Vow, for his own self is the greatest possession which anyone has, and this self he foregoes and puts himself outside it. [249]When he has made the vow, the lawgiver gives him the following instructions. First, he must not take any strong drink nor anything "which he makes from the grape" nor drink any other intoxicant to overthrow his reason [ἐπὶ καθαιρέσει λογισμοῦ], but hold himself to be serving as priest during that time [νομίζοντα τὸν χρόνον ἐκεῖνον ἱερᾶσθαι]. For indeed such priests as are performing the rites have to quench their thirst with water and are forbidden intoxicants. [250]Secondly, he must not shave the hairs of his head, thus giving a clear symbol [σύμβολον] to the eye that he does not debase the sterling coinage of his vow. Thirdly, he must keep his body pure and undefiled to the extent of abstaining from contact with parents or brothers after death, thus letting his kindly affection and fellow-feeling with the closest and dearest yield to piety [νικώσης εὐσεβείας] that victory which it is both honourable and profitable that it should always win.

²⁵¹When the final day as appointed has come, the law bids him bring, to release him from his vow, three animals, a he-lamb, a ewe-lamb and a ram, the first for a whole-burnt offering, the ewe-lamb as a sin-offering, and the ram as a preservation-offering. ²⁵²For all these find their likeness in the maker of the vow: the whole-burnt offering, because he surrenders not only the other the first-fruits and gifts but also his own self; the sin-offering, because he is a man, since even the perfect man, in so far as he is a created being, never escapes from sinning; the preservation-offering, because he has acknowledged and adopted the real preserver, God, as the author of his preservation [τῆς σωτηρίας αἴτιον] instead of the physicians and their faculties of healing [ἀλλ᾽ οὐκ ἰατροὺς καὶ τὰς παρ᾽ αὐτοῖς δυνάμεις]. For the physicians are mortals ready to perish, unable to secure health even for themselves, and their faculties are not beneficial to all persons nor always to the same person, but sometimes do great harm: there is Another who is invested with lordship over such faculties and those who exercise them.

²⁵³I note, and it is a very striking point, that in the three animals brought for the different sacrifices there is no difference of species. They are all of the same species, a ram, a he-lamb and a ewe-lamb. For the law wishes to show in this way what I mentioned a little before, that the three kinds of sacrifice are sisters of one family, because the penitent is preserved and the person preserved from the maladies of his soul repents, and both of them are pressing forward to that perfect and wholly sound frame of mind of which the whole-burnt-offering is a symbol.

²⁵⁴Another point—the votary has vowed to bring himself, and while it would be sacrilege that the altar should be defiled by human blood, it was quite necessary that some part of him should be sacrificially offered. The part, therefore, which zeal prompted him to take was one which can be removed without causing either pain of mutilation. He cut off the hairs of his head, which are to the body like the superfluous branches in the vegetation of a tree, and gave them to the fire in which the flesh of the preservation-offering is cooked, a fitting proceeding to secure that at least some part of the votary's self which cannot be lawfully brought to the altar should be merged in and share the nature of sacrifice by serving as fuel to the holy flame [ὕλη φλογὸς ἱερᾶς].⁵²

It is within the context of a treatise on sacrificial offerings that Philo provides his most detailed treatment of the Nazirite vow, which he denotes as the "Great Vow" (εὐχὴ μεγάλη).⁵³ His main purpose in

---

⁵² Philo, *Spec.* 1.247–54.
⁵³ Following LXX Num. 6.2.

discussing the rite is to demonstrate how it illuminates the friendship (φίλας) and kindred relationship (συγγενεῖς) between the three sacrifices of the whole-burnt-offering (ὁλοκαύτος), the preservation-offering (σωτηρίος), and the sin-offering (ἁμαρτίας) discussed in his preceding section. The discussion closely follows the structure of Num. 6.1–21 and forms in essence a philosophical commentary on the legislation. Philo's intended purpose throughout is to find *meaning* not only in the sacrificial elements of the vow, but also in the vow's various other features, such as its name and prescribed forms of behavior.

Philo begins his discussion with a digression on the naming of the vow (248). "The Great Vow" he informs his readers, is a name derived from the amazing sanctification (ἄλεκτον ὁσιότητα) and surpassing love of God (ὑπερβολήν τινα γνώμης φιλοθέου) exhibited when people make the vow, for when they make it he says, they give and dedicate their very selves (αὐτοὺς ἀνατιθέασι καὶ καθιεροῦσιν) in addition to their first-fruit offerings. In offering first-fruits, people give of every part of their material possessions and have nothing material remaining from which to give in order to demonstrate their piety (εὐσέβειαν). Thus, according to Philo, they give themselves as an offering via the Great Vow.

Philo goes on to discuss three behavioral instructions prescribed for the votary (249–50). Paraphrasing the instructions of Num. 6.3–8, he gives the very meanings and reasons behind them. By abstaining from intoxicants and all grape produce, the votary avoids that which leads "to the overthrow of his reason" (ἐπὶ καθαιρέσει λογισμοῦ). As such, he considers his time under the vow to be priest-like (νομίζοντα τὸν χρόνον ἐκεῖνον ἱερᾶσθαι), for the priests themselves avoid intoxicants whilst administering their sacred duties. Furthermore, the votary's abstinence from cutting the hair is by reason that the hair is the very symbol (σύμβολον) of his vow. Lastly, the requirement to avoid corpse contact, even the votary's own relatives, is an act considered a "yielding to piety" (νικώσης εὐσεβείας).

Moving on to his primary discussion of sacrifices, Philo skips the regulations for the Nazirite who has acquired accidental corpse impurity (Num. 6.9–12), legislation which preoccupies him elsewhere; and he discusses the whole-burnt-offering, sin-offering and preservation-offering required of the votary when a vow is completed. Philo describes the sacrifices as those required to release an individual from his vow, and as those elements that find their likeness in, or correspondence with,[54] the very maker of the vow. The whole-burnt-offering, which is entirely consumed on the sacrificial altar, is a reflection of the votary who offers up his very self as a type of sacrifice. The sin-offering, on the other hand, corresponds with the maker of the vow in that he is a human being, and as human cannot escape sinful behavior. Finally, the preservation-offering corresponds with the votary in that by making the vow he recognizes God as the author of his preservation (τῆς σωτηρίας αἴτιον), rather than the physicians and their powers to heal (ἀλλ᾽ οὐκ ἰατροὺς καὶ τὰς παρ᾽ αὐτοῖς δυνάμεις).

Two side notes bring Philo's discussion to a conclusion (253–4). First, he states that all three sacrifices are of the same species, symbolizing, as he has mentioned on another occasion, the stages through which the penitent moves when offering them (from penance to wholeness of soul). Second, because it is appropriate that the votary sacrifice some part of himself, and that human blood is both unlawful and that which would defile the altar, the votary offers a part of himself in sacrifice that is bloodless: his hair. Philo compares the cutting and re-growth of hair to the branches or foliage on a tree that may, harmlessly, be pruned. By cutting and placing the hair in the fire under which his offering is made, the votary identifies completely with the fleshly sacrifice (the quadruped) by offering a part of himself under the altar as fuel for the sacred flame (ὕλη φλογὸς ἱερᾶς).

Summary of Evidence

Most of what Philo tells us in *Spec.* 1.247–54 is, as mentioned in the introduction to this section, rather bookish in the sense that it is primarily a commentary on the biblical text of Num. 6.1–21. Much of what he conveys may simply reflect his own individual opinion, and hence, be more reflective of solitary contemplation on the Bible than commonly held beliefs by Jews during his period. In his digression regarding the name of the vow and how it was acquired (248), it is interesting to note that Philo relates the making of the vow with the giving of first-fruits. First-fruit offerings for Jews occurred annually at the feast of First-Fruits, or Pentecost, in Jerusalem and there is no indication in the Num. legislation, the primary basis of Philo's

---

[54] See Colson in *Philo*, vol. 7, p. 244 n. 2.

discussion, that such a connection existed. The very fact that the information he provides is couched within a tangential digression indicates that his information is probably secondary, from another source than that which lies directly before him. It is possible therefore, that Philo is speaking here from common knowledge about the custom. (1) The Great Vow, or Nazirite vow, therefore, may have been commonly made when people gave their first-fruit offerings: the feast of Pentecost.[55] (2) The vow, likewise, may have been considered a form of self-offering and made as an additional token of piety concurrent to the giving of first-fruits, as Philo describes.

Other evidence from *Spec.* 1.247–54, indicating at least what Philo himself thought of the custom, includes the various meanings of the votive regulations and any reason(s) said to lay behind them. (3) Abstinence from wine, strong drink, and all grape produce was understood as a means of keeping the reasoning faculties in good order. (4) Because of the similarities to the injunctions placed on priests to avoid wine whilst in sacred service, the Nazirite's time under the vow was considered to be priest-like. (5) The hair of the Nazirite was known to be the primary symbol of the vow, and (6) the act of avoiding all contact with a corpse was regarded as an act of personal piety. Also, with respect to the various offerings incumbent upon the Nazirite at the completion of the vow, Philo interestingly mentions that the preservation-offering corresponds with the maker of the vow, in that the votary acknowledges God as the ultimate author of his preservation rather than the intermediary physicians and their claimed powers or faculties to heal. (7) Philo seems to hint by this that people may have made the vow while under some kind of physical illness. (8) Finally, Philo's commentary on the offering of the hair may be evidence that he considered the act an acceptable form of bodily self-sacrifice.

1.5.2 *Quod Deus sit immutabilis 86–90*

[86]Now let us consider what is meant by "Noah found grace before the Lord" (Gen. vi. 8). Finders sometimes find again what they possessed and have lost, sometimes what they did not own in the past and now

---

[55] Cf. Smith, 331–2, who states explicitly that there was *no* connection between the making of the Nazirite vow (the Hebrew hair-offering) and making a pilgrim festival (in contrast to later Arabic *Ihram*). Based on Philo's text here, Smith may be wrong (see my discussion of this matter in Section 3 following).

again for the first time. . . . [87]We have a very clear example of the former in the commandment of the Great Vow (Num. vi.2). Now a vow is a request for good things from God [ἔστι δὲ εὐχὴ μὲν αἴτησις ἀγαθῶν παρὰ θεοῦ], while a "great vow" is to hold that God Himself and by Himself is the cause of good things, that though the earth may seem to be the mother of fruits, rain to give increase to seeds and plants, air to have the power of fostering them, husbandry to be the cause of the harvest, medicine the cause of health, marriage of childbirth, yet nothing else is His fellow-worker that we may think of them as bring us benefit. For all these things, through the power of God, admit of change and transition, so as often to produce effects quite the reverse of the ordinary . . . [88]He who makes this vow then, says Moses, must be "holy, suffering the hair of his head to grow" (Num. vi.5). This means that he must foster the young growths of virtue's truths in the mind . . . [89]But sometimes he loses these early growths, when as it were a whirlwind swoops suddenly down upon the soul and tears from it all that was beautiful in it. This whirlwind is a kind of involuntary defection straightway defiling the soul, and this he calls death (Num. vi.9). [90]He has lost, yet in time, when purified, he makes good the loss, remembers what he had forgotten for a while, and finds what he has lost, so that the "former days," the days of defection, are regarded as not to be counted (Num. vi.12) . . .[56]

In an exposition of Genesis 6.8, Philo refers to the Great Vow in Num. for the purpose of illustrating how Noah found grace in the eyes of the Lord; a grace which, according to Philo, he had previously lost, but then found once more. The commentary on Num. 6.9–12 is allegorical, and the text demonstrates not only Philo's exegetical tendencies but also his peculiar interest in the involuntary defilement of the Nazirite—here interpreted as the involuntary loss of "virtue's truths." Philo states that like Noah, who was caught in a flood, the one who makes the Great Vow places total trust in God so that if defiled by an act of accidental misfortune and forced to begin his days of piety anew, his misfortune is ultimately the cause of God who works all things for good.

Outside of Philo's allegory on Numbers 6.9–12, in a rather parenthetical statement (87) he provides a comment on vow making in general that may reflect common perception rather than his own ideology. There he states that a vow is "a request for good things from God" (ἔστι δὲ εὐχὴ μὲν αἴτησις ἀγαθῶν παρὰ θεοῦ). Making a

---

[56] Philo, *Deus* 86–90.

vow, in other words, appears to be understood as a form of making a personal petition to the divine (i.e., a form of prayer request, specifically for something good, whatever that may be).

Summary of Evidence

(1) Although this text primarily illustrates Philo's own allegorical interest in the law regarding the involuntary defilement of the Nazirite by a corpse (Num. 6.9–12), the emphasis on trust in God given such a circumstance may reflect for Philo that having to re-commence a vow due to corpse defilement was a legitimate concern for those making the Great Vow. (2) Though commonly taken to demonstrate personal piety, as was discussed in *Spec.* 1.248, Philo seems to think one could have made the Great Vow as a form of conditional petition, or prayer request, given that such was Philo's general understanding of what a *vow* is.

1.5.3 *De somniis 1.252–4*

> [252]Accordingly, after the dedication of the pillar he goes on to say, "Thou didst vow to me a vow." Now a vow in the fullest sense is a dedication [ἀνάθεσις], seeing that a man is said to give a gift to God when he renders to him not only his possessions but himself the possessor of them. For the lawgiver says,[253] "He shall be holy that letteth the locks of the hair of his head grow long" (Num. vi.5), that is, the man who has made the vow; and if he is holy, he is nothing else than a dedicated offering [ἀνάθημα], seeing that he no more comes into contact with anything unhallowed and profane. What I say is vouched for by that prophetess and mother of a prophet, Hannah, whose name is in our tongue "Grace." For she says that she is giving as a gift [δῶρον] to the Holy One her son Samuel (I Sam. i.11), not meaning a human being but rather an inspired temper possessed by a God-sent frenzy. And "Samuel" means "appointed for God."[57]

Philo again refers to the Great Vow in the first of his two treatises on dreams. In *Somn.* 1.252–4 a reference appears in context of an allegorical interpretation of Jacob's dream in Gen. 31.13 where God commands Jacob to leave the household of Laban and return to the land of his father as Jacob himself had promised (Gen. 28.18–22). Citing God's reminder to Jacob, "You vowed to me a vow," Philo

---

[57] Philo, *Somn.* 1.252–4.

digresses to explain to his readers what a vow is in its fullest sense. Such a vow, based on the law of the Great Vow in Num. 6.5 that the votary be holy, is for Philo a form of self-dedication (ἀνάθεσις), as not only material possessions, but also the very self is offered to God as a sacred gift (ἀνάθημα).

To support his interpretation, Philo alludes to the case of the prophet Samuel who was, via the vow of his mother Hannah, offered to God as a gift (δῶρον—cf. LXX 1 Sam. 1.11). That Samuel is understood here to be a Nazirite is made evident by Philo's comparison with Num. 6.5. For although the vow of dedication is made by Hannah (which Philo fails to mention), it is Samuel who is, like the one who makes the Great Vow, offered as the gift.

Summary of Evidence

Philo's understanding of the Nazirite vow in this text rests on an exegesis of Num. 6.5. In this sense his information again is primarily technical. What he does tell us, however, rings similar to what he mentions in *Spec.* 1.248 regarding the dedicated nature of the one making the Great Vow. In this sense, we may take the information as further confirmation that: (1) Philo regarded the Great Vow as an act offering the self in dedication to God. (2) Philo's use of Num. 6.5 may provide evidence, like testimony 1.2.2, that Nazirites were understood as those who were holy. (3) Philo also seems to view Samuel as a Nazirite, via the association he makes between the Great Vow and Samuel's dedication by his mother Hannah.

1.5.4   *De ebrietate 143–4*

[143]Again, it is the special task of law and instruction to "distinguish" the profane from the sacred and the impure from the pure, just as conversely it is the way of lawlessness and indiscipline to mix and confuse everything and thus force under the same head things which are in conflict with each other. Therefore [διὰ τοῦτο], Samuel too, the greatest of kings and prophets, "will never," as the scripture tells us, "drink wine or intoxicating liquor till his dying day" [οἶνον καὶ μέθυσμα ἄρχι τελευτῆς οὐ πίεται] (I Sam. i.11). For his place has been ordered [τέτακται] in the ranks [τάξει] of the divine army, and through the providence of the wise commander [ταξιάρχου] he will never leave it. Now probably there was an actual man called Samuel; but we conceive of the Samuel of the scripture, not as a living compound of soul and body, but as a mind [νοῦς] which rejoices in the service and wor-

ship of God and that only. For his name by interpretation means "appointed or ordered to God [τεταγμένος Θεῷ]," because he thinks that all actions that are based on idle opinions are grievous disorder.[58]

Philo's interest in the Nazirite Samuel appears once more in his treatise on drunkenness. Here, unlike the previous testimony discussed, Philo's concern lies particularly in Samuel's dietary avoidance of wine and strong drink (οἶνον καὶ μέθυσμα). It was asserted in testimony 1.5.1 that Philo considers Nazirites comparable to priests in that both are required to abstain from intoxicants; the latter while serving in the temple, and the former as an act of self-dedication. Here in *Ebr.* 143–4, Samuel, whom Philo considers a Nazirite (though interestingly he labels him here "the greatest of kings" and prophets), warrants mention because of these shared characteristics.

In a mixture of literal and allegorical interpretations of Lev. 10.8–11 (the law for Aaron and his sons to abstain from alcohol while serving in the temple), Philo ultimately depicts drunkenness as being caused by indiscipline and avarice toward anything promoting instruction (11ff.). In 143–4, he paints a continual contrast between the mind (νοῦς) ordered towards the service of God and the mind relaxed by wine. Whereas wine breeds confusion between opposed elements and obscures one's ability to distinguish the clean from the unclean or the sacred from the profane (143), Samuel, an exemplar of the mind well-ordered toward God, abstained from wine and strong drink until his death (ἄρχι τελευτῆς οὐ πίεται) precisely because he recognized these effects (διὰ τοῦτο). Samuel is here Philo's own Platonic ideal: a pure representation of the well-ordered mind (νοῦς). Throughout the passage, Philo relies on this ideal representation of Samuel to create a complete contrast between the notions of order and confusion, particularly the confusion caused by intoxication from wine. Samuel was ordered (τέτακται) into the ranks (τάξει) of the divine army and placed under the instruction of the wise commander (ταξιάρχου). The very name "Samuel," according to Philo, means "ordered to God" (τεταγμένος Θεῷ). The repeated use of τάξις, a military expression, cements Samuel for Philo as an archetype of the well-ordered man—in stark contrast to the undisciplined mind, state of intoxication (11ff.) and mental confusion wrought by wine (143).

---

[58] Philo, *Ebr.* 143–4.

Summary of Evidence

I believe Philo's comments on Samuel within his treatise *Ebr.* say little with respect to Nazirites. What they do suggest, however, is that, at least from Philo's perspective, abstinence from wine and strong drink, behavior exhibited by the Nazirite Samuel, is considered an act of virtuosity: virtuosity relative to the priest's ability to maintain a well-ordered mind toward God while performing his temple duties (I shall return to this thought of Philo in discussion of testimony 2.3 to follow).

1.6   *Josephus*

Josephus discusses Nazirites on a number of occasions in two of his primary literary works: once he refers to the Nazirate when narrating recent historical events in *The Jewish War* (*B. J.*); and on four occasions when discussing the lives of prominent Jewish figures of the past in his work of broader Jewish history, *Antiquities of the Jews* (*A. J.*). Overall, Josephus presents a mixed picture of Nazirites.

Because Josephus[59] remains the primary historian for Judaism in the Second Temple period, his comments regarding the Nazirate are naturally significant. Beyond historiography, however, his work in *A. J.* bases much of its early history on the sources of the Bible, and for this, Josephus is also important as a Bible interpreter. Although he states in the preface to *A. J.* that he neither adds to nor retracts from his sources but relates their content accurately,[60] Josephus often rewrites the biblical texts with a disposition toward interpretation, sometimes adding information and sometimes taking it away. Feldman has likened his interpretive methodologies as akin to the rabbinic Targum tradition:[61] Aramaic translations of the Bible that include in some instances very liberal interpretive elements in their reproduction of the biblical text (see 1.12 following). Josephus, moreover, is a valu-

---

[59] For a full treatment on Josephus' biographical details see T. Rajak, *Josephus, the Historian and His Society* (London: Duckworth, 1983), 11–45; see also Josephus, *Vita* 1–12.

[60] Josephus, *A. J.* 1.10–7.

[61] L. H. Feldman, *Josephus's Interpretation of the Bible* (Hellenistic Culture and Society 27; Berkley: University of California Press, 1998), 17. Feldman discusses many possible models for Josephus' methodology in rewriting biblical history, however "the closest analogue to Josephus' *Antiquities*, . . . is to be found in the targumim (sic)," Ibid.

able source with regard to matters sacerdotal, for he mentions in his autobiography that he was a serving priest born into a family with royal connections stemming from the daughter of Jonathan Hasmonaeus, the first of the Hasmonaeans to attain the high priesthood.[62] He also states that his family was registered to serve with the illustrious first of the twenty-four courses of priests who had the right to serve in the temple.[63]

Modern critics of Josephus have well recognized that as a writer he has his biases and composes biblical, as well as contemporary history, often with the aim of delivering a pre-determined agenda.[64] Scholars differ on his reliability as a historian, and such concerns must always be considered when approaching a particular topic discussed by the writer, including the topic at hand. From a critical point of view, what Josephus tells us about Nazirites and the Nazirite vow is likely very reliable, as much of his information is parenthetical to the other details occupying his principal concerns. What he tells his readers, like the author of I Macc., is based largely on his own tacit assumptions about the Nazirate. It is highly likely therefore, that these assumptions reflect how votaries were typically perceived and how the Nazirate was commonly observed.

1.6.1 *Bellum judaicum 2.313–4*

[313]She was visiting Jerusalem to discharge a vow to God; for it is customary [ἔθος] for those suffering from illness or other affliction to make a vow to abstain from wine and to shave their heads [καὶ ξυρήσεσθαι] during the thirty days preceding that on which they must offer sacrifices [πρὸ τριάκοντα ἡμερῶν ἧς ἀποδώσειν μέλλοειν θυσίας]. [314]These rites Bernice was then undergoing, and she would come barefoot before the tribunal and make supplication to Florus, without any respect being shown to her, and even at the peril of her life.[65]

Josephus' account of Bernice, sister of King Agrippa II, in *B. J.* 2.313–4, contains the most detailed description of the Nazirite vow in any historical narrative pertaining to the period under study. The

---

[62] Josephus, *Vita* 1–6.

[63] Ibid.

[64] See Feldman, 74–220; and J. S. McLaren, *Turbulent Times? Josephus and Scholarship on Judaea in the First Century CE* (JSPsup 29; Sheffield, Eng.: Sheffield Academic Press, 1998).

[65] Josephus, *B. J.* 2.313–4.

vow mentioned is not explicitly labeled a Nazirite vow, but contextually it is certainly implied to be one. No other vow practiced among the Jews included the combined elements of abstaining from wine, shaving the hair of the head, and offering sacrifices at the end of an avowed period than that which is described in sources as the Nazirite vow.[66] Moreover, LXX Num. 6.1–21 (discussed previously) bears witness to the fact that the Nazirate may be described in a source without actually utilizing the religious technical term in the process, particularly where an author felt his readership unversed in relevant technical jargon. That this is the case with Josephus may be supported not only by the detailed nature of his description, but by the fact that the account as we have it is written in Greek primarily for a Graeco-Roman readership, which likely was unfamiliar with the particular Jewish custom (cf. *B. J.* 1.1ff.).

The context in which the account is found is Josephus' narrative of the tumult in Jerusalem under the Roman procurator Florus in AD 66, a major episode in a series of events leading to the outbreak of war between the Jews and Rome. Josephus states that on the occasion of Agrippa's absence from Jerusalem, Florus took up residence in the royal palace, plundered the city and slew over 3,000 of the city's inhabitants (Agrippa, Josephus tells us, was in Alexandria on an errand to congratulate Bernice's brother-in-law, Tiberias Alexander, on his appointment by the emperor Nero to the office of prefect of Egypt). Bernice, however, happened to be in Jerusalem to witness Florus' atrocities—even at the peril of her life.

Josephus' mention of the vow within this narrative context anticipates the begging of two questions: if Agrippa was in Alexandria to congratulate Bernice's own brother-in-law on the occasion of such a significant appointment as head of the Egyptian government, what was *she* doing in Jerusalem? Moreover, why, given the tumultuous events taking place in Jerusalem, did she remain in the city at the peril of her very life? Josephus' answer is that Bernice was under a vow she had made to God, a peculiar type of vow that required her to be present in Jerusalem for its completion.

In an effort to more fully explain why the vow required her to be in the city, Josephus rather parenthetically provides a detailed description of the custom. He informs his readers that those who

---

[66] Cartledge, *The Vow in the Hebrew Bible*, 32.

typically made it included the sick and those suffering from some other form of affliction. By implication this included Bernice, although Josephus provides no indication as to what Bernice's ailment might have been. The custom also, he says, incorporated a certain manner of behavior, namely abstaining from wine and from cutting the hair. The conjunctive plus the infinitive καὶ ξυρήσεσθαι in, "to abstain from wine *and to cut their hair*," seems to imply a vow *to* cut the hair for thirty days. It is likely, however, the phrase is inclusive of the previous action, ἀφέξεσθαι, "to abstain." When Josephus mentions Nazirites elsewhere, he consistently discusses the cutting of the hair in context of the temple (*A. J.* 4.72; 19.294), and, as is likely the case with Bernice, the cutting of the hair was probably an act to be done only at the moment the vow was completed. Finally, Josephus tells his readers that the vow was typically observed for a thirty-day period, after which time sacrifices had to be offered (by implication at the temple in Jerusalem).

It is not entirely clear which of these last two elements accounts for Bernice's need to be in the city at such a time. Josephus may mean by the phrase πρὸ τριάκοντα ἡμερῶν ἧς ἀποδώσειν μέλλοειν θυσίας, "for thirty days prior to that on which they are to offer sacrifices," that those who made the vow had to offer sacrifices immediately after the thirty days were completed. Bernice, then, would have been in Jerusalem primarily to ensure that her timing was right when partaking of the sacrificial ritual.[67] He states at the end of his account that she was "then undergoing these rites, even at the peril of her life" and seems to indicate by this that she was in the city for the entire duration of the thirty days. Alternatively, the emphasis of the phrase may lie simply on the requirement to offer sacrifices. Bernice then, having fulfilled her thirty days at some point prior to, or perhaps even partially during her visit, would have been in Jerusalem primarily to be released from her vow—the sacrifices being the emancipating agent. The latter of the two interpretations seems the more plausible, as Josephus introduces the account by informing his readers that she was in Jerusalem "discharging (ἐκτελοῦσα)

---

[67] Cf. W. Whiston who translates the phrase more loosely, "... for thirty days before they are to offer their sacrifices." Whiston, however, believes Bernice was in Jerusalem for the entire duration of the thirty-day period, see *The Complete Works of Josephus* (trans. by W. Whiston; New Updated ed.; Peabody, Mass.: Hendrickson Publishers, 1987), 618, n. a.

a vow to God" or "bringing to an end a vow," not fulfilling the full regime of its requirements. Moreover, if she intended to go to Alexandria (which, admittedly, Josephus says nothing of), being released from her vow beforehand would certainly have been optimal.

Josephus gives no explicit indication as to what the precise significance of the thirty-day period for observing the vow might have been. However, it is interesting that he describes Bernice as being clad in bare feet when approaching Florus and his tribunal; a state that Josephus says ought to have gained her some respect. Josephus provides no further description of Bernice's attire, but perhaps traversing barefoot was an outward means of expressing that she was under the vow.[68] Given that thirty days would have allowed for an insignificant growth of hair, particularly for a woman, walking barefoot may have been a means of accentuating her status as a Nazirite. Moreover, it might have been a way of partially expressing a personal state of affliction or illness, since Josephus says that these were motivations for making the vow. Taking this description of Bernice into consideration with the other behavioral elements incorporated in the vow, particularly the thirty-day observance period, the vow is reminiscent of similar patterns of behavior witnessed in the Jewish rite of mourning known from rabbinic sources as the *Shloshim*, (שלשים), "thirty days."[69] During the *Shloshim*, a mourner abstained from cutting the hair and nails, wore rent clothing, and for at least a portion of the thirty-day period abstained from drinking wine.[70] The similarities between the two customs are rather striking and may demonstrate some common relationship between them. The thirty-day period for the temporary Nazirite vow, together with the custom of undertaking the vow during a time of illness or other affliction, abstaining from wine, and demonstrating such a status through other outward means, may indicate that the significance of the thirty days lies in an amalgamation of features shared with late Second Temple mourning rites.[71]

---

[68] Ibid.; Whiston sees Bernice's barefoot gesture as in relation to her being under the vow as well. However, he sees the behavior, as well as the thirty-day requirement, as possibly originating with the Pharisees, a suggestion I find highly unlikely as there is no evidence for this in any surviving source which speaks of the Pharisees.

[69] I would like to thank Prof. Martin Goodman for suggesting that there might be a connection between the two rites.

[70] *Sifre* to Num. 23.1; *m. Taan.* 4.7; *m. M. Kat.* 3.5, 7; *m. Hor.* 3.4.

[71] There appears to have been multiple forms of outward expression to signify

Summary of Evidence

Based on Josephus' description of the Nazirite vow, (1) it was customary to take it up in a time of illness or other affliction in this period. (2) It was also customary to observe the rite for thirty days. (3) According to Josephus the vow involved abstaining from wine, cutting one's hair and perhaps some additional form of outward expression as a means of demonstrating that the rite was being observed, such as traversing barefoot. (4) At the end of thirty days, sacrifices were offered, and by textual implication, (5) the vow was discharged in Jerusalem and (7) observed in one instance by a woman among the socially elite.

1.6.2 *Antiquitates judaicae 4.72 (70–2)*

[70]Moreover, the people are required to offer to God first-fruits [ἀπαρχὰς] of all the produce of the soil, and again of those quadrupeds which the law sanctions as sacrifices they are to present the firstborn, if a male, to the priests for sacrifice, to be consumed by them with their families in the holy city. [71]In the case of creatures which they are forbidden to eat in compliance with their ancestral laws, the owners thereof must pay to the priests a shekel and a half, and for the first born of man five shekels. To them too fall first-fruits of the shearing [κουρᾶς] of the sheep; and when the corn is baked and made into bread, some of these cakes must be supplied to them. [72]All who consecrate themselves [αὐτοὺς καθιερῶσιν] in fulfillment of a vow—Nazirites as they are called [ναζιραῖοι καλοῦνται], people who grow long hair and abstain from wine [κομῶντες καὶ οἶνον οὐ προσφερόμενοι]—these too, when they dedicate their hair and offer it in sacrifice assign their shorn locks to the priests [δρῶσι τὰς κουρὰς νέμεσθαι πρὸς τοὺς ἱερέας].[72]

Josephus introduces Nazirites for the first time in book four of *A. J.* in context of a discussion on priestly dues. He informs his readers that in addition to the wool shorn from sheep, the Hebrew priests receive as part of the annual first-fruit income (ἀπαρχὰς) the hair shorn from Nazirites. Such a gift seems odd given its seeming

---

mourning behavior during this period, in addition to the rites described in the custom of the *Shloshim*. In the book of Ezekiel, a text read at this time, for instance, mourning behavior included traversing barefoot, like Bernice, and unbinding the turban. In the Greek version of Esther, the queen is described as putting on specific clothing that signified "distress and mourning," and covering her head with ashes and dung (14.2 NRSV); cf. I Macc. 3.47; and *Test. 12 Patr.* 1.10.

[72] Josephus, *A. J.* 4.70–2.

impracticality, not to mention its apparent contradiction with the biblical law (Num. 6.18). Josephus may be interpreting the custom in a way more comprehendible to his Graeco-Roman readership, but there is evidence both in Philo and in the Mishnah that suggests his depiction is rather accurate of the custom as it was commonly observed by Jews in this period (to be explained following).

It is possible, as suggested by Whiston, that the phrase "assign their shorn locks to the priests" (δρῶσι τὰς κουρὰς νέμεσθαι πρὸς τοὺς ἱερέας) is a reference to the casting of the hair on the sacrificial fire (cf. Num. 6.18). That Josephus intends instead to mean, however, that Nazirites literally gave their shorn hair to the priests when it was cut is supported by the general context. He mentions Nazirites as an afterthought to his mention of the wool shorn from sheep. Just as the priests receive as a first-fruit offering the hair shorn from sheep (κουρᾶς), so too do they receive the hair (κουρᾶς) shorn from Nazirites. The two hair-offerings for Josephus, in other words, are analogous. Moreover, hair consumed on the sacrificial fire would be of no benefit to the priests.

When explaining to his foreign readers who Nazirites are (ναζιραῖοι καλοῦνται), Josephus says they comprise all who dedicate, or consecrate, themselves (αὐτοὺς καθιερῶσιν) in order to fulfil a vow. He furthermore states, and this in order to clarify their relevance to the present context, that they are those who *grow long hair* and do not take wine (κομῶντες καὶ οἶνον οὐ προσφερόμενοι). Josephus says nothing regarding the Nazirite's required abstinence from corpse impurity (Num. 6.5–8), and nothing, surprisingly given the context, of the Nazirite's required sacrifices (Num. 6.13–21). This is peculiar in that the author's main source is the Bible (cf. *A. J.* 1.1ff.). Josephus' comments are rather parenthetical in context, however, and he appears to be revealing only what is essential and beneficial to his present discussion.

On the basis of his description, like the vow of Bernice in *B. J.* 2.313–4, it may be the case that Josephus is referring to Nazirites of a temporary duration. The element of assigning shorn hair to the priests as a sacrificial offering seems to imply a sense of purpose or goal behind the act of shaving the head, something Nazirites of a lifelong duration might not do.[73] This being said, evidence in the

---

[73] Gray, 204.

Mishnah, and possibly the *Mekhilta*, suggests some making lifelong vows may have cut their hair periodically, possibly even annually (see 1.8.1 and 1.10.1, following).

In general it is possible, as mentioned previously, that Josephus is interpreting the Nazirite custom in a way more palatable and understandable to his Greek and Roman readers. It was perhaps the case, however, that common Greek practice bore an influence on the Nazirite custom in this period, and that Jews, therefore, saw the hair as an object of some sacred use, particularly in the context of first-fruit offerings (see 3.2.12 following). Discussed in testimony 1.5.1, Philo asserts that Jews made the Great Vow when they gave their annual first-fruits. This is very similar to what Josephus mentions of Nazirites here in *A. J.* 4.72. Furthermore, there is evidence in the Mishnah that Nazirite hair, in addition to the hair shorn from the firstborn of sheep, may have been woven together and used for sacks (see testimony 1.8 following).[74]

Summary of Evidence

According to Josephus's brief description of Nazirites in *A. J.* 4.72, Nazirites were individuals who consecrated themselves in fulfillment of a vow. (2) Two marks, namely abstinence from wine and the growth of long hair, identified them. (3) They offered their hair as a first-fruit offering to the administering priests when it was shorn.

1.6.3 *Antiquitates judaicae 5.277–8, 285, 312*

[277]Now once when his wife was alone, a spectre appeared to her from God, in the likeness of a comely and tall youth, bringing her the good news of the approaching birth of a son through God's good providence [κατὰ θεοῦ πρόνοιαν καλοῦ]—a son goodly and illustrious for strength [ῥώμην ἐπιφανοῦς], by whom on reaching man's estate, the Philistines would be afflicted. [278]He further charged her not to cut the lad's locks, and that he was to renounce all other forms of drink (so God commanded) and to accustom himself to water only [ἔσται δ' αὐτῷ πρὸς ἄλλο μὲν ποτὸν ἀποστροφὴ τοῦ θεοῦ τοῦτο προστάσσοντος, πρὸς ὕδωρ δὲ μόνον οἰκειότηξ]. And having thus spoken the visitor departed, having come but to execute God's will.

[285]And the woman conceived and paid good heed to the injunctions laid upon her; and when the infant was born they called him Samson, a name which means "strong." And the child grew apace and it was

---

[74] *m. Orl.* 3.3.

plain [δῆλος] from the frugality of his diet [δίαιταν σωφροσύνης] and
his loosely flowing locks [τριχῶν ἀνέσεως] that he was to be a prophet
[ἦν προφητεύσων].

³¹²But when even by this experiment the truth was not discovered, at
last, at her petitions, Samson—since he must needs [ἔδει] fall a vic-
tim to calamity—wishing to humor Dalala said: "I am under God's
care and under His providence since birth [ἐμοῦ φησίν ὁ θεὸς κήδεται
καὶ κατὰ τὴν ἐκείνου πρόνοιαν γεννηθείς], I nurse these locks, God having enjoined upon me not to cut them, for that my strength is mea-
sured by their growth and preservation."⁷⁵

In retelling the story of Samson, Josephus in book five of *A. J.* oddly
refrains from calling Samson a Nazirite, but instead, refers to him
as a prophet (προφητεύσων). Josephus' interpretation of the biblical
figure is most peculiar given that Samson is the only person named
a Nazirite in the Bible, and Samson in the Bible is never called a
prophet. Josephus, moreover, has promised his readers in book one
of *A. J.* neither to add to nor detract from his source (the Bible) in
any way, but only to relay it accurately. Some special reason(s), therefore, must account for his peculiar portrayal. For the purposes of the
present study, two things about Josephus' rendition of Samson are
of interest: namely, what Josephus thinks about Samson *as a Nazirite*
that might reflect his own thoughts about Nazirites, and what it is
that causes him to refrain from naming Samson a Nazirite in light
of his previous introduction of these figures in book four (4.72).

First, with respect to Josephus' version of Samson's vocation, he
nowhere names Samson a Nazirite. The author loosely follows the
narrative structure of his source (the Bible), and in the two places
where such a reference might be expected, that is in the annuncia-
tion of Samson's birth and commissioning by the angel (5.277–8)
and Samson's admission of the secret source of his power to Delilah
(5.312), he does not use the religious technical term. Rather, in
Josephus' version an angel merely commands that the child refrain
from cutting his hair and avoid all forms of drink but water, and
Samson, when declaring the source of his strength to the Philistine
harlot, merely mentions that he is a man "under God's care and
providence since birth" (ἐμοῦ ὁ θεὸς κήδεται καὶ κατὰ τὴν ἐκείνου
πρόνοιαν γεννηθείς). What readers *are* told of Samson's vocation is

---

⁷⁵ Josephus, *A. J.* 5.277–8, 285, 312.

that it was revealed early on—I take this to mean to his parents—by his prudent diet (δίαιταν σωφροσύνης) and flowing, uncut locks (τριχῶν ἀνέσεως), that he was to be a prophet.

By the very manner in which Josephus describes Samson's behavior in his version, he reveals that he *does* see Samson as a Nazirite despite his seeming ignorance of the term. The commandment for Samson never to cut his hair, namely the only proscription originally given to Samson in relation to his Nazirite status in Judg. 13.5, 7 and 16.17, is retained in Josephus' account; yet, the injunction to avoid wine and strong drink (originally placed upon Samson's mother [Judg. 13.5, 7]) is instead applied to Samson, albeit subliminally via the command that he abstain from all forms of drink but water. Josephus even provides the editorial remark that this commandment was from God (τοῦ θεοῦ τοῦτο προστασσοντος). Josephus' application of such an injunction to Samson might be inspired by Num. 6.3–4. Such an association between Samson and the Nazirite vow of Num. 6.1–21 was witnessed in the LXX[B] version of Samson (see testimony 1.2.2), and Josephus as well may have viewed Samson as one under a Nazirite *vow*. Furthermore, given its place in the narrative, Josephus appears to provide a translation of the very word נזיר/ναζιρ when narrating Samson's revelation of the secret of his power in 5.312; namely, that a Nazirite is one under God's care and providence, "I am a man under God's care and providence since birth" (cf. "I am a Nazirite (נזיר) to God from birth"—MT; "I am a holy one (ἅγιος = ναζιρ) of God from birth"—LXX[B]).

Reading between the lines of his description then, Josephus probably thinks of Samson as a Nazirite, but purposefully masks this knowledge not only by means of associating Samson's behavior with that of a prophet, but by avoiding specific lexical terminology respecting Samson's diet and that used of Nazirites elsewhere in his history. In *A. J.* 4.72, just one book prior, Josephus informed his readers that Nazirites are those who grow long hair and abstain from wine. Samson in 5.278 is a figure who grows long hair and is commanded to turn away from all forms of drink but water (ἔσται δ' αὐτῷ πρὸς ἄλλο μὲν ποτὸν ἀποστροφὴ τοῦ θεοῦ τοῦτο προστάσσοντος, πρὸς ὕδωρ δὲ μόνον οἰκειότης). Though semantically the dietary habits appear similar, lexically the descriptions are slightly different, and Josephus' readers, only now vaguely familiar with who Nazirites are, would likely have failed to make any immediate and certain connection between the two accounts without due pondering or further discourse.

Why Josephus depicts Samson in this way, omitting as he does any reference to him as a Nazirite and blurring any concrete indication that he was one, might possibly be explained when comparing what he has said about Nazirites previously in *A. J.* to what he says about Samson in his complete version of the Judg. story. Essentially, Josephus tends to depict Samson in a manner with which his Graeco-Roman readers might readily identify. First, in *A. J.* 4.72 Josephus has told his readers that Nazirites offer their hair to the administering priests as a first-fruit offering when it is shorn (like the hair shorn from sheep). For Samson, however, cutting the hair is precisely what he is commanded *not* to do in the narrative. In fact, when Samson is bereft of his hair it ultimately leads to his downfall. In light of such a disparity, Josephus may have altered the vocation of Samson in part to avoid undue confusion over these disparate treatments of the hair. Secondly, his alterations to the biblical story extend beyond Samson's vocation. Portions of the narrative are omitted, and features absent in the biblical account are added to such a degree that Josephus, in effect, has portrayed Samson in a manner more identifiable with his primarily Hellenistic audience: elements of romance absent in the biblical story are introduced, and an emphasis in the story is placed on the human traits of Samson. Rather than the Spirit of the Lord as in the biblical account, for instance, it is Samson's illustrious bodily strength (ῥώμην ἐπιφανοῦς) that enables him to perform his miraculous feats; the role of the Spirit, so crucial to the biblical version, is reduced to acts of mere providence (πρόνοια). In general, as noted by Feldman, Josephus has presented Samson as a figure praiseworthy in Greek minds and one akin to an Israelite Achilles or Heracles.[76] Because of this overriding agenda, Josephus may have wished to avoid Samson's religious technical identification as found in the Bible so as to disassociate him from the contemporary figures introduced just one book previously (4.72).

Summary of Evidence

In terms of what can be gathered from Josephus' rendition of Samson for historical purposes pertaining to Nazirites in the late Second

---

[76] Feldman sees this particularly in the aspect of Samson's tempestuous nature, 489.

Temple period, although Josephus masked Samson's biblical vocation, (1) he nonetheless thought of him as under a Nazirite vow in
the likeness of Num. 6.1–21. Furthermore, (2) he appears to understand the term "Nazirite" as meaning "one under God's special care
and providence."

1.6.4 *Antiquitates judaicae 5.344, 346–7*

[344]And, her grief proving stronger than her husband's consolation, she
went off to the tabernacle, to beseech God to grant her offspring and
to make her a mother, promising that her first-born should be consecrated to the service of God [καθιερώσειν ἐπὶ διακονίᾳ τοῦ θεοῦ] and
that his manner of life should be unlike that of ordinary men.

[346]They came therefore again to offer sacrifices for the birth of the
child and brought their tithes also [δεκατας τ' ἔφερον]. [347]And the woman,
mindful of the vow which she made concerning the child, delivered
him to Eli, dedicating him to God to be a prophet; so his locks were
left to grow and his drink was water [κόμη τε οὖν αὐτῷ ἀνεῖτο καὶ ποτὸν
ἦν ὕδωρ].[77]

Similar to the manner in which Josephus represents Samson, though
there is good indication that he understands Samuel to be a Nazirite,
he once again appears to purposefully blur any clear indication of
this for his readers. The narrative idiosyncrasies facing Josephus in
I Sam. are substantially different from those in the book of Judges.
Alterations to the general character of Samuel are, therefore, less
drastic than in the case of Samson, yet in terms of vocational status,
there is evidence that Josephus consciously reworks the details of his
source material, I believe, to avoid possible confusion over the disparate treatments of the hair between Samuel and Nazirites as they
were, again, described just one book prior in *A. J.* 4.72.

In his paraphrase of I Sam. 1.11, 21, Josephus describes Samuel
as allowing his hair to grow long and maintaining a diet free of
intoxicants. Josephus' source must be the LXX where, in contrast
to MT, the addition of abstinence from wine and strong drink is
made explicit in Hannah's vow (I Sam. 1.11). That Josephus' text
is the LXX is also indicated by the mention that Hannah and her
husband brought with them their tithes (δεκατας τ' ἔφερον) when they
brought the child Samuel to Eli.

---

[77] Josephus, *A. J.* 5.344, 346–7.

Because of the dual proscription against cutting the hair and drinking intoxicants, Josephus likely understands Samuel to be a Nazirite and this may be evidenced in his paraphrase of Hannah's vow. If granted a child, he tells us, Hannah promises that the child will be dedicated to the service of the Lord (καθιερώσειν ἐπὶ διακονίᾳ τοῦ θεοῦ). In *A. J.* 4.72, Josephus describes Nazirites as those who consecrate or dedicate themselves (καθιερῶσιν) in fulfillment of a vow. Josephus' description of Samuel may be a subliminal indication that he sees him as a Nazirite; i.e., that Samuel was one dedicated by means of a vow (in this case the vow of Samuel's mother). Samuel's status as a Nazirite may also be witnessed in Josephus' alteration to the account of Agag's execution much later in his narrative (6.155). In the biblical episode, Samuel hacks Agag to pieces with the king's own sword (I Sam. 15.33), but according to Josephus, Samuel instead *orders* Agag's execution. It is possible, in other words, that he saw the episode as problematic for Samuel as a Nazirite due to the injunction to remain pure from corpse contamination (Num. 6.6–8).

Similar to his representation of Samson, however, Josephus avoids using dietary lexicography identical to that used within his source or used of Nazirites elsewhere in *A. J.* Rather than avoiding οἶνον (as do Nazirites in 4.72) or οἶνον καὶ μέθυσμα (as does Samuel in LXX I Sam. 1.11), Samuel's abstinence from intoxicants is oddly rendered as "his drink was water" (ποτὸν ἦν ὕδωρ). This seems to be an intentional obscuring of the dietary injunction and follows the same principle as that used to describe Samson in the previous testimony: Josephus may wish to subtly blur any clear indication that Samuel was a Nazirite.

Why Josephus reworks his source in such a manner may follow, in part, what was said regarding Samson; namely, he may wish to avoid possible confusion on the part of his readers over the disparate treatments of the hair between Samuel on the one hand, whose locks were allowed to grow (κόμη τε οὖν αὐτῷ ἀνεῖτο), and Nazirites on the other, as described earlier in 4.72, who offer their hair to the priests when it is shorn.

Summary of Evidence

I believe two things may be gathered from Josephus' rendition of Samuel. (1) Although he appears to blur any clear indication that Samuel was a Nazirite, read between the lines of his narrative,

Josephus nonetheless appears to see Samuel as one under a Nazirite vow. (2) Secondly, likely based on the LXX of I Sam. 1.21, Josephus understands Samuel's dedication as having occurred at the time Hannah and Elkanah gave the tenths of the produce of their land.

1.6.5 *Antiquitates judaicae 19.294 (293–4)*

[293]Agrippa, naturally, since he was to go back with improved fortunes, turned quickly homewards. On entering Jerusalem, he offered sacrifices of thanksgiving, omitting none of the ritual enjoined by our law. [294]Accordingly he also arranged for a considerable number of nazirites (sic) to be shorn [ναζιραίων ξυρᾶσθαι].[78]

Josephus mentions Nazirites explicitly for the second time in book nineteen of *A. J.* When Agrippa I received confirmation of his kingship over Judaea and Samaria from Claudius Caesar in AD 41,[79] Josephus describes his return to Jerusalem from Egypt as a joyous occasion. In addition to offering thanksgiving sacrifices as a public display of his elation, Agrippa, Josephus tells his readers, arranged for a considerable number of Nazirites to be shorn (ναζιραίων ξυρᾶσθαι).

"To be shaved" (ξυρᾶσθαι) is most likely an idiomatic expression referring to the payment of sacrifices on behalf of the Nazirites. Alternatively, the term may denote the act of merely cutting the hair. With regard to the latter, Josephus has already introduced Nazirites as those who offer their shorn locks (κουρὰς) to the temple priests as a first-fruit offering (*A. J.* 4.72). Read in light of this information ξυρᾶσθαι may denote this same activity (i.e., the very literal act of cutting the hair). Such an interpretation must at least be allowed, given that the commentary in 4.72 is the only other reference to ναζιραῖοι in *A. J.* There is no mention of first-fruit offerings in this passage, however, and the only festive activity described is that instigated by Agrippa himself. The sense of the Greek verb is similar, furthermore, to the Hebrew idiom לגלח, "to shave": an expression found in early rabbinic literature and one which refers not merely to the shaving of the Nazirite's hair, but to the whole of the votary's offerings given when the hair is cut (cf. Num. 6.13–21).[80]

---

[78] Josephus, *A. J.* 19.293–4.
[79] Schürer (vol. 1; Edinburgh: T&T Clark, 1973), 444–6.
[80] See n. 127, p. 83.

Josephus is drawing attention to the magnanimity of Agrippa's sacrificial activity and if Josephus means by ξυρᾶσθαι that Agrippa paid for the many sacrifices incumbent upon the Nazirites, this would befit such a context. Josephus is well aware of the sacrificial obligations of Nazirites, as stated with respect to the vow of Bernice in *B. J.* 2.313–4, and, since the comment on Nazirites is exceedingly pithy and parenthetical to the surrounding context, Josephus has likely allowed an expression familiar to himself but unknown to his audience to slip into his narration.

Because of the emphasis on sacrificial offerings, the good number of "Nazirites" (ναζιραίων) mentioned by Josephus may refer here, like 4.72, to Nazirites of the temporary type. Such sacrifices would have been numerous and the offer to pay for them would likewise have been a generous gift befitting, as mentioned previously, the general context and flow of Josephus' narrative.

That these were poor Nazirites, as Feldman asserts,[81] is nowhere stated. The emphasis of the text is simply the fact that payment of the sacrificial offerings on behalf of a great number of Nazirites was demonstrative of the sheer magnitude of Agrippa's religious devotion and thanksgiving.

Summary of Evidence

In similar fashion as I Macc. 3.49, this text attests (1) to the popularity of the custom. (2) As in I Macc., Josephus' account also bears witness of a case in which Nazirites appeared together as a large group. (3) Significance is also placed by Josephus in this text on the element of sacrifice incumbent upon Nazirites. (4) I take Josephus' comments as evidence that making the Nazirite vow was common in the first century AD.

---

[81] Feldman states that these must have been poor Nazirites due to the impracticality of the timing involved: ". . . there is no indication that the time limit of all these Nazirites had simultaneously expired," *Josephus*, vol. 9, p. 353. The text says nothing of the Nazirites being poor, however, and I see no problem with Nazirites appearing in Jerusalem in large numbers here (for a more likely explanation see Chapter 3).

1.7 *Nazirite Tomb*

An accidental discovery on Hebrew University's Mount Scopus campus in 1967 unveiled the remains of a burial vault thought by archaeologists to be the tomb of a first-century AD Nazirite and his family.[82] The excavation of the vault was documented and published four years later by N. Avigad in an article appearing in the *Israel Exploration Journal.*

From the details of Avigad's report, the vault's designation as a Nazirite tomb is based on the discovery of inscriptions etched on the sides of two ossuaries found within the tomb. The inscriptions, written in cursive Aramaic,[83] refer to a certain "Jonathan the Nazirite." One ossuary is labeled "Hanania son of Jonathan the Nazirite," חנניה בר יהונתן הנזר, and the other "Salome wife of Hanania son of the Nazirite," שלום אנתת חניה בר הנזיר.[84]

In addition to the ossuaries, other significant discoveries from inside the tomb include two sarcophagi.[85] The smaller of the two is decorated with Hellenistic vine patterns and Jewish Second Temple style grape clusters amounting to what Avigad describes as "one of the most aesthetically pleasing Jewish sarcophagi known."[86] The larger sarcophagus is plain and without ornamentation.[87]

In general, the burial vault and the artifacts discovered therein are comparable in their quality of craftsmanship to both the tomb of the Herodians and the tomb of Queen Helena of Adiabene (the "Tomb of the Kings").[88] The owner of the tomb would certainly be considered among the wealthy of Palestine.

Summary of Evidence

At least two characteristics of late Second Temple Nazirites may be evidenced from the discovery of the Nazirite burial vault. (1) The use of the appellative form of the technical term נזיר is probably evidence

---

[82] N. Avigad, "The Burial Vault of a Nazirite Family on Mount Scopus," *IEJ* 21 (1971): 185.
[83] Ibid., 196–7.
[84] Ibid.
[85] Ibid., 191–3.
[86] Ibid., 191.
[87] Ibid., 192.
[88] Ibid., 191.

of a Nazirite of lifelong duration, though admittedly this is conjectural. (2) Given the craftsmanship of the tomb and the quality of design on the decorated sarcophagus, it would appear that at least one Nazirite would rank among the socially elite.

1.8   *The Mishnah*

How Nazirites should behave in light of biblical law and the changing circumstances of daily life (a concept known in rabbinic sources as *halakhah*) is a topic addressed in the Mishnah. The Mishnah,[89] a collection of oral tradition finally redacted at the turn of third century AD, contains an entire tractate devoted to the topic, as well as numerous other references to Nazirite halakhah within tractates treating related subject matters.

Halakhah, as contained in the Mishnah, spans the entire spectrum of Pentateuchal law; its six orders (*sedarim*) and sixty-three individual tractates (*massekhtot*) cover topics that range from the use of agricultural produce to matters affecting purity. Of these various orders and tractates, Nazirite Halakhah, as mentioned, occupies a treatise of its own: a tractate within the Mishnah's third order, the order on laws affecting women (*Nashim*). Nazirite halakhah also features as a topic of discussion within other Mishnaic tractates dealing with related legal subject matters, such as vow making, the use of forbidden fruit, the giving of offerings and sacrifices, and matters affecting purity among others.

Much attention has been paid to the Mishnaic material in previous studies on Nazirites, particularly for the purpose of identifying what the *rules* of Nazirite behavior were at the time of and prior to the Mishnah's composition. Rabbinic decisions on matters have often been viewed as the basis for the way Nazirites typically behaved. When the School of Shammai debated with the School of Hillel

---

[89] Introductions to the Mishnah and other rabbinic literature may be found in a number of works. For a large bibliography see G. Stemberger, *Introduction to the Talmud and Midrash* (2nd ed.; trans. and ed. by M. Bockmuehl; Edinburgh: T&T Clark, 1996), esp. 108–48; Some of the more helpful works include the following: G. F. Moore, "The Sources," in *Judaism in the First Centuries of the Christian Era: The Age of the Tannaim* (vol. 1; Cambridge, Eng.: Cambridge University Press, 1958), 125–219; and J. Bowker, *The Targums and Rabbinic Literature: An Introduction to Jewish Interpretations of Scripture* (Cambridge, Eng.: Cambridge University Press, 1969).

over the required period a Nazirite had to re-observe his/her vow when entering the land of Palestine from abroad (*m. Naz.* 3.6), for instance, scholars have often taken the decision as evidence that Nazirites regularly observed an additional period of sanctity when entering the land from abroad. Why? To borrow a phrase of Ed Sanders, ". . . because the Rabbis laid it down."[90]

Such an approach to the Mishnaic material is rather unfortunate, for it assumes the Mishnah comprises an all-embracing law code to which Jews commonly adhered. A safer take on the material is that rabbinic discussions in the Mishnah reflect common Nazirite behavior only potentially, and not in the decisions of the rabbis per se, but in the tacit assumptions they make regarding the way people could have behaved when making these vows. As will be shown, the Mishnah provides evidence to suggest the rabbis held little influence over people when making Nazirite vows, and the purpose of the Mishnah when discussing Nazirite halakhah is far from that of a code of law.[91]

In treating the Mishnaic evidence, I will first discuss the content of tractate *Nazir*, followed by a critical evaluation of how I believe it represents Nazirite behavior respecting the period under study. I will then follow this with a discussion of key references to Nazirite halakhah found in other Mishnaic tractates, and finally, in keeping with the procedure of source examination thus far, I will provide a brief section summarizing what I believe the Mishnah reveals regarding common Nazirite behavior in the period at hand.

---

[90] E. P. Sanders, *Judaism: Practice and Belief, 63 BCE—66 CE* (London: SCM, 1992), 458ff.

[91] What the general purpose of the Mishnah is, as a redacted body of tradition, is a topic of frequent discussion among scholars. It would seem, given its accretion as an authoritative collection of oral law, that its purpose was intended to be a type of Jewish law code. There are a variety of genres in which halakhah is communicated in the Mishnah, however, such as debates, Bible interpretation, conundrums, etc., and by comparison, it differs substantially from other known law codes of the period; its closest analogy perhaps being the much later Justinian's Digest of Roman law. Scholars have been divided on this issue since the rise of modern critical theory; some hold that the Mishnah was intended as a law code, others a mere collection of halakhic tradition, or even a study manual of halakhah (the views are presented and evaluated by Stemberger, pp. 135–9). Though the work as a whole, as asserted by Stemberger, probably has some elements of all three of these functions, the portion of material to be examined at present is foremost pedagogical. Rather than a code of law or mere collection of halakhic decisions made by rabbis of succeeding generations, with respect to Nazirite halakhah *m. Naz.* resembles a type of study manual (see "Assessment" following on pp. 108ff.).

Tractate Mishnah Nazir

Tractate *Mishnah Nazir* (*m. Naz.*) appears, as mentioned, within the
Mishnah's third order: the order on laws affecting women (*Nashim*).
In terms of the transmission history of the Mishnah, *m. Naz.* has always
been in the order on women. Why it is accorded such a place is
not exactly clear. It is suggested in the Babylonian Talmud[92] that its
inclusion in *Nashim* is due to the biblical juxtaposition of the law for
the Nazirite vow (Num. 6.1–21) against the law for the adulterous
woman (Num. 5.11–31). Such a rationale is conceivable, but it seems
more plausible that its placement is due, like its preceding and related
tractate *Nedarim* (*vows*), to the special case of a woman's vow and the
right of a husband or father to annul it (cf. Num. 30.3–16).[93] Why,
too, the topic is accorded its own tractate is likely founded on the
Bible. Since the Bible contains a special law for the Nazirite vow
(Num. 6.1–21) in relation to ordinary vows (Num. 30.1–16), the rabbis probably followed suit by shaping and ordering Nazirite halakhah
separately from ordinary votive tradition (i.e., *m. Nedarim*).[94]

The final redaction of tractate *m. Naz.* presumably stems from the
hand of Rabbi, the redactor of the Mishnah. Its content, on the
other hand, originates from previous collections of halakhah, a
significant portion of which dates back to R. Akiba (AD 90–130)[95]
and possibly earlier.[96] Within the context of a discussion on how
much grape produce renders a Nazirite culpable of breaking his/her
vow, *m. Naz.* 6.1 makes reference to a teaching in "the First Mishnah,"

---

[92] *b. Naz.* 2a; see also *Tg. Ps.-J.* on Num. 6.2.

[93] Though admittedly such a matter is only discussed in *m. Naz.* 4.2–7 and 9.1;
Stemberger holds that its inclusion is based primarily on its being an extension of
tractate *m. Ned.* (i.e., *m. Naz.* represents a special kind of vow), 122; Similarly, M.
Boertien states that the vow of *m. Naz.* is a special vow and belongs with *m. Ned.*,
see *Nazir: Text, Übersetzung und Erklärung nebst textkritischen Anhang* (vol. 3:4 of *Die
Mischna: Text, Übersetzung und ausfürliche Erklärung*; eds. K. H. Rengstorf, L. Rost, and
S. Herrmann; Berlin: Walter de Gruyter, 1971), 1; cf. J. Neusner, *A History of the
Mishnaic Law of Women* (SJLA 33:3; Leiden: Brill, 1980), 112–3. Neusner holds that
although based on scripture the tractate would be expected in the order *Qodashim*
(*Holy Things*), its placement in *Nashim* is logically due, like *m. Ned.*, to the interests
of the rabbis in the effects of language on the relationships between the sexes.

[94] That *m. Naz.* is to be recognized as connected with *m. Ned.* may be seen in
the opening discussion of *m. Naz.* 1.1.

[95] Scholars tend to use different systems for dating the rabbis. I follow here the
practice of dating the rabbis according to their respective generations; cf. Stemberger,
56–83; and Bowker, 323, n. a.

[96] Boertien, 5.

a likely reference to an early collection of Nazirite tradition, and one possibly in a form similar to the present work. Boertien, following Epstein, attributes many of the anonymous sayings in *m. Naz.*, sayings amounting to roughly half the total content of the tractate, to R. Judah b. Ilai (AD 130–60), the third generation Tanna and student of Akiba.[97] R. Judah is cited seven times in the tractate,[98] and within sources outside the Mishnah many anonymous sayings are attributed to him.[99] Later rabbinic tradition also, however, ascribes the anonymous material in the Mishnah, presumably including tractate *m. Naz.*, to R. Meir (AD 130–60), another prominent student of Akiba.[100] Either of the two possibilities suggests the use of a previous collection(s) by Rabbi, likely originating in some fashion with Akiba at the turn of the first to second century AD.

With respect to the dating of the material, a significant portion, as mentioned, likely dates back to Akiba and possibly earlier. Sayings attributed to particular rabbis stem primarily from Tannaim of the second and third generations after the destruction of the temple (AD 90–160), and attributions to figures active during the temple's lifetime are few, numbering twenty-two in total. Twenty-one of these comprise opposite opinions in debates and are ascribed to the Schools of Hillel and Shammai.[101] One saying is attributed to Nahum the Mede, a figure active at the time of the temple's destruction.[102]

The present form of the tractate if not original is certainly old; its division into nine chapters and subdivision into individual laws, or *mishnayot*, are presupposed in the Talmuds.[103] Logical arrangement on a grand scale is avoided and although the material follows the general scheme of the law for the Nazirite vow in Num. 6.1–21, it does so only very loosely. Reasons behind the various chapter divisions, therefore, are not always apparent. Minor divisions, on the other hand, appear rather naturally as the content tends to coagulate into groups of mishnayot sharing a similar purpose or topic. These in turn are linked together by a variety of redactional principles including associations of literary form, sub-topic or rabbinic citation.

---

[97] See *m. Gitt.* 5.6; *m. Sanh.* 3.4; *m. Eduy.* 7.2; see also Bowker, 57.
[98] *m. Naz.* 1.7; 2.1,2; 3.6; 4.3; 6.2,7.
[99] Boertien, 5.
[100] *b. Sanh.* 86a.
[101] *m. Naz.* 2.1,2; 3.6,7; 5.1, 2, 3, 5.
[102] *m. Naz.* 5.4.
[103] Stemberger, 121.

1.8.1   *Mishnah Nazir 1.1–7*

The tractate opens with the introductory declaration that "all substitute forms of words connoting a Nazirite vow are binding as a
Nazirite vow" (כל כנויי נזירות כנזירות).[104] This is then followed by a
series of hypothetical expressions illustrating what does or does not
constitute substitute forms of words:[105]

> If one says, "I will be,"[106] he is a Nazirite; "I will be comely," he becomes
> a Nazirite; or, "Nazik," or "Naziakh," or "Paziakh,"[107] he becomes a
> Nazirite. "I will be as this one," or "I will plait [my hair]," or "I will
> grow a crown of hair," or "I undertake to let my hair grow unkempt,"
> he becomes a Nazirite. "I undertake to bring birds," R. Meir says,
> "He is a Nazirite"; but the Sages say, "He is not a Nazirite."[108]

The mishnah, as stated, is general and introductory and links tractate *m. Naz.* with tractate *m. Ned.* which opens with a similar declaration (*m. Ned.* 1.1–2).[109] In this manner, the Mishnah introduces the
Nazirite vow as a special type of vow and, like all vows, generally
declares all forms, whether explicit or implied, binding. One debate
appears at the end of the periscope: a debate between R. Meir and

---

[104] כנויים, from the Pi. pl. of כנה, is rendered into English with some clumsiness.
The verb carries the meaning "to qualify, define; to surname, to nickname; to mod-
ify an expression," see M. Jastrow, *Dictionary of the Targumim, the Talmud Babli and
Yerushalmi, and the Midrashic Literature, with an Index of Scriptural Quotations* (New York:
Judaica Press, 1996), 648; Danby translates the nominal form as a "substitute [for
the form of words used to utter] a vow," *The Mishnah* (Oxford: Oxford University
Press, 1933), 280 (cf. 264, nos. 1–5), and Neusner the pl. as "euphemisms," *Mishnaic
Law*, 114; cf. Boertien, "Nebenbennungen," 38–9.

[105] Neusner and Danby see a lemma in the halakhah following the Gemara (*b.
Ned.* 2b; *b. Naz.* 2b,) and state that only the three terms Nazik, Naziakh and Paziakh
(1.1b) constitute actual כנויים. All other expressions comprise "handles" for the
Nazirite vow, Danby, ibid., and Neusner, ibid, 115; The Tosefta, however, sees no
distinction when labeling Samson-vows כנויים (cf. *m. Naz.* 1.2 and *t. Naz.* 1.5).

[106] This expression probably assumes a hypothetical context in which a Nazirite
is in visual sight of the one uttering the words (i.e., it is likely a shortened version
of the following expression, "I will be like this one"); see Ch. Albeck, *Shishah sidre
Mishnah* (vol. 3; Jerusalem: Mosad Byalik, 1952–8), 195.

[107] These terms likely represent pronounced mutilations of the term נזיר, to which
they are phonologically similar (cf. the parallel citation in the context of *m. Ned.*
1.2). They may be accidental or intended mutilations, either because of a speech
impediment (such as stuttering [see the Gemara of R. Jose in *y. Ned.* 37a; *y. Naz.*
51a. 55]) or perhaps because of the use of slang.

[108] All English citations from the Mishnah are adapted from the translation by
Danby, *The Mishnah*, as well as P. Blackman, *Mishnayoth* (7 vols.; London: Mishna
Press, 1951–6).

[109] *m. Ned.* 1.1: כל כנויי נדרים כנדרים, "All substitute forms of words connoting a
vow, are binding as a vow."

the Sages over the binding nature of a promise to bring birds.[110] The Mishnah appears to side with the opinion of the Sages in declaring such a promise non-connotative of a Nazirite vow.

Mishnah Nazir 1.1 also sets the tone for the manner in which the first chapter of the tractate is laid out. *Mishnah Nazir* 1.2 and 1.3–7 serve as introductory rulings as well: 1.2 introduces the various rules of behavior required of Nazirites and 1.3–7 the length of time a Nazirate without a specified duration is to be observed.

> If one says, "I will be a Nazirite from grape-stones," or[111] "from grape-skins," or "from cutting my hair," or "from uncleanness," he becomes a Nazirite and all the rules of Naziriteship [דקדוקי נזירות] apply to him. "I will be like Samson," or "like the son of Manoah," or "like the husband of Delilah," or "like him who tore out the gates of Gaza," or "like him whose eyes the Philistines put out," then he becomes a Nazirite like Samson [נזיר שמשון]. What is the difference between a lifelong Nazirite [נזיר עולם] and a Nazirite like Samson? If the hair of a lifelong Nazirite becomes too heavy he may lighten it with a razor, and he must bring the three offerings of cattle, and if he becomes unclean he brings the offering for uncleanness; a Nazirite like Samson, if his hair becomes heavy he may not lighten it, and if he becomes unclean he does not bring the offering for uncleanness. (*m. Naz.* 1.2)

Establishing various *rules* (דקדוקים) of Naziriteship is an attempt to deal with possible exemptions to normative Nazirite behavior (Num. 6.1–21). Though scripture is taken for granted, the Mishnah appears to harmonize in this halakhah the apparent disparities between the behavior required of Nazirites in the law of Num. 6.1–21 and the behavior exhibited by Nazirites known in the Bible, Samson (Judg. 13–16), and in this case Absalom (rather than Samuel, cf. *Mekh. Shirata* 2; II Sam. 14.26). Behavior observed while under a vow is contingent upon a person's frame of reference when making the vow.

---

[110] Although forming part of the required offerings of a Nazirite, birds are offered only when a Nazirite is rendered unclean because of a corpse (Num. 6.9–12); see Albeck, 195; and Boertien, 43; see also P. Kehati, *The Mishnah: A New Translation* (vol. 3:2; Jerusalem: Eliner Library, 1994), 3.

[111] The ו in ומן, "and/or from," may be translated as either consecutive or conjunctive. Most scholars opt for the latter. The pericope deals with the issue of exemptions, e.g. the case of the Nazirite like Samson who is allowed an exemption to the Law's proscription against corpse contact (Num. 6.9–12), and the conjunctive use of ומן makes best sense in light of such a context; see Neusner on "the point of A-B," *Mishnaic Law*, 116; and Boertien, 45; see also Albeck, 195; cf. Danby, 281, who opts for the former.

Such is the principle the Mishnah wishes to communicate. If a votary utters any form of words relative to the activities prohibited in the Num. 6.1–21 (esp. vv. 2–8) legislation (e.g., abstinence from grape produce, cutting the hair, or contacting a corpse), then the law for the Nazirite vow, together with all[112] its regulations, is the pattern of behavior to which the votary must adhere.[113] If reference is made instead, however, to Samson when making a vow, then the votary must pattern his behavior after the Nazirite Samson whose lifestyle exhibited certain exemptions to the law in Num.

Reference to lifelong Naziriteship is secondary in the mishnah and is used primarily as a means of delineating how exactly a נזיר שמשון behaves. Like a lifelong Nazirite (נזיר עולם), a Samson-Nazirite is under the obligation of abstinence for a lifetime. Unlike the lifelong Nazirite, however, he must refrain from cutting his hair even if it becomes too heavy for him (cf. Judg. 13.5; 16.17), and, like Samson, he is exempt from the Law's proscription against corpse impurity (Num. 6.9–12). A lifelong Nazirite, on the other hand, may trim his hair if it becomes too heavy,[114] provided he offers the sacrifices appropriate for cutting his hair in cleanness (Num. 6.13–21). Like an ordinary Nazirite he must also observe the rite of purification if rendered unclean because of a corpse (Num. 6.9–12).

Of added interest, the Mishnah utilizes in this halakhah a principle already elucidated in the previous pericope (m. Naz. 1.1); namely, care is taken to include as examples of Samson-Nazirite vows promises made with only implicit reference to Samson, such as "I will be like the son of Manoah," or "like the husband of Delilah," etc. In this respect, even substitute forms of words for Samson-Nazirite vows are binding as Samson-Nazirite vows.[115]

Mishnah Nazir 1.3–7 in similar fashion introduces the סתם נזירות, or "Naziriteship of unspecified duration." Mishnah Nazir 1.3 unambiguously states that "a Naziriteship of unspecified duration is binding for thirty days" (סתם נזירות שלשים יום). Like m. Naz. 1.1, the laconic comment is then followed by a series of hypothetical vows.

---

[112] "Detailed, minute points of the law," see דקדוק, דיק in Jastrow, Dictionary, 318.
[113] Kehati, 5.
[114] Cf. II Sam. 14.26 where Absalom's hair is described as "heavy upon him" (עליו כי כבד). Absalom, however, is never named a Nazirite, nor is he described as offering sacrifices when he cut his hair.
[115] t. Naz. 1.5; Albeck, 195.

In this respect, vows are adjudicated either binding for thirty days, more than thirty days, a series of sequential thirty-day periods, or for the duration of a lifetime depending on what a person utters when making a vow.

> If one says, "I will be a Nazirite for one long term," or "for one short term," or even "from now until the end of the world," he is a Nazirite for thirty days. "I will be a Nazirite and for one more day," or "I will be a Nazirite and for one hour more," or "I will be a Nazirite for one term and a half," he must be a Nazirite for two terms. "I will be a Nazirite for thirty days and one hour more," he must be a Nazirite for thirty-one days, because Naziriteship is not measured by hours. (*m. Naz.* 1.3).

> "I will be a Nazirite as the hairs of my head," or "as the dust of the earth," or "as the sand of the sea," then he becomes a lifelong Nazirite and must cut his hair off every thirty days. Rabbi says, "Such a one does not cut his hair every thirty days; but who is the one who cuts his hair every thirty days? One who says, 'I undertake to observe as many Nazirite vows as the hairs of my head,' or 'as the dust of the earth,' or 'as the sand of the sea.'" (*m. Naz.* 1.4)

> "I will be a Nazirite a house-full," or "a basket-full," they must inquire of him searchingly; If he said, "I vowed to abstain for one long term," he becomes a Nazirite for thirty days; But if he said, "I vowed unspecified," then they look upon the basket as if it were filled with mustard seed and he must be a Nazirite all the days of his life. (*m. Naz.* 1.5)

> "I will be a Nazirite from here to such-and-such a place," they must calculate how many days' journey it is from here to such-and-such a place. If less than thirty days, he is a Nazirite for thirty days, but if more he is a Nazirite for as many days as the days of the journey. (*m. Naz.* 1.6)

> "I will be a Nazirite as the number of days in the solar year," he must count as many Naziriteships as the number of days in the solar year. R. Judah said, "Such a case once happened, and when he completed his vow he died." (*m. Naz.* 1.7)

Ambiguity of time in Num. 6.1–21 and the specifics of spoken language are of central concern.[116] The section addresses in progressive fashion a series of hyperbolic expressions, each representing a different standard for measuring time. Decisions in each case are based on two primary principles: (1) if a vow is articulated without expressing

---

[116] Neusner, *Mishnaic Law*, 118ff.; and Kehati, 7.

a time limit, it is binding for thirty days (*why* thirty is the standard
is undisclosed); and (2) if the length of time for a vow is unspecified
according to numbers of "days" (the unit of measurement assumed
to be the standard for making Nazirite vows in Num. 6.1–21 [cf.
Num. 6.4, 8]),[117] then whatever expression *is* used is to be broken
down into such units: either a number equaling at least thirty, but
possibly more (such as when using an expression measurable in terms
of days, like days required for a journey [*m. Naz.* 1.6]), or units of
thirty-day periods (such as when using generally immeasurable expressions like "one long spell," or "one short spell" [*m. Naz.* 1.3], or "as
the hairs of my head" [*m. Naz.* 1.7]).

Only one debate appears in the section, a debate between the
anonymous source and Rabbi over who it is that cuts his hair off
every thirty days (*m. Naz.* 1.4). The Mishnah appears to side with Rabbi,
and the delineation serves to illumine one of the two principles at
hand: decision rests on specificity of language. Following the halakhah
that a vow unspecified according to numbers of days is binding for
thirty days (*m. Naz.* 1.3), the one who vows to be a Nazirite as the
hairs of his head, dust of the earth, or sand of the sea does not cut
his hair off every thirty days, but only the one who promises specifically
to observe "as many Nazirite vows [הרי עלי נזירות]" as the hairs of
his head, the dust of the earth, or the sands of the sea.[118]

Why the rabbis determine a length of thirty days as a general and
minimum period for a Nazirite vow, as noted previously, is never
stated. It is possible, as some have suggested, that an exegetical principle lies behind the decision.[119] The numeric value of "he will be"
(יהיה) in Num. 6.5, "he will be holy, allowing his hair to grow long,"
is thirty, and the rabbis may have followed such a hermeneutic when
deciding the general length of a Nazirite vow. It is more likely, however, that here, as with so many decisions in the tractate, the rabbis have simply adopted a tradition already extant.[120] I will leave the
significance of the thirty days for further discussion in Section 3.

---

[117] Albeck, 197.

[118] In other words, a thirty-day period for each hair, granule of dust, or grain
of sand; see Kehati, 9.

[119] Salmanowitsch, 53; see *b. Naz.* 5a, *y. Naz.* 51c, *Sifre Zutta* on Num. 6.5, and
Num. R. 10; see also Boertien, 50.

[120] Josephus states that thirty days was the customary period for observing the
vow (*B. J.* 2.313–14); cf. Maimonides, *Nezirut 3.2*, who states that the Sages received
this concept from oral tradition (מפי קבלה); see also Salmanowitsch, 53; and Kehati,
p. 7.

1.8.2 *Mishnah Nazir 2.1–3*

Terminologically, "nazir" simply means "one who abstains."[121] Given common spoken usage of the term, together with a certain imme-diate context in which it might be mentioned, one may imagine how an ordinary vow to be an "abstain*er*" from certain item(s) might be confused with intent to make a Nazirite vow. Such cases are addressed in *m. Naz.* 2.1–3.

> If one said, "I will be a nazirite [הריני נזיר] from dried figs and from fig-cakes," the School of Shammai say, "he is a Nazirite"; the School of Hillel say, "he is not a Nazirite." R. Judah said, "Although the School of Shammai spoke in this way, they meant it to refer to one who said, "May they be to me as *Korban!*" (*m. Naz.* 2.1)

> If one said, "This cow thinks it will be a Nazirite if it stands up," or "This door thinks it will be a Nazirite if it opens," the School of Shammai say, "he is a Nazirite"; but the School of Hillel say, "He is not a Nazirite." R. Judah said, "Although the School of Shammai spoke in this way, they meant it to refer to one who said, "May this cow be to me as *Korban!*" (*m. Naz.* 2.2)

> If they filled a cup for one and he said, "I will be a Nazirite from it!"—then he becomes a Nazirite. It once happened that a certain woman was intoxicated and they filled the cup for her, and she said, "I will be a Nazirite from it [הריני נזירה ממנו]!" The Sages said, "She only intended to say, "Let it be me as *Korban!*" (*m. Naz.* 2.3)

The section involves a series of debates between the Schools of Hillel and Shammai with the final pericope comprising a case decided by the Sages. Clarification of the Shammaite position is supplied by R. Judah,[122] and as a whole, the series presents a single unified princi-ple: where there is confusion of intent, sensitivity to context is the determining factor.[123] The vow to be a "nazir" from dried figs or fig-cakes is ruled an ordinary vow in the likeness of vows of *Korban*[124]

---

[121] See the Introduction, pp. 2–3.

[122] Albeck, 197; and Kehati, 15; cf. Neusner, who asserts that R. Judah's explanation is an attempt to bring the Shammaites over to the Hillelite position, against the intended meaning of the logion, *Mishnaic Law*, 122–3; I believe the explanation of Judah is didactic of the principle at hand: even the Shammaites' use of the term was confusing; cf. Boertien, "R. Jehuda ist somit der Meinung, daß nach der Schule Scham-mais der Gelobende das Wort נזיר als ein כנוי des Worte קרבן benutzt habe," 62.

[123] Neusner, *Mishnaic Law*, 121–4.

[124] An expression connoting one's desire to remain separate from someone or some material thing in imitation of an item dedicated to the temple as an offering (and which, thereby, is set apart from common use); cf. *m. Ned.* 1.4.

since such items, although similar in appearance to raisins and raisin-cakes, are not forbidden to the Nazirite. Similarly, when spoken in reference to animals or inanimate objects (*m. Naz.* 2.2) or in the context of one vowing to abstain from a cup of wine while already drunk (*m. Naz.* 2.3), "nazir" spoken in such contexts must be taken to denote an ordinary vow of abstention, not a Nazirite vow since only humans may become Nazirites, and a state of intoxication certainly precludes any intention to abstain.

1.8.3   *Mishnah Nazir 2.4*

Following the mention of "wine" in *m. Naz.* 2.3, *m. Naz.* 2.4 addresses cases involving possible exemptions to the Law's proscriptions against wine and corpse impurity (Num. 6.2–8).

> "I will be a Nazirite on condition that I be allowed to drink wine and become unclean because of the dead," he becomes a Nazirite and is forbidden all of them. "I know there are vows of Naziriteship, but I did not know a Nazirite is forbidden wine," he is bound; but R. Simeon permits it. "I know the Nazirite is forbidden wine, but I thought the Sages permit it to me because I cannot live without wine," or "because I have to bury the dead," then he is permitted, but R. Simeon prohibits it. (*m. Naz.* 2.4)

The pericope involves a series of debates between the anonymous source and R. Simeon, and decisions are based on what a person *knows* about such proscriptions when uttering a vow. If a votary understands the proscriptions before making the vow (*m. Naz.* 2.4a), he is allowed no exemptions and his vow remains binding.[125] If ignorant, however, or his life circumstances prohibit proper observance (i.e., if his life depends upon drinking wine, or his occupation depends on contacting a corpse [e.g., a gravedigger]), he may be allowed such exemptions—though such decisions are conjectured.[126]

1.8.4   *Mishnah Nazir 2.5–6*

> "I will be a Nazirite and I undertake to bring the offerings of another Nazirite [לנלח נזיר]," and his fellow heard him and said, "And I, too, and I will bring the offerings of another Nazirite," if they are shrewd,

---

[125] Cf. *m. Naz.* 1.2; and Kehati, 19–20.
[126] Kehati, following the Gemara (*b. Naz.* 3.1–3), holds that מתיר, "permits," refers to the annulment of the vows, 20.

they bring one another's offerings, but if not, they must bring the offerings of other Nazirites. (*m. Naz.* 2.5)

"I undertake to bring half the offerings of another Nazirite," and his fellow heard him and said, "And I, too, undertake to bring half the offerings of another Nazirite," each must bring the whole offerings of a Nazirite. So says R. Meir. But the Sages say, one brings half the offerings of a Nazirite, and the other half the offerings of a Nazirite (*m. Naz.* 2.6)

Mishnah Nazir 2.5–6 contain two, perhaps, humorous cases involving companions vowing to become Nazirites in one another's presence; both of whom agree to bring as an additional token of piety either the whole (*m. Naz.* 2.5) or half (*m. Naz.* 2.6) of another's Nazirite offerings.[127] If the companions are shrewd, so the Mishnah asserts, when the time for giving offerings is upon them, they will either simply bring one another's offerings to the altar (*m. Naz.* 2.5), or, though debated, share one whole set of offerings between them (*m. Naz.* 2.6).

1.8.5 *Mishnah Nazir 2.7–10*

Nazirite vows made on the condition of childbirth occupies the topic of discussion in the following section. *Mishnah Nazir* 2.7–8 deal with cases involving a single vow and *m. Naz.* 9–10 with those involving multiple or sequential vows.

"I will be a Nazirite when a son is born to me," and a son is born to him, he is a Nazirite; If a daughter, one of indeterminate sex, or androgynous, he is not a Nazirite. If he said, "When I see that I have a child," even if a daughter is born to him, or one of indeterminate sex, or androgynous, he becomes a Nazirite. (*m. Naz.* 2.7)

If his wife miscarried, he does not become a Nazirite. R. Simeon says, "He should say, 'If it it is a child likely to live, I will be a Nazirite by obligation [נזיר הובה], but if not, I will be a Nazirite of free will [נזיר נדבה]'" If she afterward gave birth to a child, he becomes a Nazirite. R. Simeon says, "He should say, 'If the first were a child likely to live, my first Nazirite vow will be obligatory, and this one by

---

[127] By way of context, this is the meaning of לגלה, literally "to shave." The term implies the promise to bring the offerings, or pay for the cost of the offerings, which accompany the shaving of the hair at the conclusion of a vow (Num. 6.13–21), and not simply the shaven hair itself (cf. the use of the term ξυρᾶσθαι in Josephus' *A. J.* 19.294, testimony 1.6.5); cf. Boertien who translates the term "Ausweihungskosten," literally "de-sanctification cost," 71ff.

free will, but if not, the first be of free will and the second by obligation.'" (m. Naz. 2.8)

"I will be a Nazirite and a Nazirite when I have a son," if he began to
count his own vow and then a son was born to him, he fulfills his own
and after that counts the vow for his son. "I will be a Nazirite when
a son is born to me, and a Nazirite," if he began counting his own
and after that a son was born to him, he sets aside his own and counts
the vow for his son, and after that fulfills his own vow. (m. Naz. 2.9)

"I will be a Nazirite when I have a son and a Nazirite for one-hundred days," and a son was born to him, if before seventy days, he has
suffered no loss, but if after seventy days it makes the following days
of no effect since the hair may not be cut within less than thirty days.
(m. Naz. 2.10)

Motivation for making a Nazirite vow is a concept taken for granted
in Num. 6.1–21, yet making a Nazirite vow on the condition of
childbirth is a concept familiar to biblical narrative (I Sam. 1.11).
The guiding principle underlying rabbinic halakhah in such circumstances appears to be Num. 30.2, "when a man makes a vow . . . he
must do according to all that proceeds out of his mouth." *Mishnah
Nazir* 2.7–8 are fairly straight forward. If one promises to be a Nazirite
when a son is born and a son is born, then he must fulfill his words
and become a Nazirite. If a child other than a son is born to him,
however, the conditional arrangement has not been met and the
votary is free from any obligation. If the votary simply promised to
become a Nazirite when a child of unspecified sex was born, then
no matter what the sex of the child, so long as it lives, he is bound
by his vow and must become a Nazirite. The Mishnah is quick to
cover all possible scenarios, and states in the case of a miscarriage
that if *after* the miscarriage a child was born (the case of twins?),[128]
the votary must become a Nazirite since the arrangement was met—
albeit in an unexpected manner. Additional commentary is added
by R. Simeon regarding the issue of motivation in such circumstances (m. Naz. 2.8).[129] Preference is given to making the Nazirite
vow voluntarily, or out of free will (נדבה), rather than strictly by
obligation (חובה) in fulfillment of a conditional arrangement.

---

[128] הורי וילדה—It is not clear whether this mean immediately afterwards, very
soon afterwards, or simply *whenever* the wife has another child.

[129] *Tosefta Nezirut* 2.8–9 suggests R. Simeon's commentary pertains to cases of
doubt, Neusner, *Mishnaic Law*, 128; see also Kehati, 26–7.

Again, the principle is exercised when making multiple or sequential Nazirite vows (*m. Naz.* 2.9–10). If one vowed to be a Nazirite (perhaps out of excitement over a wife's pregnancy) on condition of the birth of a son, the votary must complete his own spell of Naziriteship (presumably thirty days)[130] before beginning the second term, even if a son was born while in the midst of observing his first spell. The reason for this is the specific *order* of terms articulated when the vow was spoken. Conversely, if the promised order of observance was reversed, and a son was born while observing the first spell, the votary must interrupt the first spell, observe the term taken on the condition of childbirth, and once completed, take up again the initial spell (*m. Naz.* 2.9). The principle is applied in the final pericope with some lack of clarity. If one made a one hundred-day vow plus an additional unspecified vow, and a child was born in the midst of observing the lengthy term, an uninterrupted thirty-day period must remain in order for the Nazirite to cut his hair after the appropriate number of days. It is not clear what is meant by "the following days are no effect." It may mean either the remaining days of the lengthy vow are forfeited without loss to the votary (i.e., he simply neglects them); or he must observe a thirty-day period once the second vow is completed, no matter how few days he has remaining in his original vow.[131]

1.8.6 *Mishnah Nazir 3.1–2*

> If one said, "I will be a Nazirite," he cuts his hair off on the thirty-first day, but if he cut it off on the thirtieth day, he has fulfilled his obligation. "I will be a Nazirite for thirty days," if he cut his hair off on the thirtieth day, he has not fulfilled his obligation. (*m. Naz.* 3.1)

> One who made two Nazirite vows must cut his hair off for the first term on the thirty-first day and for the second on the sixty-first day; but if he cut off his hair of the first term on the thirtieth day, he must cut his hair for the second on the sixtieth day, and if he cut his hair on the fifty-ninth day, he has fulfilled his obligation. R. Papias testified regarding one who made two Nazirite vows that if he cut his hair for the first term on the thirtieth day, he should cut off his hair for the second on the sixtieth day, and that if he cut his hair off on the fifty-ninth day, he has fulfilled his obligation because the thirtieth day may be counted for him among the number. (*m. Naz.* 3.2)

---

[130] Cf. *m. Naz.* 1.3ff.

[131] This is the position of Maimonides (*Naziriteship* 4.3–5), cited in Neusner, *Mishnaic Law*, 130–1.

Following the mention of the cutting of the hair in *m. Naz.* 2.10, *m. Naz.* 3.1–2 address in similar fashion the issue of what *day* the hair must be cut when a vow is completed (cf. Num. 6.13–21). *Mishnah Nazir* 3.1 deals with cases involving a single vow, and *m. Naz.* 3.2 with cases involving multiple or sequential vows. The adjudicating principle is the same in both: the number of "days" specified in a vow, or series of vows, cannot be encroached upon when cutting the hair because, again, a man must fulfill his vow according to his explicit words (cf. Num. 30.3). If one said, "I will be a Nazirite," when uttering a vow, although the vow is to be observed for thirty days (cf. *m. Naz.* 1.3), the actual phrase "thirty days" was not articulated. If the votary then cut his hair on the thirtieth day, he has acted appropriately. But if he said specifically, "I will be a Nazirite *for thirty days*," the thirtieth day must be observed completely. Similarly if one vowed to be a Nazirite for two spells, a period equal to a total of sixty days (cf. *m. Naz.* 1.3ff.), it is preferred that the votary cut his hair off for the first term on the thirty-first day and for the second on the sixty-first day, so that the total number of days for observing the Nazirite vows are not encroached upon (*m. Naz.* 3.2). But since "sixty days" was not actually articulated in the vow, the votary is accorded leeway in calculation, even to the point of cutting the hair for the first term on the thirtieth day itself and on the fifty-ninth day for the second term (a scenario supported by R. Papias).

1.8.7   *Mishnah Nazir 3.3–6*

If a Nazirite becomes unclean because of accidental contact with a corpse, the law requires the votary to undergo a seven-day rite of purification (cf. Num. 19.11–19), after which the defiled hair must be shaved. Once appropriate offerings are given on the following day, the votary must then start the vow over again, "counting the former days as void" (Num. 6.9–12). Precisely how many days are void if uncleanness is acquired at the very point a vow is completed (yet before sacrifices are actually given), is the subject of concern in *m. Naz.* 3.3–6.

> If one who said, "I will be a Nazirite," became unclean on the thirtieth day, he forfeits the whole. R. Eliezer says, "He forfeits only seven days." If he says, "I will be a Nazirite for thirty days," and he became unclean on the thirtieth day, he renders the whole of no effect. (*m. Naz.* 3.3)

> "I will be a Nazirite for a hundred days," and he became unclean on the hundredth day, he renders the whole period of no effect. R. Eliezer

says, "He forfeits only thirty-days." If he became unclean on the one hundred and first day, he forgoes thirty days. R. Eliezer says, "He forfeits only seven days." (*m. Naz.* 3.4)

One who made the Nazirite vow while in a cemetery, even if he were there for thirty days, these are not reckoned to him among the number of days, neither does he bring the offering of uncleanness. But if he went out and came back in again, they do reckon to him the number of days and he must bring the offering for uncleanness. R. Eliezer says, "Not if on the same day, as it says, 'and the former days shall be void,' so only until he has acquired 'former days.'" (*m. Naz.* 3.5)

One who made a vow for a long period and completed it and afterwards came to the Land, the School of Shammai say, "He must be a Nazirite again for thirty days"; but the School of Hillel say, "He must be a Nazirite from the beginning." It once happened that Queen Helena, whose son went to war, said, "If my son returns home safely from the war, I will be a Nazirite for seven years!" and her son returned home from the war and she was a Nazirite for seven years; and at the end of the seven years she came up to the Land, and the School of Hillel instructed her that she must be a Nazirite for seven more years; but at the end of those seven years she became unclean, and she found herself a Nazirite for twenty-one years. R. Judah said, "She was a Nazirite for only fourteen years." (*m. Naz.* 3.6)

A number of principles are communicated in this section, the primary concern being the vow of prolonged duration (*m. Naz.* 3.4 and 3.6). Regarding the thirty-day vow, similar to previous decisions respecting what day a Nazirite should cut his hair, the basis for determining how much time is lost if impurity is obtained is the words a person specifically uttered when making the vow. If it is a סתם נזירות, or Naziriteship of unspecified "days," only the seven days required to observe the rite of purification are forfeit, according to R. Eliezer. Again, however, if "thirty days" was actually articulated in the vow, even if the votary became unclean on the thirtieth day, the whole period is rendered of no effect (*m. Naz.* 3.3).

In the case of one who made a vow for a prolonged period, such as a hundred days, if corpse uncleanness is acquired on the one-hundredth day, according to the anonymous source, the votary must renew the entire period. For R. Eliezer only a general period of thirty days is lost.[132]

---

[132] Why R. Eliezer rules in such a way is likely due to an association between the term "days" and a general period of thirty days. "Counting the former days as void" (Num. 6.12) then, on exegetical grounds, is taken to imply a standard value of thirty no matter what the initial length of a vow.

The Mishnah continues and addresses the scenario in which the same votary was rendered unclean on the one hundred and first day. The anonymous source decides that an additional period of thirty days is required. For R. Eliezer, as with the previous case involving the סתם נזירות, because the number of avowed days was actually fulfilled, only the seven days attendant to the rite of purification are required (*m. Naz.* 3.4).[133]

The final two pericopae are related in such a way that the former (*m. Naz.* 3.5) serves as a clever introduction to the latter (*m. Naz.* 3.6).[134] The latter serves in turn as the climax of the entire section. Days observed while in a cemetery (an incredible scenario) are ruled insufficient as credit towards completing a vow. Only when the votary leaves the unclean region do the promised days begin to accumulate (*m. Naz.* 3.5). In like manner, one who observes a prolonged vow while in a country of the non-Jews and then enters the land, presumably to discharge it, must renew the avowed period— the original term being considered as performed in a state of uncleanness (like one in a cemetery). Precisely how much of the initial period should be renewed is debated, and the decisions of *m. Naz.* 3.4 are repeated. Whereas the School of Shammai decide only a thirty-day period should be renewed, the School of Hillel assert the entire avowed period should be renewed. As an illustration of one who followed the more stringent ruling of the School of Hillel, the Mishnah relates the story of Queen Helena (of Adiabene) who was supposedly, according to one tradition, a Nazirite for twenty-one years. Following an original avowed period of seven years, taken on the condition that her son return home safe from war, when Helena entered the land (of the Jews) to discharge her vow, she heeded the advice of the School of Hillel and observed her vow again for another seven years. Unfortunately, at the conclusion of the second term, she acquired uncleanness because of a corpse and observed her vow again for another seven years, totaling twenty-one in all. R. Judah, however, disagrees on the facts of the case and asserts she was a Nazirite for no more than fourteen years.

Josephus mentions Queen Helena (wife of Monobazus I and mother

---

[133] Because he said, "I will be a Nazirite for one-hundred days."
[134] Kehati, 42.

of Izates II and Monobazus II, kings of Adiabene)[135] in book twenty of *A. J.* (20.17–96). He discusses in some detail the affairs accompanying her conversion to Judaism in the ca. AD 40's, yet says nothing of her supposed term as a Nazirite. The Mishnah's account of Queen Helena is problematic in that the facts are inconsistent. The rabbis disagree over the number of years she was under her vow, and the disagreement raises suspicion of embellishment. Rather than reporting with any degree of historical accuracy, the rabbis may be conforming the facts to fit their own respective points of view in the halakhic debate. Given the piety, however, that Josephus ascribes to Helena, and the military encounters which Izates I (who was first in the family to convert to Judaism) faced, the Mishnah's depiction is not implausible and may contain at least some degree of accuracy in depicting Helena as a Nazirite, although the details of the account remain speculative.

1.8.8 *Mishnah Nazir 3.7*

Following the citations of the School of Hillel and the School of Shammai, *m. Naz.* 3.7 provides the first of several rabbinic conundrums found in tractate *m. Naz.* The conundrum consists of a case in which there are multiple witnesses testifying at variance against one who made multiple Nazirite vows.

> If two pairs of witnesses testified against a man, one testifying that he vowed two Nazirite vows and the other that he vowed five, the School of Shammai say, "The evidence is at variance, and the Nazirite vows are not binding"; but the School of Hillel say, "With the five the two are included and so he must be a Nazirite for two terms."

The conundrum appears to be nothing more than a display of rabbinic wisdom; in both scholastic opinions a variety of interpretations of the law of Deut. 19.15 are applied (a law which states that there must be agreement between two or more [in this case two *pairs* of] witnesses for an accusation to stand as valid). Lev 5.4, "if a person swears thoughtlessly with his lips . . . and it is hidden from him, and he then comes to know it, he will be guilty . . ." may also stand behind this mishnah.

---

[135] Boertien, 95–6.

1.8.9   *Mishnah Nazir 4.1–7*

Chapter four of tractate *m. Naz.* (4.1–7) deals with the issue of the Nazirite vow and women and introduces some of the more complex matters of Nazirite halakhah. *Mishnah Nazir* 4.1–5 concern cases involving the annulment of a woman's vow by her husband, and *m. Naz.* 4.6–7 with a variety of issues relating to the assumption of the Nazirate by a son, either by compulsion of a father while the son is under age (*m. Naz.* 4.6), or when come of age to stand in place of a father who is unable to complete a vow by reason of death (*m. Naz.* 4.7). The Mishnah in these cases is concerned with yet a further issue: what to do with dedicated offerings when a vow has been annulled or unfulfilled.

> If one said, "I will be a Nazirite," and his fellow heard and said, "And I, too," and another, "And I, also," they all become Nazirites. If the first one were absolved they are all absolved; if the last one were released, the last one is released but all the others are forbidden. If one said, "I will be a Nazirite," and his fellow heard and said, "My mouth be as his mouth," or "My hair be as his hair," then he becomes a Nazirite. "I will be a Nazirite," and his wife heard it and said, "And I, also," he may annul her vow but his own is binding. "I will be a Nazirite," and her husband heard it and said, "And I, also," he cannot annul her vow. (*m. Naz.* 4.1)

> "I will be a Nazirite, and will you?" And she said, "Amen!" He may revoke her vow, but his own is binding. "I will be a Nazirite and will you?" And he said, "Amen!" He cannot annul her vow. (*m. Naz.* 4.2)

> If the blood of any one of the offerings were sprinkled for her, he cannot annul. R. Akiba says, "Even if one of all the beasts were slaughtered for her, he cannot cancel her vow." When is this the case? When it concerns the cutting off of the hair in cleanness, but concerning the cutting off of the hair in uncleanness he may annul, because he may say, "I have no pleasure in an untidy woman [אשה מנולת]." Rabbi says, "He may annul even in the case involving cutting off the hair in cleanness, since he may say, "I have no delight in a shorn woman [אשה מנולדת]." (*m. Naz.* 4.5)

Mishnah Nazir 4.1–2 and 5[136] address circumstances in which a husband is and is *not* permitted to annul his wife's vow, the primary

---

[136] I treat these mishnayot together and out of sequence because of they relate topically. All three deal with the issue of allowed or disallowed annulment of a wife's vow, whereas *m. Naz.* 4.3 deals primarily with the issue of the wife who rebels from her vow.

interest lying in the latter.[137] *Mishnah Nazir* 4.1–2 contain a series of
related cases in which two or more vows are mutually dependent.
The principle involved is that when a vow is uttered by one individual, and another makes the same vow by way of agreement with
the other, using such phrases as, "And I, also" or such words as
"Amen," the latter's vow is mutually dependent upon the former's
by reason that the former vow contains the actual spoken words, "*I
will be a Nazirite.*" What happens in the case of the former then happens to the latter. If the former is valid, then all vows dependent
on it are valid. If the former is annulled, then all vows dependent
upon it are annulled. The same stands in the case of Nazirite vows
made between a husband and a wife. If the husband's vow is dependent upon the actual wording of his wife's vow, then he cannot
annul it because in doing so he would annul his very own vow.

At what point in time is too late for a husband to annul his wife's
vow, is the topic of concern in *m. Naz.* 4.5. According to Num.
30.6–8, a husband may annul his wife's vow on "the day he hears
of it." However, if he says nothing to her on that day, "her vow
shall stand." Nothing is mentioned with respect to when it is too
late for a husband to annul his wife's vow even on "that day," however, and the rabbis debate whether a wife's vow may be cancelled
even at the point of sacrifice (Num. 6.9–12, 13–21). According to
the anonymous source and R. Akiba, it is too late when at the completion of a vow the blood of even one animal is sacrificed in behalf
of the wife's vow. In the case of the slaughtering of an animal because
of uncleanness (Num. 6.9–12), however, a husband may annul his
wife's vow by stating that he has no joy in an untidy or impure
woman (אשה מנולת).[138] Rabbi, however, states that a man may cancel
his wife's vow even at the point of sacrificing in cleanness, since a
man may say, "I have no pleasure in a shorn woman (אשה מנולחת)."

> If a woman vowed to become a Nazirite, and she drank wine or
> became unclean because of the dead, she must receive the forty-stripes.
> If her husband absolved her, but she did not know that her husband

---

[137] Boertien divides this mishnah into two parts: *m. Naz.* 4.1a-b (comprising the
vows of the various individuals) and 4.1c-d (comprising the vows of the husband
and wife), 101–3.

[138] מנולת carries the meaning "nasty, filthy, or muddy," and refers to the woman's
impurity because of a corpse.

absolved her, and she drank wine or became unclean because of the
dead, she does not suffer the forty-stripes. R. Judah says, "If she did
not suffer the forty-stripes, she must suffer the punishment for rebellion." (m. Naz. 4.3)

Mishnah Nazir 4.3 decides a case involving a rebellious wife who will-
fully breaks her vow to abstain from wine and uncleanness because
of a corpse (m. Naz. 4.3). Nothing is said regarding the cutting of
the hair, but the topic is discussed elsewhere in m. Naz.[139] Punishment
for disobedience is not a topic consigned to women, but is discussed
here because of the wider context. In line with Deut. 25.2ff., the
Mishnah decides that in such a case the wife receives the punishment of forty lashes.[140] If her husband absolved her vow without her
knowing it, however, she is free from castigation. The Mishnah
capitalizes on the intention of the wife, however, and according to
Rabbi, the wife should at least receive the lesser punishment of lashes
for rebellion.[141]

> If a woman vowed to become a Nazirite and had set aside her beast,
> and then her husband absolved her, if her beast were his it must go
> forth and pasture with the herd, but if her beast were hers the sin-
> offering must be kept until it dies, and the burnt-offering must be
> offered as a burnt-offering, and the peace-offering offered as a peace-
> offering and they must be consumed on the same day, but they do
> not require the bread-offering. If she had unspecified money, it must
> fall as a free will offering; if the money were specified, the money for
> the sin-offering must be thrown into the Salt Sea, no one may derive
> benefit from it but no one is liable to the law of sacrilege because of
> it; with the money set apart for a burnt-offering they must bring a
> burnt-offering, and they are liable to the law of sacrilege for it; and
> with the money meant for a peace-offering they must bring a peace-
> offering; and they must be consumed on the same day, but they do
> not require the bread-offering. (m. Naz. 4.4)

Proper behavior respecting objects dedicated to the temple is a concern of an entire tractate in the Mishnah (m. Meilah), including animals dedicated or set apart for offerings. Animals already dedicated
as Nazirite offerings when a wife's vow is annulled is here a topic
of concern in m. Naz. 4.4. Following the law of Lev. 27.9–10, that
whatever animal is dedicated remains holy to the Lord, the decision

---

[139] Cf. m. Naz. 6.3.
[140] The Mishnah devotes an entire tractate to the issue of the forty-lashes punishment, see m. Makk.; cf. Josephus A. J. 4.248; and 2 Cor. 2.24.
[141] A lesser number of lashes.

follows the principle that whatever is dedicated remains dedicated even if a wife's Nazirite vow has been annulled. If a beast was not actually hers by ownership, then the beast is released; and if money was set aside to purchase offerings but not assigned to any *specific* offering, then that money is to fall as a free will offering to the temple. If while under her vow a beast or money to purchase a beast was already set apart and designated for a specific type of offering, however (such as a male lamb for a burnt-offering, a ewe-lamb for a sin-offering, or a ram for a peace-offering [cf. Num. 6.14]), then the burnt-offering and the peace-offering must be offered, or purchased and offered at the temple and "consumed on the same day." The sin-offering, however, must be kept until it dies, and any money set aside to purchase the sin-offering must be "cast into the Salt Sea" so that no one may receive benefit from it. The bread-offerings of the Nazirite (Num. 6.15) are not required in such a case.

> A man may place his son under a Nazirite vow, but a woman may not place her son under a Nazirite vow. What shall they do with the offerings if his son cut his hair off, or if his relatives cut off his hair, or if he objected, or his kindred objected for him? If he had cattle set apart, the sin-offering must be kept until it dies, and the burnt-offering must be offered as a burnt-offering, and the peace-offering must be offered as a peace-offering, and they must be consumed on the same day, but they they do not require the bread-offering. If he had any unassigned money, it must fall as a free-will-offering; if the money were specified, the money for the sin-offering must be thrown into the Salt Sea, none may derive benefit from it but none is liable to the law of sacrilege because of it; with the money assigned for a burnt-offering they must bring a burnt-offering, and they are liable to the law of sacrilege for it; and with the money designated for a peace-offering they must bring a peace-offering; and they must be consumed on the same day, but they do not require the bread-offering. (*m. Naz.* 4.6)

> A man may shave his hair and bring the offerings of a Nazirite for his father's vow, but a woman may not shave her hair and bring the offerings for her father's Nazirite vow. How so? If one's father were a Nazirite and had set aside money unassigned for his Nazirite vow, and he died, and he said, "I will be a Nazirite on the condition that I may cut off my hair and bring the offerings from my father's money," R. Jose said, "This must fall as a free-will-offering and this man may not cut off his hair and bring the offerings for the Nazirite vow of his father." Who then may cut off his hair and bring the offerings for his father's Nazirite vow? In the case where the man and his father were Nazirites, and his father had set apart unassigned money for his Nazirite vow and then died; that son may cut off his hair and bring the offerings for the Nazirite vow of his father. (*m. Naz.* 4.7)

Mishnah Nazir 4.6–7 are related to the general topic of the Nazirite
vow and women, but only to a minor degree. A man may place his
son under a Nazirite vow, but a woman may not (*m. Naz.* 4.6).
Neither may a woman take up the Nazirate of a dying father, though
a son is permitted to do so (*m. Naz.* 4.7). Beyond these rather curt
decisions, the Mishnah is concerned, again, with what to do with
dedicated offerings. In the case where a son is placed involuntarily
under a Nazirite vow by his father and he refuses to observe it
(either by objecting or cutting his own hair), or where relatives protest
on his behalf, if offerings were dedicated or money was set aside to
purchase offerings, the principle exhibited in *m. Naz.* 4.4 is maintained.
Similarly, in the case of a son wishing to complete his father's Nazirite
vow, provided that he himself was a Nazirite and his father's money
was set apart but unassigned (for use to purchase offerings for his
own vow), then the son may use his father's money and cut off his
hair and bring the required offering in behalf of his father's vow.

1.8.10   *Mishnah Nazir 5.1–3*

> The School of Shammai say, "Whatever is dedicated in error remains
> dedicated"; but the School of Hillel say, "It is not dedicated." How
> is this so? If one said, "The black ox that first comes out of my house
> shall be dedicated," and a white one comes out. The School of Shammai
> say, "It is dedicated"; but the School of Hillel say, "It is not dedi-
> cated." (*m. Naz.* 5.1)

> "The gold denar that first comes into my hand shall be dedicated,"
> and a silver denar came to hand. The School of Shammai say, "It is
> dedicated"; but the School of Hillel say, "It is not dedicated." "The
> cask of wine that first comes to my hand shall be dedicated," and one
> of oil came to hand. The School of Shammai say, "It is dedicated";
> but the School of Hillel say, "It is not dedicated." (*m. Naz.* 5.2)

> One who vowed to be a Nazirite, and inquired of a Sage who declared
> the vow binding, he must count from the hour when he vowed. If he
> inquired of a Sage who released him from his vow, and he had a
> beast dedicated, it may go forth and pasture with the herd. The School
> of Hillel said to the the School of Shammai, "Do you not admit in
> this case, that what is dedicated in error must go forth and pasture
> with the herd?" The School of Shammai replied to them, "Do you not
> admit that if one erred and called the ninth the tenth, or the tenth the
> ninth, or the eleventh the tenth, that it is sanctified?" The School of
> Hillel made answer to them, "The staff did not hallow it; and what if
> he did err and laid the staff upon the eighth or the twelfth, would he
> perhaps have affected aught?—but the law which proclaimed the tenth
> hallowed has also declared the ninth and the eleventh holy." (*m. Naz.* 5.3)

The topic of dedicated offerings discussed in the previous mishnayot leads to the question of what to do with offerings dedicated in error. Leviticus 27.9–10 mandates that when an offering is dedicated to the Lord, it becomes holy and cannot be exchanged "either good for a bad, or bad for a good." However, if an offering is replaced, then "both it and its substitute become holy." The Mishnah is concerned with the status of offerings initially dedicated, yet because of a mishap, the votary is unable to complete his obligation, such as when offerings are already dedicated and a Sage declares his vow invalid (*m. Naz.* 5.3). The question raised is whether such offerings must remain dedicated even if based on such an erroneous circumstance. The Mishnah rules that offerings dedicated in such a case are free from obligation and may return to pasture (*m. Naz.* 5.3a).[142] The case forms the crux of debate between the Schools of Hillel and Shammai, and is illustrative of the decision of the School of Hillel that offerings dedicated in error are free from any obligation (*m. Naz.* 5.1–2).

1.8.11   *Mishnah Nazir 5.4*

Mishnah Nazir 5.4 follows the topic of offerings dedicated in error with an interesting case involving one who went to collect his Nazirite offerings (presumably to offer them in the temple) only to discover that they had been stolen.

> One who vowed to be a Nazirite, and he went to bring his cattle and found that they had been stolen, if he made the Nazirite vow before his cattle were stolen, then he remains a Nazirite; but if he vowed to be a Nazirite after his cattle had been stolen, he is not a Nazirite. And such was an error which Nahum the Mede made when the Nazirites came up from the Exile and found the temple destroyed. Nahum the Mede said to them, "If you had known that the temple was destroyed would you have vowed to be Nazirites?" They replied to him, "No," and Nahum the Mede released them. And when the matter came before the Sages they said to him, "Anyone who made the Nazirite vow before the temple was destroyed is a Nazirite, but if after the temple was destroyed he is not a Nazirite." (*m. Naz.* 5.4)

The Mishnah asks whether such a person's vow remains binding, and the halakhah is dependent upon the timing of the vow in relation to the theft of the offerings. If the vow was made before the

---

[142] Cf. *m. Naz.* 4.4a.

offerings were stolen, then the vow is declared binding and the man
remains a Nazirite despite his inability to offer sacrifice. If the vow
was made after the offerings were stolen, however, then his vow is
declared in error, and he is free from obligation. The principle behind
this mishnah is illustrated by an historical case involving Nazirites
entering the land from abroad to discharge their vows only to discover the temple razed when they entered Jerusalem. Nahum the
Mede released the Nazirites from their vows upon hearing of their
intentions had they known the temple was destroyed: had they known,
they would not have made their vows. The Mishnah errs on the
side of the Sages, however, who deem Nahum's question irrelevant.
The Nazirites obviously made their vows while the temple stood,
and like the man who found his offerings stolen, their original intent
renders their vows binding despite their inability to offer sacrifice:
". . . anyone who made a Nazirite vow before the temple was destroyed
must remain a Nazirite, but if after the temple was destroyed he is
not a Nazirite."

1.8.12   *Mishnah Nazir 5.5–7*

> If people were walking along on the road and another came towards
> them, and one of them said, "I will be a Nazirite if this man be so-
> and-so," and another said, "I will be a Nazirite if this man be not so-
> and-so,"—"I will be a Nazirite if one of you be a Nazirite,"—"that
> one of you be not a Nazirite,"—"that if two of you be Nazirites,"—
> "if all of you be Nazirites," the School of Shammai say, "They are
> all Nazirites"; but the School of Hillel say, "No one is a Nazirite save
> he whose words are not confirmed." But R. Tarfon says, "None of
> them is a Nazirite." (*m. Naz.* 5.5)

> If he retired, none of them is a Nazirite. R. Simeon says, "Each one
> should say, 'If it were in accordance with my words, I will be a Nazirite
> by obligation, but if not, I will be a Nazirite by free will.'" (*m. Naz.* 5.6)

> If one saw a *koy* and said, "I will be a Nazirite if this be a wild ani-
> mal,"—"I will be a Nazirite if this be not a wild animal,"—"I will be
> a Nazirite if this be a domestic beast,"—"I will be a Nazirite if this
> be not a domestic beast,"—"I will be a Nazirite if this be both a wild
> and domestic beast,"—"I will be a Nazirite if this be neither a wild
> nor domestic beast,"—"I will be a Nazirite if one of you be a Nazirite,"—
> "I will be a Nazirite if none of you be Nazirites,"—"I will be a Nazirite
> if all of you be Nazirites,"—then all of them are Nazirites. (*m. Naz.* 5.7)

Following the mention of one who "went" (הלך) to collect his offering
and found them stolen, two conundrums involving a group who

became Nazirites "walking along the road" (הלכין בדרך) encompasses
m. Naz. 5.5–7. Both address the circumstance of individuals (six in
total) making Nazirite vows on the whim of a bet; the first hinging
on the identity of a person seen at a distance (*m. Naz.* 5.5–6); the
other on the identity of the *koy*, an animal whose precise nature is
unknown (*m. Naz.* 5.7).[143] In both cases, as with the previous conundrum (*m. Naz.* 3.7), the primary point is to demonstrate the wisdom
of the Sages who can decide cases involving even the most complex
of scenarios.

1.8.13   *Mishnah Nazir 6.1–4*

Three things are forbidden to a Nazirite: uncleanness, cutting off the
hair, and whatever comes from the vine—and everything that comes
from the vine may be included together, and one is not culpable until
he eats what comes from the grapes a quantity equal to that of an
olive's bulk, but according to the first mishnah until one drinks a quarter log of wine. R. Akiba says, "Even if he soaked his bread in wine,
and there be enough of it to equal an olive's bulk, he is culpable."
(*m. Naz.* 6.1)

One is culpable by reason of wine itself, or by reason of grapes themselves, or of grape seeds by themselves, or because of grape skins by
themselves. R. Elazar ben Azariah says, "One is not culpable until he
eats two grape seeds and the skins." These are what is meant by
hartzannim, and these are what is meant by *zagim: hartzannim* are what
are outside, *zagim* are what are inside, according to R. Judah; but
R. Jose says, "That you may not err—it is, rather, as the bell (*zug*) of
cattle: what is outside is called the *zug*, and what is inside is called
inbal (the clapper). (*m. Naz.* 6.2)

A Nazirite vow without a specified time limit is binding for thirty days.
If he himself cut off his hair, or if robbers cut it off, he forfeits thirty
days. If a Nazirite cut off his hair, whether with shears or with a razor
or plucked out any hair whatsoever, he is culpable. A Nazirite may
rub or scratch his hair, but he may not comb it [לא סורק]. R. Ishmael
says, "He may not rub it with earth since it makes the hair fall out."
(*m. Naz.* 6.3)

If a Nazirite drank wine for one whole day he is guilty on only one
count. If they said to him, "Do not drink!"—"Do not drink!"—and
he still drank, he is culpable on each count. If he cut off his hair

---

[143] The animal may have been a cross between a sheep and gazelle, or some
other animal whose wild or domesticated nature was unknown.

> throughout the day, he is culpable only on one count. If they said to
> him, "Do not cut it off!"—"Do not cut it off!"—but he cut it off, he
> is culpable on each count. If he became defiled because of the dead
> the whole day through, he is guilty on only one count. But if they
> said to him, "Do not become unclean!"—"Do not become unclean!"—
> and he became unclean, he is culpable on every count. (*m. Naz.* 6.4)

Although the law provides some detail as to what a Nazirite is to
avoid when abstaining from produce of the vine, cutting the hair
and contacting a corpse, precisely *how much* of a substance renders
a Nazirite guilty of breaking his or her vow is a subject taken for
granted in the Num. legislation. *Mishnah Nazir* 6.1–3 pick up where
scripture is ambiguous, and determine that an olive's bulk of vine
produce, either by accumulation of various fruit components, wine
by itself, or the constituents of the grape by themselves, renders a
Nazirite guilty of breaking his vow. As to the cutting of the hair, if
a Nazirite purposefully removes any hair, whether with shears, a
razor, or even by plucking, he is culpable to the forty stripes, and
so is prohibited from even rubbing, scratching, or combing his hair.
Mishnah Nazir 6.4 then addresses the issue of on how many counts
a Nazirite may be culpable and determines that a Nazirite is culpable for every count he is warned.

1.8.14 *Mishnah Nazir 6.5*

> Three things are forbidden to the Nazirite: uncleanness, cutting off the
> hair, and whatever comes from the vine. Greater strictness applies to
> defilement and cutting off the hair than to what comes from the vine,
> as defilement and cutting off the hair entail forfeiture, but what comes
> from the vine does not entail forfeiture. Greater strictness applies to
> what comes from the vine than to defilement and cutting off the hair,
> as no exception is allowed for whatever comes from the vine but excep-
> tions are permitted for defilement and cutting off the hair, as when
> cutting off the hair or burying a corpse are enjoined by the law. And
> greater strictness exists in the case of defilement than in the cutting
> off the hair, since defilement renders the whole forfeit and one is liable
> to an offering because of it, but cutting off the hair causes only thirty
> days forfeiture, and one is not liable to an offering because of it.

Mishnah Nazir 6.5 consists of another conundrum, this one identifying in rather tactful manner varying degrees of stringency between
the three things forbidden to a Nazirite: produce of the vine, cutting the hair, and uncleanness because of a corpse. Little is communicated beyond a demonstration of clever rabbinic hermeneutics.

1.8.15 *Mishnah Nazir 6.6–9*

What was the ritual procedure for cutting off the hair in uncleanness? One was sprinkled on the third and seventh day, and cut off his hair on the seventh day and brought his offering on the eighth day; but if he cut off his hair on the eighth day he brought his offering on that same day; this is the opinion of R. Akiba. R. Tarfon said to him, "What difference is there between this man and that of the leper?" He replied to him, "In the case of this one his purification is made dependent on the days prescribed for him, whereas the cleansing of the leper is made dependent upon the cutting off of his hair, and he must not bring the offering before the sun has set." (*m. Naz.* 6.6)

What was the ritual procedure for cutting off the hair in cleanness? One brought three beasts, a sin-offering, a burnt-offering, and a peace-offering; and he slaughtered the peace-offering and followed that by cutting off his hair. This is the view of R. Judah. R. Elazar says, "He had to cut off his hair only following the sin-offering, because the sin-offering precedes on every occasion; but if he cut his hair off after any one of the three of them, he has carried out his obligation." (*m. Naz.* 6.7)

Rabban Simeon ben Gamaliel says, "If one brought three beasts but did not designate, what is suitable as a sin-offering shall be offered as a sin-offering, for a burnt-offering what is suitable as a burnt-offering, and for a peace-offering what is suitable for a peace-offering. Then he took the hair he cut off and placed it beneath the cauldron. But if he cut his hair off in the capital, he did not cast his hair under the cauldron. When is this the case? When the cutting off the hair is performed in cleanness, but he did not cast the hair cut off in uncleanness under the cauldron." R. Meir says, "All cast it under the cauldron except him that was unclean and in the capital." (*m. Naz.* 6.8)

When he had cooked the peace-offering, or had seethed it, the priest took the cooked shoulder of the ram and one loaf of unleavened bread from the basket and one wafer of unleavened bread from and placed them upon the palms of the Nazirite and waved them. And after that the Nazirite is permitted to drink wine and to become unclean because of the dead. R. Simeon says, "As soon as the blood of any one offering had been sprinkled for him the Nazirite is allowed to drink wine and to become unclean because of the dead." (*m. Naz.* 6.9)

Mishnah Nazir 6.6–9 concern the order of ritual procedure when shaving the hair and offering sacrifices. *Mishnah Nazir* 6.6 deals with the procedure for cutting off the hair in uncleanness (Num. 6.9–12), and *m. Naz.* 6.7–9 with cutting off the hair in cleanness (Num. 6.13–21). Scripture is repeated in the mishnah with few addenda. According to the recollection of R. Akiba, the cutting of the hair in uncleanness took place on either the seventh or the eighth day; sacrifices

accompanying the act if completed on the eighth. Attention is then
drawn to a question of interpretation regarding differences between a
Nazirite who cuts off his hair in uncleanness, and the leper who must
also shave his hair because of uncleanness. With respect to cutting
off the hair in cleanness, there is debate regarding when in relation
to the three offerings the Nazirite cuts his hair. According to R. Judah,
the cutting of the hair took place once the peace offering had been
slaughtered. According to R. Elazar, however, the cutting of the hair
took place at any point after the sin offering had been slaughtered.

Mishnah Nazir 6.8–9 continue the topic of ritual procedure at the
point of completion of the vow. Central interest in *m. Naz.* 6.8 is
whether there were exceptions to the general order of procedure
that the Nazirite shave his hair and place it on the fire cooking the
peace-offering (Num. 6.18). R. Meir states that all cast the hair under
the cauldron except him that cut off his hair in uncleanness and
within the environs of the capital city (rather then in the temple
precincts). *Mishnah Nazir* 6.9 then states that the Nazirite is permitted to drink wine and become unclean because of a corpse once the
blood of any one offering was sprinkled for him.

1.8.16   *Mishnah Nazir 6.10–1*

> If one cut off his hair after the offering and it were found invalid, the
> cutting off of the hair is invalid too and his offerings are not counted
> to his credit. If one cut off his hair following the sin-offering which
> had not been thus designated, and he brought his other offerings cor-
> rectly assigned, the cutting off of his hair is disqualified and his offerings
> are not reckoned to his credit. If one cut off his hair following a burnt-
> offering or after a peace-offering that were not assigned for that pur-
> pose, and after that he brought his offerings for there express purpose,
> the cutting off of the hair is not licit and his offerings do not count
> to his credit. R. Simeon says, "That particular offering does not count
> to his credit but the rest of the offerings are reckoned to his credit.
> But if one cut off his hair following the three of them, and one of
> them was found valid, the cutting off of his hair is valid, but he must
> bring anew the rest of his offerings." (*m. Naz.* 6.10)

> If one had the blood of one of the offerings sprinkled for him, and
> he then became unclean, R. Eleazer says, "This causes the whole to
> become forfeit." But the Sages say, "He needs only to bring the rest
> of his offerings when he has become clean." They said to him, "It
> once happened to Miriam of Tadmor that the blood of one of the
> offerings was sprinkled for her, and some people came to her and told

her that her daughter was in danger, and she went and found that
she was dead, and the Sages said, 'Let her bring the rest of the offerings
when she has become clean.'" (*m. Naz.* 6.11)

Chapter six concludes by addressing the issue of errors encountered
in ritual procedure and their consequent effect upon a Nazirite's status. In *m. Naz.* 6.10 the anonymous source decides in rather straight-
forward terms that if the Nazirite cuts off his hair and offers sacrifices
(Num. 6.13–21) only to realize afterwards that either an offering was
found invalid (perhaps because of a blemish?) or one of the offerings
was incorrectly designated (cf. Lev. 27.9–10), then both the cutting
of the hair and the offering of sacrifices are deemed ineffectual.
R. Simeon disagrees and decides that in such a case only the offerings
discovered as invalid are of no effect; the haircut remains effective,
but the Nazirite must replace the erroneous offerings with acceptable ones. *Mishnah Nazir* 6.11 then comprises a debate over what is
lost to the Nazirite if s/he becomes unclean in the very midst of
offering sacrifices to complete a vow. R. Eleazer decides in such a
case that the whole is of none effect—the ritual ceremony and the
initial spell of Naziriteship—but the Sages rule that offerings already
slaughtered remain effective, and the Nazirite loses only the time
allotted for the rite of purification (seven days, cf. *m. Naz.* 3.3–6).
Once purified, the Nazirite may then return to complete the remaining portion of his/her ceremony to discharge the vow. Though seemingly an incomprehensible scenario, an actual historic case involving
such an encounter in ritual procedure is drawn up in support of the
Sages' decision. A figure by the name of Miriam of Tadmor[144] was
supposedly rendered unclean while in the very midst of her ritual
ceremony to complete her vow. At the report that her daughter was
in immediate danger, she left the ceremony only to find her daughter already dead. By way of contact with her daughter's corpse,
Miriam was rendered impure.

1.8.17 *Mishnah Nazir 7.1*

A High Priest and a Nazirite may not become unclean because of
their kindred, but they may become unclean because of a corpse as
commanded by the Law. If they were on a journey and discovered a

---

[144] Or Palmyra.

dead body to be dealt with as commanded by the Law, R. Eliezer says, "The High Priest may become defiled, but the Nazirite may not become defiled"; but the Sages say, "A Nazirite may contract uncleanness, but the High Priest may not contract uncleanness." R. Eliezer said to them, "Let the priest contract defilement because he does not have to bring an offering because of defilement, but let not a Nazirite become unclean because he has to bring an offering because of defilement." They made reply to him, "Let a Nazirite become unclean as his sanctity is not an everlasting sanctity, but let not a priest become unclean as his sanctity is a perpetual sanctity."

Topical association links *m. Naz.* 7.1 with the previous mishnah. Here concern lies in harmonizing the Nazirite's proscription against corpse impurity (Num. 6.8) with the *met mitzvah*, or law for the abandoned corpse (Lev. 21). The mishnah is marked by debate, as in previous mishnayot addressing the matter of corpse impurity, and decision pivots on the interpretive comparison between the law for the Nazirite vow and the law for the High Priest (Lev. 21.11), who like the Nazirite is forbidden contact with a corpse even for closest kin. Although debated, the anonymous source states at the outset that while both the Nazirite and the High Priest are forbidden contact with a corpse, they are exempt from the proscription in the case of the discovered corpse, which must be removed and buried according to the mandate of the law.

1.8.18   *Mishnah Nazir 7.2–4*

The Nazirite must cut off his hair because of these defilements: because of a corpse, or because of an olive's bulk of a corpse, or because of an olive's bulk of matter exuding from a corpse, or of a ladleful of the mould of a decayed corpse, or because of the spinal column, or because of the skull, or because of any limb of a corpse, or because of a limb of a living person which still has on it its proper flesh, or because of a half-*kab* of bones, or because of a half-*log* of blood, whether from actual contact with them or from carrying them or from being present in the same room with them, or because of a barleycorn's bulk of bone whether by touching it or carrying it. Because of these the Nazirite must cut off his hair and be sprinkled on the third day and on the seventh day. And he forfeits the foregoing days and must not begin to count again until he becomes clean and brings his offerings. (*m. Naz.* 7.2)

But because of overhanging boughs, or protruding stones, or a grave-space, or a country of the non-Jews, or the top stone-covering of a tomb, or the supporting tomb stone, or a quarter-*log* of blood, or a tent, of a quarter-*kab* of bones, or utensils that have touched a corpse, or the days which he is certified a leper, in all these cases the Nazirite does not have to cut his hair off, but he must be sprinkled on the third and seventh day and he does not forfeit the preceding days, and he begins to count straightway and he does not have to bring the offering. In fact they say the days of uncleanness of a man afflicted with an issue or a woman suffering with an issue and the days of the shutting up of a leper—these are counted to his credit. (*m. Naz.* 7.3)

R. Eliezer said in the name of R. Joshua, "For whatever defilement from a corpse that a Nazirite must cut his hair off, for such people are liable if they enter the temple; but for any uncleanness from a corpse that a Nazirite does not have to cut off his hair, for such persons are not culpable for entering the temple. R. Meir said, "Would this not be more lenient than for a creeping thing?" R. Akiba said, "I dispute before R. Eliezer, seeing that a bone the size of a barley-corn, which does not defile a man by overshadowing, a Nazirite must cut off his hair if he touch it or carry it, then how much more in the case of a quarter-*log* of blood, which does render a man unclean by over-shadowing ought the Nazirite to cut his hair off because of the contact with it or because of carrying it! He made reply to him, 'What is this, Akiba? We cannot here make an inference from minor to major!' And when I came and related these words before R. Joshua he said to me, 'You have spoken well, but thus have they enjoined as *halakhah*.'" (*m. Naz.* 7.4)

The topic of defilement because of a corpse continues in *m. Naz.* 7.2–4. The intent is to identify specifics regarding what material substances do and do not render a Nazirite unclean *so that he must shave his hair and count his previous days as forfeit*. The practical concerns of *m. Naz.* 7.2–3 are left behind in *m. Naz.* 7.4, where the topic is expanded into a debate regarding the similarities between the unclean Nazirite and one who enters the temple precincts. Specifics are listed and various measurements are applied throughout *m. Naz.* 7.2–3. Degree of uncleanness is what the Mishnah wishes to draw attention to, and this is brought forth particularly in *m. Naz.* 7.3. Lists are given of those items rendering the Nazirite unclean, but to the degree that the Nazirite requires only the rite of purification and does not have to shave his hair or renew his avowed days in accordance with Num. 6.9–12. According to Num. 19, there are varying degrees of uncleanness caused by a corpse, expressed in terms of secondary and tertiary remove. The further removed a person is from someone or some object, either in direct contact or in an enclosed space with a corpse, the less stringent the requirement for purification. The Mishnah here attempts to adjudicate in such circumstances with respect to the Nazirite, a subject taken for granted in Num. 6.9–12.

One matter worthy of special attention is the rather obvious discrepancy between *m. Naz.* 7.3 and *m. Naz.* 3.6 regarding the issue of uncleanness and time lost due to a country of the non-Jews (ארץ העמים). According to *m. Naz.* 3.6, either thirty days (the School of Shammai), or the Nazirite's entire avowed period (the School of Hillel) must be observed when a Nazirite enters the land of Palestine from abroad. Here, however, a Nazirite is declared unclean with the only consequence being the loss of the seven days required for the rite of purification.

1.8.19 *Mishnah Nazir 8.1–2*

If there were two Nazirites to whom one man said, "I saw that one of you had become unclean but I know not which one of you,"—they must cut their hair off and bring one offering for uncleanness, and one offering for cleanness, and each says, "If I be the one unclean, let the offering for uncleanness be mine and yours be the offering for cleanness, but if I be the one clean, may mine be the offering in cleanness and yours be the offering in uncleanness." And they must count thirty days and bring one offering in cleanness, and each says, "If I be the one unclean, let the offering in uncleanness be mine and the offering in cleanness be yours, and this offering in cleanness be mine; but if I be the one clean, let the offering in cleanness be mine and may the offering in uncleanness be yours, and this offering in cleanness be yours." R. Joshua said, "Let him seek the one from the public place to vow to become a Nazirite in the other's stead and let him say, 'If it were I that was unclean, then you be a Nazirite straightway, but if I were the one clean, then you be a Nazirite after thirty days. And they count thirty days and bring an offering for uncleanness and an offering in cleanness, and he says, 'If I were the one that became unclean, may the offering for uncleanness be mine, and the offering in cleanness be yours, but if I were the one clean, let the offering in cleanness be mine and the offering in uncleanness be in doubt,' and they count thirty days and bring an offering in cleanness, and he says, 'If I were the unclean one, may the offering in uncleanness be mine and the offering in cleanness be yours, and this be my offering in cleanness, but if I were the one clean, let the offering in cleanness be mine and the offering in uncleanness be in doubt and let the offering for cleanness be yours.'" Ben Zoma said to him, "But who would listen to him to take the vow of the Nazirite in the other's place? But let him bring a bird as a sin-offering and a beast as a burnt-offering, and say, 'If I were unclean, the sin-offering be duty bound and the burnt-offering be voluntary, if I were clean, let the burnt-offering be in duty bound and the sin-offering by reason of uncertainty.' And he counts thirty days and brings an offering in cleanness, and he say, 'If I were unclean, the first burnt-offering be of free will and this one in duty bound, but if I were clean, let the first burnt-offering be in duty bound and this one out of free will, and this is the rest of my offering.'" R. Joshua said, "It would be found then that this man would be bringing his own offerings piecemeal!" But the Sages agreed with Ben Zoma. (*m. Naz.* 8.1)

If there is a doubt whether a Nazirite were unclean, and there is doubt whether he be declared a leper, he may eat of sacrifices after sixty days, and he may drink wine and become unclean because of a corpse after one-hundred and twenty days, because the cutting off of the hair for leprosy overrides the cutting off of the hair for the Nazirite vow so long as it is certain, but when there is a doubt it must not supercede it. (*m. Naz.* 8.2)

Chapter eight consists of two conundrums[145] both addressing the issue of doubt regarding cases of uncleanness; the former with respect to a corpse, and the latter with respect to a combined case of corpse uncleanness and impurity due to leprosy. In typical rabbinic fashion, there is a greater concern in these cases to exert to the full rabbinic juristic wisdom in complex circumstances than in communicating anything of immediate practical concern.

1.8.20   *Mishnah Nazir 9.1*

The Nazirite vow does not apply to non-Jews. Women and slaves may take the Nazirite vow. Greater strictness applies to women than to slaves, since one may force his slave but cannot compel his wife. Greater strictness applies to slaves than to women, because one can disannul his wife's vows, but he cannot disannul his slave's vows. If one annulled his wife's vow, he has annulled it absolutely, but if he absolved his slave's vow who was then set free, he must then complete his Nazirite vow. If he escaped from him, R. Meir says, "He may not drink," but R. Jose says, "He may drink."

Numbers 6.1–2 opens with the instructions of the Lord to Moses saying, "Speak to the sons of Israel and say to them, 'If any man or woman makes the vow of the Nazirite . . .'" The vow, according

---

[145] I classify these as conundrums because of the manner in which the issues are dealt. The cases are theoretical, and the Mishnah purposefully creates unnecessary complexity (i.e., the former case involving not just a single individual but two, and the latter with a mixture of cases with many parallel legal ramifications).

to the Mishnah, is therefore applicable only to Jews who are the
"sons of Israel." Slaves are also included by way of household membership (cf. Ex. 21.2ff.; Deut. 15.12,18; Lev. 25.35ff.), and, likewise,
may take up the Nazirate. Beyond this reiteration, the Mishnah
expands the topic into a conundrum in the likeness of *m. Naz.* 6.5
and asks of the Naziriteship of women and slaves, which has the
greater stringency. Clever hermeneutics is the primary interest.

1.8.21   *Mishnah Nazir 9.2–4*

If a Nazirite cut off his hair, and it became known to him that he
had become unclean, if it were a known uncleanness, it renders forfeiture, but if it were an uncleanness from a hidden source, it does
not render forfeiture; if before he cut off his hair, then in either case
it renders forfeiture. How so? If one descended into a cave to immerse
himself, and a corpse was found floating at the mouth of the cave, he
becomes unclean; if it were found sunk in the floor of the cave, and
he had only gone down to cool himself, he is clean, but if to cleanse
himself from the uncleanness because of a corpse, then he is unclean,
for he that was unclean is presumed to be still unclean and one who
was clean is assumed to be still clean, for there is evidence in support
of this matter. (*m. Naz.* 9.2)

If one discovers a corpse on a spot for the first time lying in its ordinary manner, he may remove it together with the soil around it. If
one found two, he may remove them and the soil around them. If
one found three—if there be between one and the other a space of
four cubits to eight cubits, then this must be considered a grave yard,
and he must examine the ground from there onward for a space of
twenty cubits; if he found a corpse twenty cubits away, he must search
from it and around for a space of twenty cubits for there is evidence
in support of this subject, even though if one found it on a spot for
the first time, he may remove it and the soil around it. (*m. Naz.* 9.3)

Every condition of doubt at the outset concerning leprosy symptoms
is considered clean before it has been declared within the status of
uncleanness; but when it has already been placed in the category of
uncleanness, despite any doubt concerning it, it remains unclean. Under
seven headings do they examine one afflicted with an issue before he
has been pronounced within the status of uncleanness as one suffering
from an issue: regarding what he had eaten and concerning what he
had drunk, concerning any load, and regarding jumping, and concerning any illness, and with regard to any scene, and concerning any
impure thoughts. After one has been declared to be within the status
as one afflicted with an issue they do not examine him; if one's affliction
with an issue be through a mishap or is in doubt, or in the case of
a discharge of seminal fluid, such are deemed unclean, since there is

evidence in support of the matter. If one struck his fellow, and they considered that he would die, but he then improved and afterwards became worse and died, he is guilty. R. Nehemiah says, "He is exempt as there is no proof in support of the matter." (*m. Naz.* 9.4)

Mishnah Nazir 9.2–4 provide some difficulty with respect to redactional structure. *Mishnah Nazir* 9.2 clearly refers to the topic of the Nazirite since the Nazirite surfaces as the primary subject of interest. *Mishnah Nazir* 9.3–4, however, neither make reference to the Nazirite nor form any unequivocal continuity of thought between themselves or with the previous mishnah. I treat them as a sub-unit together with *m. Naz.* 9.2, because they do address the shared topic of *uncleanness*, albeit redactionally 9.3 would seemingly have been better placed after *m. Naz.* 7.1 (which addresses the topic of the *met mitzvah*) and 9.4 after 8.2 (which addresses the topic of doubt concerning uncleanness due to leprosy).

Uncleanness caused by a corpse first hidden to the Nazirite but later revealed, is the principle subject of concern in *m. Naz.* 9.2. The Mishnah is concerned with timing and errs on the side of the completed vow. If a Nazirite had already cut his hair and it was brought to his attention that he had beforehand spent some time in an area where a corpse was discovered (i.e., in an enclosed space such as a cave), if the corpse was in plain sight (although unnoticed by the Nazirite) then the completion of his vow is deemed illicit. If, however, the corpse was hidden from plain sight (such as submerged in a body of water), then the Nazirite is declared clean (even if he immersed himself in the water to cool himself). If such a circumstance was brought to the Nazirite's attention before he cut his hair, however, then "in either case it renders forfeiture (of the vow)."

Mishnah Nazir 9.3–4 then follow with halakhah respecting the removal of an abandoned corpse (*m. Naz.* 9.3) and cases of doubt regarding leprosy. The pericope has nothing of direct relevance to the topic of the Nazirite vow and reason behind its inclusion is suspect. It is possible its inclusion is due to the parallels shared between the leper and the unclean Nazirite (as discussed in previous mishnayot).

1.8.22 *Mishnah Nazir 9.5*

Samuel was a Nazirite, according to the opinion of R. Nehorai—as it is said, "and a razor shall not cross over his head." It is said of Samson, "and a razor," and it is said of Samuel, "and a razor"; just as the "razor" spoken of in the case of Samson means that he was to be a

Nazirite so "razor" spoken of regarding Samuel shows that he was to be a Nazirite." R. Jose said, "But does not *morah* refer to one of flesh and blood? R. Nehorai replied to him, "But has is not already been said, 'And Samuel said, 'How can I go? If Saul hears it he will slay me.' Thus already had there come upon him the fear of flesh and blood."

The tractate closes with a debate on the Nazirite status of Samuel and comprises a series of disparate midrashic interpretations of I Sam. 1.11. Debate centers on the interpretation of the term מורה, a term meaning either "razor" or "fear."[146] In *gezerah shewa* fashion (i.e., what is meant in one usage likely means the same in another) R. Nehorai decides that since מורה means "razor" when used of Samson (who was a Nazirite [Judg. 13.5]), the term must also mean "razor" when used of Samuel. Samuel is, therefore, a Nazirite by implication. R. Jose disagrees, suggesting rhetorically that the term can refer to "one of flesh and blood" (i.e., "and no fear [of man] shall come upon his head"). R. Nehorai, in response, then cites I Sam. 16.2, which describes Samuel's fear that Saul would slay him if he followed the Lord's command to head for Bethlehem and anoint another king over Israel. Samuel's fear of Saul thereby substantiates R. Nehorai's opinion that מורה in I Sam. 1.11 must refer to a "razor."

Assessment of Tractate Mishnah Nazir

In terms of the general content of *m. Naz.*, the tractate deals primarily with ambiguities in the biblical law of Num. 6.1–21 (though on occasion other related topics are discussed). Matters such as how long a Nazirite vow should be, when precisely a votary should cut his or her hair, or what happens if a votary intentionally breaks his/her vow among others, are issues taken for granted in the Num. legislation. From this perspective the tractate is an expansion on biblical law; an expansion which, in the spirit of the Oral Law, serves as a type of "fence around the Torah" (cf. *m. Aboth* 1.1); a fence not merely comprising an addition of rules for its own sake, but an enclosure reaching out to encompass those points where reality, in all its varieties of experience, meets the static, and in this case, very general regulations of Mosaic Law. Nazirite halakhah in tractate *m. Naz.* is, therefore, both pragmatic and formative. It is *pragmatic* in that

---

[146] Jastrow, *Dictionary*, 749; cf. Danby who translates מורה as "authority," but who describes the term as meaning "fear" in this context, p. 293 n. 3; see also the translation of the term in *Tg. J.* discussed in testimony 1.12.5 following).

many of the issues addressed appear reflective of very real and practical concerns, yet *formative* in that lying behind it is a tradition already
extant; a tradition that the rabbis wish to conform or shape to meet
their own halakhic ideal.

In terms of the overall function or purpose of the tractate, it is
foremost pedagogical. It serves neither as a code of law nor as a mere
collection of rabbinic tradition, but as a type of study manual; a manual intended to prepare one in a position to grant advice on Nazirite
matters either unclear or unspecified in biblical law. This makes best
sense of the theoretical nature of so much of the material, as well
as takes into account the general tendency of the tractate to communicate halakhic principles on issues rather than merely collating
disparate legal opinions. In *m. Naz.* 1.3–7 for example, which addresses
the סתם נזירות, or Nazirite vow of unspecified duration, cases depicted
are in no way exhaustive, yet they cover a wide range of possible
scenarios involving various ways of expressing a length of time for
a vow. The same decisions are repeated throughout the section, and
this repetition serves to convey a basic principle: since "days" is
assumed as the standard measurement of time for a Nazirite vow in
Num. 6.1–21, then a vow of unspecified duration should be assigned
a length in days, either thirty or more, depending on what words a
person actually spoke when making the vow. One might imagine,
by way of illustration, a Nazirite approaching a Sage to whom the
question is asked, "How long must I be a Nazirite?" Based on the
principle learned from *m. Naz.* 1.3–7, the Sage would then reply
with an immediate question, "Well, what exactly did you *say* when
you made your vow?" Depending on the Nazirite's response, the
Sage would then advise him/her to remain a Nazirite for at least
thirty days but possibly longer. This same pedagogical tendency is
witnessed throughout the tractate, covering issues such as the use of
substitute expressions for a Nazirite vow, discernment of the intended
meaning of "nazir" when spoken in a given context, proper behavior in the case of a vow made on the condition of childbirth, what
to do with offerings when a vow is being annulled or unfulfilled,
and so on, and is intensified with the presence of debates, periodic
conundrums, and exegetical motifs.

The question of ultimate concern then, is how the material relates
to, or reflects, common Nazirite behavior and, in particular, such
behavior within the period prior to the destruction of the temple in
AD 70—some 130 years before the Mishnah's final redaction. As

was stated in the introductory section to the tractate, much of the material originates from Tannaim of the second and third generations after the destruction of the temple (AD 90–160). Such a period is distant from the period of interest, but not too distant. It was also asserted that at least some portion of the tractate may be earlier than the second-generation Tannaim, including those cases describing historic individuals said to be Nazirites prior to or at the time of the temple's destruction, such as Queen Helena of Adiabene, Miriam of Tadmor, and the case decided by Nahum the Mede. The content of *m. Naz.* as a whole, then, does have a reasonable chance of representing, at least with some degree of accuracy, the circumstances in the period under investigation.

In terms of genre, however, what is certain of the material is that the decisions of the rabbis do not in themselves reflect the *rules* to which Jews in Palestine commonly adhered, but rather halakhah to which Jews, in the eyes of the rabbis, *ought* to adhere. The material is idealistic and formative, rather than representative of generally accepted norms. On only a few occasions are the rabbis actually depicted in *m. Naz.* as giving advice on matters, and even where these instances occur, the appropriateness of the advice given is often debated. Furthermore, rabbinic decisions, as discussed, typically serve as a means of getting across certain halakhic principles in the material rather than forming mere constituents of a collection of halakhah, such as in a legal canon (they are didactic rather than exhaustive). More importantly, although the decisions of the rabbis themselves are of minimal significance, the delineation of behavior forming the basis of those decisions does at least represent what the rabbis assumed people *could* do and say when making Nazirite vows, and there is some possibility that these assumptions reflect how people, in fact, would have behaved. In the opening pericope of *m. Naz.* 1.1, for example, a series of substitute forms of words adjudicated either binding or not binding as a Nazirite vow were given. According to a study by Saul Lieberman, the practice of making substitute expressions for oaths and vows was common in the wider Graeco-Roman culture of the period.[147] The Mishnah, therefore, may provide very real evidence of a similar practice in Jewish Palestine respecting

---

[147] S. Lieberman, *Greek in Jewish Palestine: Studies in the Life and Manners of Jewish Palestine in the II–IV Centuries C.E.* (2nd ed.; New York: P. Feldheim, 1965), 115–41.

Nazirite vows. Whereas the decisions of the rabbis in declaring the various expressions as binding or not binding, in other words, represent the ideal world under the auspices of the rabbinate, the behavior serving as the basis for those decisions may reflect the real or actual world and provide examples of what people said when making their vows: "I will be like this one," or "I will let my hair grow unkempt," or "I will be a Nazik", ". . . Naziakh" or ". . . Paziakh."

Certainly with respect to a portion of the material, the rabbis do move well beyond the realm of reality and into the sphere of the tangential—such as in those sections comprising conundrums or possibly humorous cases of one kind or another. As juristic exercises, these pericopae probably bear little relationship to the outside world, but possibly do shed at least some light on common behavior. Some votaries, for instance, may have taken the vow lightly and made it on the whim of a bet as the rabbis anticipate (*m. Naz.* 5.5–7); others may have made multiple vows, giving little recourse to the seriousness of their words (*m. Naz.* 3.7); and some may have offered to cover the expenses of another's Nazirite offerings as an additional token of piety (*m. Naz.* 2.5–6), a scenario similar to behavior witnessed in other literary sources of the period.[148] Also, where the rabbis are concerned with providing halakhah on specific measurements and orders of procedure, though these decisions appear trivial, the concerns of the rabbis may reflect some element of actual behavioral and cult ritual experience among those making Nazirite vows. Some may have soaked their bread in wine only to question afterwards whether they had partaken enough of the substance to break their vow. Some, likewise, may never have combed or tended their hair while under a vow. According to the law's regulations, the Nazirite renewing or completing a vow was required to offer a significant number of offerings and sacrifices, and the process of working through them at the altar may have proven rather clumsy or cumbersome.

Other references to Nazirite halakhah in the Mishnah
References to Nazirite halakhah outside tractate *m. Naz.* appear primarily for the purpose of harmonizing various laws relating to or

---

[148] Cf. the cases of Agrippa I in *A. J.* 19.294 and Paul in Acts 21.23–27a, where the act of paying for Nazirites to have their offerings made is perceived as a token of piety.

possibly affecting the Nazirite. Some comprise mere parallel citations from *m. Naz.*, others are fresh and innovative, and some more elaborate than others.[149] Those that add significantly to the discussion of *m. Naz.* include the following.

1.8.23   *Mishnah Orlah 3.3*

> If a man wove into a garment one *sit*'s length of wool from a firstling, the garment must be burnt; and if he wove into a sack a Nazirite's hair [שׂעֵר הַנָּזִיר בְּשַׂק] or hair from the firstborn of an ass, the sack must be burnt. And in the case of other hallowed things, they render the rest hallowed in any quantity whatsoever.

Halakhah in tractate *Mishnah Orlah* (*m. Orl.*)[150] concerns the use of forbidden fruit, fruit deemed unusable in the first three years of planting and "holy as an offering of praise to the Lord" in its fourth (cf. Lev. 19.23–4). The citation above forms part of a greater context involving a debate between R. Meir and the Sages over whether even a single strand of wool dyed with the shells of Orlah-fruit renders the entire garment of which it is a constituent unusable (*m. Orl.* 3.1–2). *Mishnah Orlah* 3.3 then concerns the use of wool shorn from firstborn animals: wool forbidden under the law because of the sacred status of such animals (Deut. 15.19). The content is an argument from analogy in support of the position of R. Meir in stating that any mixture of a sacred substance with common substance renders sanctified the whole of which it is a part, and, therefore, unavailable for common use.[151] Interestingly, the hair (שׂעֵר) of the Nazirite, who is no firstborn animal, is brought up in this context. If the hair of a Nazirite, which like the hair of firstborn animals is regarded as

---

[149] Halakhah in the Mishnah pertaining to the various aspects of the Nazirate may be categorized accordingly: the vow: *m. Ned.* 1.1–2, 2.3, 11.5, 9, *m. Eduy.* 4.11, *m. Toh.* 4.11; the use of grape produce: *m. Orl.* 1.7–8, *m. Erub.* 3.1; the growth or cutting of the hair: *m. Orl.* 3.3, *m. M. Kat.* 3.1, *m. Eduy.* 7.5, *m. Tem.* 7.4, *m. Neg.* 14.4; corpse impurity: *m. Pes.* 7.7, *m. Ohol.* 18.4, *m. Toh.* 4.7, *m. Makk.* 3.9; the various offerings incumbent upon a Nazirite: *m. Hall.* 1.6, *m. Pes.* 2.5, *m. Shek.* 2.5, *m. Kidd.* 1.8, *m. A. Zar.* 5.9, *m. Zeb.* 5.5–6, 10.2, 5, *m. Men.* 3.6, 7.2, 9.3, 13.10, *m. Hull.* 10.4, *m. Ker.* 2.1, 2.2–3, *m. Meil.* 3.2, *m. Midd.* 2.5, *m. Par.* 1.4; and other related halakhot: *m. Bikk.* 2.11, *m. Makk.* 3.7, *m. Kel.* 6.2.

[150] Literally, "uncircumcised fruit."

[151] K. Albrecht, '*Orla: Text, Übersetzung und Erklärung nebst textkritischen Anhang* (vol. 1:10 of *Die Mischna: Text, Übersetzung und ausführliche Erklärung*, eds. K. H. Rengstorf, L. Rost, and S. Herrmann; Gießen: Alfred Töpelmann [vormals J. Ricker], 1916), 29.

holy to the Lord (Num. 6.9), is woven into a sack (שׂק), the Mishnah declares that the sack must be burnt.

Both the context and content of the comment are reminiscent of the statement of Josephus in *A. J.* 4.72 that Nazirites offered their hair to the priests when it was shorn.[152] *Mishnah Orlah* suggests, via its assumption of common behavior, that people (priests?) wove Nazirite hair into sacks. This is odd, as is with the description given by Josephus, given the Law's requirement that such hair is to be placed on the fire under the peace offering (cf. Num. 6.18). It also suggests, like Josephus, that there was some form of correlation between the sacred status of Nazirite hair and the wool of firstborn male-animals.

1.8.24 *Mishnah Pesachim 2.5*

> These are the things which eaten unleavened at Passover a man fulfills his obligation: wheat, barley, spelt, goat-grass, and oats. The obligation is fulfilled if they are demai-produce, First Tithe from which heave-offering has been taken, Second Tithe or dedicated produce which has been redeemed; and the priest—dough-offering or heave-offering. But the obligation is not fulfilled if they are untithed produce, or First Tithe from which heave-offering has not been taken, or Second Tithe or dedicated produce which have not been redeemed. A man cannot fulfill his obligation by eating the cakes for the thank-offerings or the wafers of the Nazirite if he made them for himself; but if he made them to sell in the market he can fulfill his obligation therewith.

Exodus 12.15–20 and 23.15 command that during the festival of Passover, or the feast of Unleavened Bread, the sons of Israel are to eat unleavened bread for seven days. What substances may be used to make the unleavened bread, or what types of unleavened bread may be used as the unleavened bread for the feast, are issues taken for granted in the Law. The Mishnah, therefore, concerns itself with these gray areas in *Mishnah Pesachim* (*m. Pes.*)[153] 2.5. The pericope is divided into two primary parts: (a) a listing of those items whereby when eaten a man fulfills his obligation to eat the unleavened bread for Passover, and (b) those items whereby when eaten a man does not fulfill his obligation to eat the unleavened bread for Passover. The Mishnah decides that Nazirite wafers (cf. Num. 6.15) may be used for Passover bread provided they are made to be sold in the marketplace

---

[152] See testimony 1.6.2.
[153] "Passover."

rather than for personal use (i.e., the baker was not himself a Nazirite, in which case the wafers would already be assigned for a purpose other than the Paschal meal).[154] The passage suggests that Nazirite wafers could be sold and purchased in the market place, and, implies in turn, that there must have been some level of public demand for them—perhaps even during the festival period.

1.8.25   *Mishnah Shekalim 2.5*

> The surplus of money assigned to Shekel dues is free for common use, but the surplus of the price of the tenth of the ephaph, of the bird offering of a man or woman that have a flux, or of a woman after childbirth, or of sin-offerings or guilt-offerings, their surplus falls to the temple fund. This is the general rule: the surplus of what had been assigned as the price of sin-offering or guilt-offering falls to the temple fund. The surplus of money assigned to a whole-offering must be used for a whole-offering; the surplus of money assigned to a meal-offering must be used for a meal-offering; the surplus of money assigned to a peace-offering must be used for a peace-offering; the surplus of money assigned to a Passover-offering must be used for a Passover-offering; the surplus of money assigned to Nazirite offerings must be used for Nazirite offerings; the surplus of money assigned to one Nazirite's offerings falls to the temple fund; the surplus of money collected for the poor, must must be used for the poor; the surplus of money collected for one poor man must be given to that poor man; the surplus of money collected to ransom captives must be used for captives; the surplus of money assigned to ransom one captive must be used for that captive; the surplus of money collected for the purpose of burying the dead must be used for the dead; the surplus of money collected for the purpose of burying one dead person must be used for his heirs. R. Meir says, "The surplus of money collected for the burial of one dead person must be left until Elijah comes." R. Nathan says, "It is used to build a monument over his grave."

Tractate *Mishnah Shekalim* (*m. Shek.*) deals with the annual temple tax of the half-shekel: a tax incumbent upon every Israelite male twenty-years old and upwards (Ex. 30.13ff.). It is in this context that the surplus of money assigned to Nazirite offerings is discussed. In like manner, as other funds circulated in the temple treasury, the Mishnah declares that money designated for the purpose of purchasing Nazirite

---

[154] Cf. G. Beer, *Pesachim: Text, Übersetzung und Erklärung nebst textkritischen Anhang* (vol. 2:3 of *Die Mischna: Text, Übersetzung und ausführliche Erklärung*, eds. K. H. Rengstorf, L. Rost, and S. Herrmann; Gießen: Alfred Töpelmann [vormals J. Ricker], 1912), 121.

offerings must be used only for that purpose, even where there is money left over once those offerings have been purchased. The surplus of money given to purchase any number of Nazirite offerings may continue to be used for that purpose. However, the case in which funds were designated for the purchase of offerings for a single Nazirite, since that must remain so dedicated even where money is left over, it cannot be used by other Nazirites. What is left over falls to the general temple fund (as a free-will offering).

The significance of this passage is that it envisages Nazirites individually and collectively purchasing their offerings at the temple, and that there was a general fund at the temple for the purpose of purchasing those offerings, a portion of which could be used freely by Nazirites. Contributions underlie the halakhah, and contributions for the purchase of Nazirite offerings is reminiscent of such cases as the Nazirite who promised to pay for the offerings of another Nazirite in addition to his own (*m. Naz.* 2.5), and King Agrippa I, discussed by Josephus, who paid for a significant number of Nazirites to be shaved on a single occasion (*A. J.* 19.294).

1.8.26 *Mishnah Menahot 13.10*

> If one said, "I pledge myself to offer a whole-offering," he must offer it in the temple. And if he offered it in the House of Onias he has not fulfilled his obligation. "I will offer it in the House of Onias," he should offer it in the temple, but if he offered it in the House of Onias he has fulfilled his obligation. R. Simeon says, "Such is not accounted as a whole-offering." If one said, "I will be a Nazirite," he must offer the hair-offering in the temple; and if he offered it in the House of Onias he has not fulfilled his obligation. "I will offer the hair-offering in the House of Onias," he should offer it in the temple; but if he offered it in the House of Onias he has fulfilled his obligation. R. Simeon says, "Such a one is not accounted a Nazirite." If priests have ministered in the House of Onias they may not minister in the temple in Jerusalem; still more does this apply to priests in that other matter; for it is written, "Nevertheless the priests of the high places came not up to the altar of the Lord in Jerusalem, but they did eat unleavened bread among their brethren"; thus they were like them that have a blemish: they may share and they may eat but they may not offer sacrifice.

Mishnah Menahot (*m. Men.*) 13.10 contains a series of debates between the anonymous material and R. Simeon regarding the legitimacy of offerings made in the Temple of Onias: the Jewish temple in Leontopolis, Egypt (active between ca. 165 BC and AD 70). As is the case with all vows, decisions are based on what a person utters when making his promise to deliver an offering (Num. 30.2). If a vow was made to provide an offering with no explicit mention of *where* it would be offered, then it must be given in the temple at Jerusalem. However, if one promised expressly to offer it "in the Temple of Onias" then, although he *should* offer it in the Jerusalem temple, if he offered it in the Temple of Onias he has fulfilled his obligation. The same principle applies for one vowing to bring his Nazirite offerings to the temple.

The bias of the rabbis toward the Jerusalem sanctuary is made obvious by R. Simeon's rejecting the legitimacy of any offering made at the Egyptian temple. Further, priests who serve in the Egyptian sanctuary are said to be like priests "who have a blemish" and are no longer permitted to serve in Jerusalem. For our purposes, the opinions of the rabbis are secondary to the assumption they make regarding Nazirites and the rival temple in Egypt. The rabbis seem to assume that people could complete their vows in the Temple of Onias rather than in Jerusalem. It is at least possible that such activity was going on, especially perhaps amongst those making Nazirite vows in Egypt.[155]

1.8.27   *Mishnah Temurah 7.4*[156]

> These must be buried: miscarriages of animal offerings must be buried; if they cast an afterbirth it must be buried; the ox that is condemned to be stoned, the heifer whose neck is to be broken, the bird offerings of the leper, the hair of the Nazirite [שְׂעַר נָזִיר], the firstling of an ass, flesh seethed in milk, and unconsecrated beasts slaughtered in the temple court. R. Simeon says, "Unconsecrated beasts slaughtered in the temple court must be burnt; so, too, a wild animal that was slaughtered in the temple court."

Although Num. 6.18 states that the Nazirite shall place his shaven hair on the fire under the peace offering when the vow is completed, what to do with the hair shaven in the case of uncleanness is not discussed in the Law (cf. Num. 6.9–12). Surprisingly, nothing of this is addressed in tractate *m. Naz. Mishnah Temurah* (*m. Tem.*) 7.4, however, declares that such hair should be buried. The context in which

---

[155] Boertien remarks, "Dieser Abschnitt mach klar, daß Juden in Ägypten Nasiräergeübde ablegten und sogar eine Ausweihe in Leontopolis vornahmen," 93.
[156] Cf. *m. A. Zar.* 5.9.

Nazirite hair (שְׂעַר נְזִיר) is mentioned addresses those items requiring burial because in one manner or another they constitute a carcass and therefore convey uncleanness. שְׂעַר, therefore, refers to the hair of the Nazirite when shaven in a state of uncleanness and not at the point of completion of a vow (Num. 6.13–21).

1.8.28 *Mishnah Middoth 2.5*

> The Court of Women was one-hundred and thirty-five cubits long and one-hundred and thirty-five cubits wide. At its four corners were four chambers each of forty cubits; and they had no roofs. And so shall they be hereafter, for it is written, "Then he brought me forth into the outer court and caused me to pass by the four corners of the court; and behold, in every corner of the court there was a court. In the four corners of the court there were courts enclosed"; and "enclosed" means only that they were not roofed. And what was their use? That to the south-east was the Chamber of the Nazirites, for there the Nazirites cooked their peace-offerings and cut off their hair and threw it under the pot. That to the north-east was the Chamber of the Wood-shed, for there the priests that were blemished examined the wood for worms, since any wood wherein was found a worm was invalid upon the altar. That to the north-west was the Chamber of the Lepers. That to the south-west—R. Eliezer ben Jacob said, "I forgot what it was used for." Abba Saul said, "There they put the wine and the oil, and it was called the Chamber of Oil." Before-time the Court of Women was free from buildings and afterward they surrounded it with a gallery, so that the women should behold from above and the men from below and that they should not mingle together. Fifteen steps led up from within it to the Court of the Israelites, corresponding to the fifteen Songs of Ascents in the Psalms, and upon them the levites used to sing. They were not four-square, but rounded like the half of a round threshing-floor.

Mishnah Middoth (m. Midd.)[157] is a tractate concerned with the dimensions of the temple as it stood before the destruction of AD 70. *Mishnah Middoth* 2.5 describes in some detail the Court of Women, the second of the four[158] successive courtyards surrounding the temple sanctuary. Besides describing the very dimensions of the court, the Mishnah includes the names and purposes of four inner chambers said to adorn the four-corners of the court; the southeast being

---

[157] "Measurements."

[158] *Mishnah Middoth* only describes the three inner courts of the temple and fails to mention the Court of the Gentiles.

named as the Chamber of the Nazirites: "There the Nazirites cooked their peace-offerings, cut their hair and threw it under the pot" (cf. Num. 6.18).

According to the Law (Num. 6.13, 18), the cutting of the hair and sacrificing of the peace offering was to take place "at the doorway of the tent of meeting," a place inaccessible to women. Only Israelite males, whose own courtyard immediately preceded that of the priests, could draw near the place where sacrificial rites were typically carried out. A chamber for Nazirites as described here, however, would allow women a place in the precincts to fulfill such rites.

The reference is fraught with a number of difficulties. The chamber, as well as the other three said to adorn the women's court, is never mentioned in other sources of the period. Josephus describes the women's court on a number of occasions, in significant detail as well, and says nothing of any inner chambers. His account is probably more trustworthy than that of the Mishnah for three reasons. First, since he was a priest who served in the temple, his familiarity with the layout of the court is firsthand and likely to be true. Second, he probably utilized Roman records when describing the temple, at least in his account of the Jewish War (*B. J.* 5.198ff.).[159] Third, the manner in which the Mishnah introduces its version calls for some initial suspicion. The chambers are introduced by means of a midrash on Ezekiel 46.22, which describes the outer court of the temple as adorned with separately enclosed chambers, one in each corner. The question for the historian is whether rabbinic recollection here is merely late idealistic representation based on the prophetic description of the messianic temple in the Bible,[160] or if it does in fact contain some true historical reminiscences not found in other sources. I believe there may be a mixture of the two. It is possible Nazirites used the Court of Women as the Mishnah describes, for it would have been a good place for both sexes to carry out their rites, particularly if Nazirites appeared simultaneously in large numbers, as other sources describe, and space was needed. It may

---

[159] Sanders, 59–60.
[160] O. Holtzmann, *Middot: Text, Übersetzung und Erklärung nebst textkritischen Anhang* (vol. 5:10 of *Die Mischna: Text, Übersetzung und ausführliche Erklärung*, eds. K. H. Rengstorf, L. Rost, and S. Herrmann; Gießen: Alfred Töpelmann [vormals J. Ricker], 1913), 67.

have even acquired an unofficial name, like the "Chamber of the Nazirites," but that this was an official, architecturally distinct part of the Court of Women in Herod's temple remains speculative.

1.8.29 *Mishnah Kelim 6.2*

> A stone on which a cooking-pot is so set that it resets both on the stone and on an oven or a double stove or a single stove, is susceptible to uncleanness. If the cooking pot rested on this stone and also on another stone or on a rock or on a wall, such is not susceptible to uncleanness. This was the kind of stove put against a rock used by the Nazirites in Jerusalem. If stones were set side by side for a butcher's stove, and one of them became unclean, all of them do not become unclean.

In addition to the reference in *m. Midd.* 2.5, *Mishnah Kelim* (*m. Kel.*) 6.2 claims knowledge of the type of pot used by the Nazirites in Jerusalem, presumably to cook their peace offerings. Nothing of the kind is discussed in other sources, and so, though possibly reliable, I approach this reference with some caution.

Summary of Evidence

Taking the results of this examination into consideration, the Mishnah offers a wide range of possibilities respecting Nazirite behavior in the period under discussion. Based on the vision of the rabbis, the evidence suggests most of all that behind the veil of formative rabbinic tradition there lay a religious custom abounding with great variety and personal freedom of expression.

In terms of the vow itself, Nazirite practices likely varied greatly. (1) People probably made vows for a variety of reasons: either out of free will or out of duty[161] to fulfill a promise made to God for his help in some circumstance (whether for the successful birth of a child, deliverance from danger, or any number of likely scenarios),[162] and (2) used all manners of expression when making vows, possibly even employing the use of slang.[163] (3) Though the customary period for observing a Nazirite vow was for thirty days,[164] people likely observed the vow for whatever period they wanted, whether for more, though

---

[161] See 1.8.5.
[162] See 1.8.5.
[163] See 1.8.1.
[164] See 1.8.1.

probably not less, than thirty days.[165] Some potentially continued in the state of consecration throughout their entire life, emulating such biblical figures as Samson, Samuel and possibly Absalom.[166] (4) Some, however, may have failed to take their vows seriously, making multiple vows[167] or vows even on the whim of a bet.[168]

With respect to who typically made such vows and where they observed them, (5) all types of people probably made the vow: the socially elite,[169] as well as the poor,[170] male and female,[171] and perhaps even slaves.[172] Some plausibly placed their children under obligation of the vow, in which case problems occasionally arose, such as when a son rebelled against the vow and cut off his hair, or when relatives protested on his behalf.[173] (6) Among women the social effects of the vow were probably felt significantly, particularly after completion of the vow when the hair was shaved. Husbands repulsed by the thought of their wives having no hair may have protested.[174] (7) People observed the vow both in the land of Palestine and abroad, most coming to Jerusalem to dispel their vows,[175] while some may have terminated them at the temple of Onias in Egypt.[176] Some Jerusalem pilgrims may have observed the vow for an additional period of sanctity when they entered Palestine to complete their vows,[177] but most likely went straight to the temple.[178]

Appearances probably varied. (8) Most may have opted for the disheveled look; not combing or tending their hair in any way would have compensated for the insufficient growth of hair accumulated in just thirty days and, similar to one in a state of mourning, a votary could thus easily be distinguished by onlookers.[179] (9) Others, particularly those who made lifetime vows, may have allowed their hair

---

[165] See 1.8.1; and 1.8.5–7.
[166] See 1.8.1.
[167] See 1.8.8.
[168] See 1.8.12.
[169] See 1.8.7.
[170] See 1.8.25.
[171] See 1.8.7; and 1.8.9; see also 1.8.16.
[172] See 1.8.20.
[173] See 1.8.9.
[174] See 1.8.9.
[175] See 1.8.7; and 1.8.11; see also 1.8.18.
[176] See 1.8.26.
[177] See 1.8.7.
[178] See 1.8.11; and 1.8.18.
[179] See 1.8.1; and 1.8.13.

to grow long and comely.[180] (10) Such appearances could have betrayed some in neglect of their vows to the punishment of forty lashes in a local synagogue.[181]

Procedurally, (11) Nazirites probably cut their hair wherever they liked, whether in the vicinity of Jerusalem,[182] inside the temple precincts (the Court of Women)[183] or, perhaps, in any location they chose. (12) The hair shaved in cleanness was either cast on the fire under the pot cooking the peace offering in the temple,[184] or given to the priest to be used in some fashion (such as a sack).[185] (13) Hair cut in uncleanness may have been swept up and buried.[186] (14) Those who became unclean because of corpse contact potentially observed the seven-day rite of purification,[187] offered their required dues, and, for some, once the seven-day ritual was passed, proceeded to bring the required offerings for the completion of their vows.[188] Others may have waited until they observed their entire avowed period over again.[189] (15) Offerings could have been purchased in the market place[190] and the temple.[191] (16) Due to the hefty quantity of offerings and sacrifices required, when the full procedure took place at the altar, it was likely clumsy and cumbersome.[192] (17) If a vow was annulled, designated offerings either may have been donated to the temple or simply returned to common use.[193]

1.9   *The Tosefta*

The Tosefta is a collection of rabbinic halakhah compiled and redacted sometime shortly after the Mishnah (ca. 220–250 AD).[194] It is difficult

---

[180] See 1.8.1.
[181] See 1.8.9; and 1.8.13.
[182] See 1.8.15.
[183] See 1.8.28.
[184] See 1.8.15; and 1.8.28–9.
[185] See 1.8.23.
[186] See 1.8.27.
[187] See 1.8.7.
[188] See 1.8.7; and 1.8.17.
[189] See 1.8.7.
[190] See 1.8.24.
[191] See 1.8.25.
[192] See 1.8.16.
[193] See 1.8.9.
[194] Stemberger suggests the end of the third to the beginning of the fourth century AD as a date for the Tosefta, 157. I believe a date in closer proximity to the final redaction of the Mishnah is called for, hence the date suggested above.

to pinpoint the precise relationship between the two works, though traditionally as the name implies, the Tosefta has been regarded as forming a type of supplement to the Mishnah.[195] The work closely resembles the Mishnah in both form and content: halakhah is arranged according to the same six orders with the names, number, and sequences of individual tractates differing only slightly.[196]

Where Nazirite halakhah is concerned, the Tosefta functions very much like a commentary on the Mishnah: parallel passages are numerous and where they occur (a) the Tosefta often identifies an anonymous source in the Mishnah, (b) halakhah is expanded to address further ambiguities in the law of Num. 6.1–21, and (c) decisions in the Mishnah are often explained or (d) illustrated by further case examples.[197] Redactionally, the Tosefta's content is far less organized than that of the Mishnah, so much so that according to Boertien, without tractate *m. Naz.* tractate *Tosefta Nezirut (t. Naz.)* would scarcely be intelligible.[198] *Tosefta Nezirut* is, therefore, not at all like *m. Naz.* in terms of revealing any coherent and recognizable purpose, at least outside of providing the bits of commentary as described above. For the purposes of the present study, therefore, Nazirite halakhah in the Tosefta is much less significant than in the Mishnah. It is less significant first, due to the generally late date of the material; and secondly, in that very little appears to reflect actual Nazirite behavior beyond or outside of what is already envisaged in the Mishnah. Be that as it may, there are a few passages in the Tosefta unparalleled in the Mishnah that I believe are of particular interest.

1.9.1   *Tosefta Nezirut 4.7*

> Simeon the Righteous said, "In my whole life I ate the guilt-offering [אשם] of a Nazirite only one time. It once happened that a man came to me from the South, and I saw that he had beautiful eyes, a hand-

---

[195] Bowker, 61; The relationship between the Mishnah and Tosefta is a complex one. For a non-traditional perspective on how these two sources relate to one another, see the recent article by J. Hauptman, "Mishnah as a Response to 'Tosefta'," in *The Synoptic Problem in Rabbinic Literature* (ed. S. J. D. Cohen; BJS 326; Providence, R. I.: Brown Judaica Studies, 2000), 13–34.

[196] Bowker, 61.

[197] See for example the parallel passages shared between *m. Naz.* and *t. Naz.* as listed and described by Boertien, "Das Verhältnis des Mischnatraktats Nazir zum Toseftatraktat Nezirot," in *Nazir*, 8–14.

[198] *Nezirut*, "Naziriteship," is a slight variation of the Mishnaic title *Nazir*; Boertien, 13.

some face, and curly locks. I said to him, 'My son, on what account did you destroy this lovely hair?' He said to me, 'I was a shepherd in my village, and I came to draw water from the river, and I looked at my reflection and my bad impulse took hold of me and sought to drive me from the world. I said to him, 'Evil one! You should not have taken pride in something which does not belong to you, in something which is going to turn to dust, worms and corruption. Lo, I take upon myself to shave you off for the sake of Heaven.' I patted his head and kissed him and said to him, 'My son, may people like you become many, people who do the will of the Omnipresent in Israel. Through you is fulfilled the scripture, as it is said, *A man or a woman, when he will express a vow to be a Nazirite, to abstain for the sake of the Lord.*[199]

The above story, attributed to Simeon the Righteous (either son of Onias the High Priest [ca. 280 BC] or Simeon II, High Priest [ca. 200 BC]),[200] lies in the context of a debate over the correct procedure for shaving the hair in a state of corpse impurity (cf. Num. 6.9–12). The content is reminiscent of the Greek story of Narcissus, the man who supposedly became infatuated with his own reflection while peering into a stream, as well as the biblical account of Absalom, the son of King David in the Bible, whose ruddiness and length of hair was purportedly unparalleled in Israel (and which, consequently, became the very source of his downfall [cf. 2 Sam. 14.25–6; 18.9–15]).[201] The peculiar feature of the present story lies in its point of illustration. Rather than exemplifying a case in which Nazirite hair was shaven off because of uncleanness acquired from of a corpse, it reports a case in which the hair was shaven off because of remorse over sinful thought. When the man from the South, as the case relates, recognized the vanity with which he was admiring his long and comely hair (hair which belonged not to him but to God because of his consecrated status as a Nazirite), he decided to shave it off "for the sake of heaven" and bring the guilt-offering required for the Nazirite rendered unclean (Num. 6.9–12). Motivation for the man's action is of principle concern in the story, as it demonstrates his intent in making the Nazirite vow. Because the man was distraught over his vanity to the degree that he considered himself ritually impure, Simeon the Righteous recognized the man's intent as

---

[199] All citations from the Tosefta are based on the translation of Neusner, *Tosefta* (6 vols.; New York: Ktav, 1979–1986).
[200] Danby, 446.
[201] Cf. *Mekh. Shirata* 2.64–75 (discussed in testimony 1.10.1 following).

truly pious and evidence that he had separated himself truly "for the sake of the Lord" (cf. Num. 6.2).

The historical veracity of the account, as with the case of Queen Helena in the Mishnah, is suspect. The case appears to contain an element of rabbinic embellishment, as it may be no coincidence that the story, exemplifying as it does proper motivation for making the Nazirite vow (to the degree that it involved an act of supererogation), is attributed to the figure Simeon the Righteous. Taken with a degree of caution, however, the case does at least exemplify a rabbinic perspective on what the ideal motivation for making the Nazirite vow is, namely personal piety, or "for the sake of the Lord."

1.9.2 *Tosefta Niddah 5.15*

> It once happened with R. Hananiah b. Hananiah that his father set upon him the vow of the Nazirite and brought him before Rabban Gamaliel. And Rabban Gamaliel was examining him (to see) whether he had come of the age of producing tokens of maturity (R. Jose b. R. Judah says, 'Whether he was come of the age of making vows'). He said to him, 'Why are you troubled? If I am subject to the authority of my father, the authority of my father is upon me and I am a Nazirite. But if I am subject to my own authority, I am a Nazirite from now on.' He stood and kissed him on his head. He said, 'I am sure with this one that he will not die before he has taught instruction.' And he did not die before he taught instruction in Israel. R. Eliezer b. R. Sadok said, "I saw that he was teaching instruction in Israel."

The case cited is situated in the midst of a debate over whether a vow superimposed by a father on his son is annulled at the point the son reaches maturity (according to rabbinic tradition the age of 12–13). The story is a diplomatic one in that it represents a case in which a diagnosis of maturity (for the purpose of releasing a child from a vow) was ultimately unnecessary. According to the story, the boy Hananiah b. Hananiah (the future rabbi) was examined by Rabban Gamaliel to see if he had produced tokens of maturity, thereby allowing him to be released from the Nazirite vow imposed on him by his father. In response to the examination, Hananiah unexpectedly informed Rabban Gamaliel that regardless of his decision, he would remain under the Nazirite vow of his own volition (thereby relieving the master of his diagnostic task).

The case is an interesting one in that it provides an example of at least one prominent rabbinic figure observing the Nazirite vow, possibly even for the duration of a lifetime. Who precisely R. Hananiah b. Hananiah was, however, as well as which Rabban Gamaliel is referred to in this story, is difficult to determine. It is likely Rabban Gamaliel is Simeon b. Gamaliel I (active during the Jewish war against Rome in AD 66–70, as mentioned by Josephus in his *Vita* 38 [191]),[202] rather than Gamaliel the Elder or Gamaliel II of Yavneh.[203] This is suggested by parallel readings in the Jerusalem Talmud (*y. Naz.* 53c) and one MS of the Babylonian Talmud (*b. Naz.* 29b of MS Moscow-Ginsberg 4311) where the Rabban Gamaliel of this passage is specifically named Simeon b. Gamaliel. R. Hananiah might thus be the son of Hananiah, the prefect of the temple and contemporary of Rabban Simeon b. Gamaliel.[204]

The two eyewitness testimonies recorded at the end of the passage may support the historical reliability of the account. The testimonies function primarily to support the prediction of Rabban Gamaliel that Hananiah b. Hananiah would someday teach instruction; however, their presence may lend credence to the general content of the story given R. Hananiah's apparent popularity in rabbinic circles.[205]

1.9.3 *Tosefta Nedarim 1.1*

R. Judah says, . . . 'For the pious men of old used to make free-will offerings of Nazirite vows. For there is not sufficient place [on the altar] for the bringing of offerings in expiation for inadvertent sins in their behalf. So they would offer Nazirite vows as free-will offerings, so that they might bring an offering.

---

[202] Stemberger, 67.

[203] G. Lisowsky and E. Schereschewsky, *Seder VI: Tohorot: Übersetszt und ërklärt* (vol. 6:2 of *Die Tosefta: Text, Überzetsung, Erklärung*, eds. G. Kittel and K. H. Rengstorf; Rabbinische Texte, erste Reihe; Stuttgart: W. Kohlhammer Verlag, 1965), 215.

[204] Stemberger, 67; This identification seems supported by the eyewitness testimony attributed to R. Eliezer b. R. Sadok, if original (see the above paragraph on the historical reliability of the account), placed at the end of the passage: "I saw that he was teaching in Israel." R. Sadok (the father of R. Eliezer b. R. Sadok) was also a contemporary of Rabban Simeon b. Gamaliel and Hananiah the prefect of the temple; see also n. 275 below.

[205] It must be noted that the second of the two testimonies, that attributed to R. Eliezer b. R. Sadok, is problematic. It is not extant in all MSS (it is omitted in the parallel found in the Babylon Talmud, but included with a slight variation in the version in the Jerusalem Talmud). Lisowsky and Schereschewsky omit the reading. Zuckermandel, on the other hand (the version accepted in the present work), adopts the saying as original; see Lieberman, et al. *Tosefet Rishonim* (vol. 2; Jerusalem: Bamberger and Warhman, 1937–9), 272; and Lisowsky and Schereschewsky, 216.

The comment attributed to R. Judah lies in the midst of a debate regarding the status of one who makes a Nazirite vow using the particular words, "like the free-will offering of suitable folk." R. Judah states that such is a legitimate vow because the pious men of old used to make free-will offerings in the form of Nazirite vows. According to the text, the pious character of these men was in relation to their having no need to make a sin-offering (cf. Num. 6.14). Instead, in order to offer something, they would make free-will offerings in the form of Nazirite vows.

Though R. Judah's recollection is debated in the context, it is peculiarly reminiscent of the comment by Philo in *Spec.* 1.248 that people made Nazirite vows as a type of first-fruit offering. R. Judah's recollection, therefore, may have some historical merit. In any case, it shows that respecting free-will offerings R. Judah can imagine approving of the use of Nazirite vows.

1.9.4 *Tosefta Shekalim 3.7*

> Six chests for a free-will offering: for the surplus of sin-offerings, guilt-offerings, the surplus of bird-offerings for *Zabs*, bird-offerings for female *Zabs*, and bird-offerings for women after child-birth, and the surplus of the offerings of a Nazirite and those of one afflicted with leprosy.

Tosefta Shekalim (*t. Shek.*) 3.7 forms part of a commentary on *m. Shek.* 6.5, which states, "There were thirteen Shofar-chests in the Temple . . . on six of them [were inscribed] 'Freewill-offerings.'" Where the Mishnah fails to describe the designated purposes of these six chests, the Tosefta provides this information. One of the six is said to have housed the surplus of money used to purchase Nazirite offerings.

In relation to *m. Shek.* 2.5, discussed in testimony 1.8.25, the passage at hand offers a further addendum to the notion that Nazirite offerings were in significant demand in Jerusalem, to the degree that the rabbis envisage there being a chest present in the temple treasury specifically to house the surplus of money assigned to these offerings. As mentioned with respect to *m. Shek.* 2.5, the presence of such a designated fund in the temple treasury would account for other sources making mention of public contributions to cover the cost of Nazirite offerings, even to the degree of paying for the expenses of whole groups of Nazirites on a single occasion (as attributed to Agrippa I by Josephus). In the same context, Josephus also mentions Agrippa's dedication of a golden chain given to him by Gaius Caesar, an object supposedly hung "within the temple precincts, over the treasure-chamber . . ."[206] The mention of the free-will offering of the golden chain, together with Agrippa's offer to pay for the expenses of a significant number of Nazirite offerings, all in view of the temple treasury, may lend credence to the rabbi's vision of there being a designated fund for Nazirite offerings, the surplus of which may have been housed in a separate chest.[207]

Summary of Evidence

What may be cautiously gathered from the Tosefta as possible evidence of Nazirite behavior within the period at hand is the following. (1) First, in terms of the widespread practice of the Nazirite vow within the late Second Temple period, the vow was known to be practiced among the rabbis in at least one case, that of R. Hananiah b. Hananiah. (2) The case also provides evidence of at least one instance where a child was placed under the obligation of Naziriteship by a parent (in similar fashion as the biblical figure Samuel). (3) In terms of rabbinic interests, the rabbis were concerned with proper motivation when making the vow, namely that the vow be observed strictly "for the Lord." (4) R. Judah's recollection that the pious men of old made free-will offerings of Nazirite vows finds possible support in Philo. As suggested in discussion of testimony 1.5.1, Nazirite vows were made as first-fruit offerings, and this seems peculiarly similar to the behavior described by R. Judah. (5) Finally, because of the significant demand for Nazirite offerings at the temple, if the rabbis' vision is correct, there may have been a chest in the precincts of the temple treasury designated specifically to house the surplus of money used to purchase Nazirite offerings.

1.10   The Halakhic Midrashim

In the period following the redactions of the Mishnah and Tosefta, a series of exegetical works attributed to rabbis of the Tannaitic period was compiled and redacted sometime in the latter half of the

---

[206] Josephus, *A. J.* 19.294.

[207] Based on *m. Shek.* 6.5, Feldman notes when commenting on Josephus' description of Agrippa I's offering of the golden chain in *A. J.* 19.294, that there were six chests marked for free-will offerings in the temple treasury, *Josephus*, p. 353.

third century AD.[208] Known traditionally as the Halakhic Midrashim, these works comprise commentaries on the biblical books of Exodus, Leviticus, Numbers, and Deuteronomy.[209] As the traditional title implies, the subject matter with which these works are concerned is primarily (though not exclusively) *halakhah*. The Halakhic Midrashim (HM) consist of three commentaries, the last transmitted as two books in one: (a) the *Mekhilta de-Rabbi Ishmael*,[210] comprising a commentary on portions of Exodus chapters 12–35; (b) *Sifra*,[211] covering the book of Leviticus; and (c) *Sifre*,[212] containing an exegesis of the books of both Numbers and Deuteronomy.

Whereas the Mishnah and Tosefta take scripture for granted when deciding halakhah, a central purpose of the HM is to *ground* halakhah on scripture. One manner in which this is accomplished is by placing decisions paralleled in the Mishnah and Tosefta alongside relative biblical passages. The works, therefore, provide more than an exegesis of scripture in its own right: they complement, or supplement, both the Mishnah and the Tosefta. Because of this supplemental relationship, the value of these sources for the purposes of the present study, while recognized, is substantially less significant than the rabbinic material previously examined. Moreover, in terms of the nature of the HM, whereas the Mishnah (though less so the Tosefta) is generally both outward and inward looking in scope, touching as it does the actual realm of Nazirite behavior in our period and shaping it didactically for one who might grant advice on Nazirite matters, the HM, as Neusner has noted, are *inward* looking only and reflect primarily the interests of the intellectual.[213]

---

[208] Ca. AD 250–300; see Stemberger, 255, 263, 267, 273.

[209] The works are also known as Tannaitic Midrashim because of their ascription to rabbis of the Mishnaic or Tannaitic period. This is the title preferred by Bowker, 69, n. 4, and 70, n. 1.

[210] The title *Mekhilta* is derived from the Aramaic and based on the Hebrew term *kelal*, meaning "rule, or norm" (thus reflecting the *rules* of rabbinic interpretation known as *middoth*; thirteen of which are traditionally ascribed to the Tannaitic rabbi, Ishmael, a contemporary of R. Akiba); see Stemberger, 252; and Jastrow, *Dictionary*, 782; see also Bowker, 70, n. 1.

[211] From the Aramaic *sifra*, meaning "book."

[212] From the plural of *sifra* (i.e., "books").

[213] This is the assessment of Neusner when comparing and contrasting the nature of the Halakhic Midrashim, particularly *Sifra* and *Sifre*, to such works as the later Amoraic commentaries, *Genesis Rabbah* and *Leviticus Rabbah*, see *Sifré to Numbers: An American Translation and Explanation* (vol. 1; BJS 118; Atlanta, Ga.: Scholars Press, 1986), 42–3.

Because the HM have less to offer the present study, as compared to the Mishnah or even the Tosefta, I have chosen to treat them separately but under a single rubric (i.e., testimony 1.10). I will examine them in the order of the biblical books with which each is concerned, *Sifre* being divided into two separate testimonia: *Sifre* to Numbers and *Sifre* to Deuteronomy.

1.10.1 *Mekhilta de-Rabbi Ishmael*

Shirata 2.64–75[214]

> And you also find it so in the case of Absalom. By means of the very thing with which he acted proudly before Him, God punished him. For it says: "Now in all Israel there was none to be so much praised as Absalom for his beauty . . . And when he polled his head," etc. (II Sam. 14.25–26)—R. Judah says: He was a Nazirite for life and would poll his hair once in twelve months, as it is said: "And it came to pass at the end of forty years, that Absalom said," etc. (ibid., 15.7). R. Jose says: He was a Nazirite for a certain number of days and would poll his hair once every thirty days, as it is said: "Now it was after a period of days, according to the days after which he polled it," etc. (ibid., 14.26). Rabbi says: He would poll his hair every Friday. For such is the custom of princes that they poll their hair every Friday—And what is written further on? "And Absalom chanced to meet the servants of David. And Absalom was riding on his mule and his head caught hold of the terebinth," etc. (ibid., 18.19).[215]

Within the *Mekhilta* a single reference to Nazirite halakhah appears in the context of an exegetical homily on Ex. 15. The reference comprises a digression addressing what *type* of Nazirite the biblical figure Absalom was, and it arises within the sixth part of an eight part discourse illustrating the principle, "With the very thing with which the nations of the world pride themselves before Him [God], He punishes them." Absalom is included in the list of illustrations because of his pride in his comely and robust hair (I Sam. 14.25–6)— the very *thing* with which he was ensnared in a tree leading to his capture and demise at the hands of his enemies (I Sam. 18.19ff.).

---

[214] This citation is taken from the edition of J. Z. Lauterbach, *Mekilta de-Rabbi Ishmael* (vol. 2; Schiff Library of Jewish Classics; Philadelphia: Jewish Publication Society of America, 1933). Other editions place the reference in tractate *Bashalakh*, see Bowker, 71; and Stemberger, 253.

[215] Lauterbach, 16–7.

The digression is haggadic in nature, but does include the element of halakhah in that the rabbis are interested in how often Absalom cut his hair. Three interpretations are given, each based on various renderings of the temporal clause מקץ ימים לימים, "it was (lit.) *at the end of days to days* that he cut it . . ." (II Sam. 14.26).[216] According to R. Judah, the phrase should be construed "from year to year" based on Absalom's request made[217] מקץ ארבעים שנה, "at the end of forty years," for permission to leave Jerusalem in order to pay a *vow* which he made in Hebron. R. Jose disagrees, basing his opinion on a literal interpretation of the term ימים, "days," and asserts that Absalom was not a lifelong Nazirite, but a Nazirite "of days," consequently cutting his hair every *thirty* days. Rabbi disagrees with both opinions stating that Absalom merely cut his hair every Friday as was the custom of princess at the time.[218]

The primary significance of the passage lies in its apparent relationship to Mishnaic halakhah. The opinions of R. Judah and R. Jose reflect both *m. Naz.* 1.2 and *m. Naz.* 1.4, which address these same issues. According to *m. Naz.* 1.2, the lifelong Nazirite may cut his hair periodically when it becomes "too heavy" for him, a rationale based on the biblical narrative describing Absalom. In *m. Naz.* 1.4 the issue is raised over who must cut his hair every thirty days: the one who says, "I will be a Nazirite as the hairs of my head"; or the one who says, "I will observe as many Nazirite vows as the hairs of my head." The former is interpreted in the Mishnah as a lifelong Nazirite, while the latter a Nazirite of days.[219]

1.10.2 *Sifra*

Nazirite halakhah is discussed more frequently in *Sifra* than in the *Mekhilta*, but the references are of little significance to the present study. Where references do occur, they typically serve as mere analo-

---

[216] *Targum Jonathan* reads מזמן עדן לעדן, "from a period of time to time."

[217] I find it interesting that no comparison is made with I Sam. 1.3 and 7, where the phrase מימים ימימה (MT v. 3) is synonymous with שנה בשנה, "from year to year" (MT v. 7).

[218] It is unclear how this last opinion relates to the preceding argument that Absalom was a Nazirite. I am inclined to think Rabbi's interpretation represents an alternative view of Absalom from the preceding two perspectives (i.e., that he was not a Nazirite but merely following common regal custom when cutting his hair).

[219] See testimony 1.8.

gies within arguments attempting either to harmonize biblical laws relating to various offerings and sacrifices, or to justify some decision relating to a point of ambiguity in the Law. In Lev. 4.24, for example, the taxonomic traits of the sin offering required of the leader who sins against the Law are those of a male goat, with no mention of its age requirement. *Sifra* addresses the legal lacuna by posing a potential solution via an analogy with the sin offering required of the Nazirite, which, though sharing the altar with other sacrifices at the time it is given, is required to be one year old. Similarly, in an exegesis of the food laws in Lev. 11.1–8, *Sifra* raises the question as to whether or not the law prohibiting the consumption of unclean beasts extends to the use of their milk. *Sifra* poses a possible affirmative answer by drawing an analogy to Num. 6.3–4:

> It is a matter of logic [potentially]. The law has prohibited an unclean domesticated beast. In the case of the Nazirite, the law has forbidden grapes. Just as, in the case of a Nazirite and grapes, the law has forbidden what derives from grapes as much as the grapes themselves, so in the case of a domesticated beast, we should surely treat what derives from an unclean domesticated beast as equivalent to the unclean domesticated beast itself.[220]

References like these abound in *Sifra*, and as mentioned, unlike *Sifre* to Num. and Deut., they carry no real significance for the purposes of the present study, except, perhaps, to demonstrate that the rabbis assumed readers were familiar with the rules of the Nazirate.

1.10.3 Sifre *to Numbers*

Sifre to Num. provides an exegetical commentary on the entire section of the law pertaining to the Nazirite vow (Num. 6.1–21). The commentary found in §22–§38 of *Sifre* is thorough, yet for the most part unenlightening in that, although phrases and sometimes individual words are accorded separate treatment, little is communicated beyond (a) a recapitulation of what has already been stated in the Mishnah and Tosefta; and (b) what is important within the exegetical program of *Sifre*, namely (1) to demonstrate that a strict exegesis of scripture and not analogical reasoning is the arbiter of halakhah,

---

[220] *Sifra, Parashat Shemini, Pereq* 4; The translation is taken from Neusner, *Sifra: An Analytical Translation* (vol. 2; BJS 139; Atlanta, Ga.: Scholar Press, 1988), 158. The word in brackets is my own.

and (2) that scripture itself exudes certain exegetical principles. Though relatively few interpretations provided in *Sifre* to Num. prove illuminating, there are a few that are peculiar, and others that appear repeatedly throughout commentary, showing themselves to be of particular interest to the rabbis.

In *Sifre* to Num. 6.3–4, the prohibition against "wine and strong drink" is interpreted as applicable to both wine drunk for religious purposes and wine drunk for mere pleasure[221]—an issue not dealt with in either the Mishnah or Tosefta. The very terms themselves, יין ושכר, are interpreted variously as either synonyms for one another, or the former as referring to diluted wine (מזוג) and latter undiluted wine (חי).[222] "He shall separate himself" (יזיר in Num. 6.3) in this context is interpreted as meaning "abstinence," but only from drinking wine: "meaning that he is permitted to conduct trade in wine or use it for healing."[223] Also, the law is said to apply to the votary in the interim period between the day his vow is fulfilled and the moment he provides the sacrifices required to conclude his vow: for "Scripture states, 'and *after that* the Nazirite may drink wine.'" (cf. Num. 6.20).[224] Finally, in commenting on Num. 6.5, ". . . he shall let the hair of his head grow long," the thirty-day period said to be the minimum period for observing the vow is justified on the grounds that a month is required for the hair to acquire sufficient growth: "Scripture says, 'He shall let the locks of the hair of his head grow long.' And how long is a spell required for the hair to grow long? Not under thirty days."[225]

Repetition of interpretation and analogy occurs periodically within the commentary. Repeated matters include the following: (a) that the various laws in Num. 6.1–12 apply during the interim period between the day on which the vow is fulfilled and the actual point at which sacrifices are given at the temple (a point mentioned previously); (b) that the term "holy" refers to the hair of the Nazirite *and* his body, as well as (c) to a Nazirite with or without hair; and (d) that the law for the Nazarite in Num. 6.1–21 applies to both the Nazirite of

---

[221] *Sifre* to Numbers 23.1.
[222] Ibid., 23.2; Jastrow, *Dictionary*, 450b.
[223] Ibid., 23.3.
[224] Ibid., 24.6.
[225] Ibid., 25.8; The translation is taken from Neusner, *Sifré*, 149.

a specified duration, as well as the perpetual Nazirite. Analogies frequently made include comparisons between the Nazirite and the High Priest, as well as the Nazirite and the leper (for the High Priest, the comparable traits include abstinence from corpse contact; and for the leper, the prescription that the hair grow long and that the hair be cut when transferred from a state of uncleanness to a state of cleanness).

1.10.4   Sifre *to Deuteronomy*

Sifre to Deut. twice makes reference to Nazirite matters: once in a commentary on the blessings of Joseph in Deut. 33.16, and once in a parenthetical comment on the phrase "thirty days" in Deut. 34.8.

Deuteronomy 33.16 repeats the blessing bestowed on Joseph by his father Jacob (cf. Gen. 49.26), this time in the context of Moses' blessing upon the people of Israel just prior to his death. Within the blessing, Joseph is described as the *nezir* (the construct form of *nazir*) of his brothers (נזיר אחיו). The term in this context may mean "one set apart" (RSV), or "one distinguished" (NAS) from his brethren. *Sifre* to Deut. interprets the term in its religious technical sense, however, by referring to Joseph as "him whose brothers set him apart and made him a Nazirite."[226] The rationale behind this technical rendering appears to be the rejection of Joseph by his brothers as recorded in the Genesis narrative (Gen. 37.18–28), a rejection that leads to Joseph's enslavement in Egypt and separation from his kin. Rather than in the more *positive* sense of "one distinguished" or "one set apart," in other words, *nazir* appears to be construed only in the *negative* sense of "one separated" and is analogous to the separation from societal norms required of the Nazirite (e.g., wine drinking, attending funerals, and cutting the hair).

The second reference, as mentioned, appears in a parenthetical comment on Deut. 34.8. The verse states, "The Israelites mourned for Moses in the steppes of Moab for thirty days. The period of weeping and mourning for Moses came to an end." Regarding the phrase "thirty days," *Sifre* asks the following: And how on the basis of scripture do we know that the spell of a Nazirite-vow [sic] is thirty days?

---

[226] Translation is taken from Neusner, *Sifré to Deuteronomy: An Analytical Translation* (vol. 2; BJS 101; Atlanta, Ga.: Scholars Press, 1987), 436.

Here "days . . ." is stated, and elsewhere, "days . . ." (Num. 6.4 with reference to the Nazirite vow). Just as "days" here refers to thirty days, so "days" stated there involves thirty days.[227]

In *gezerah shewa* fashion (meaning, what is meant in one usage means the same in another), the thirty days during which Israel mourned for Moses is given as *the* reason for thirty days being the customary period for observing the Nazirite vow. Though significance in the text is placed merely on the temporal aspect of the vow, the analogy with the rite of mourning is reminiscent of the description of Bernice's vow given by Josephus in *B. J.* 2.313–4 (see testimony 1.6.1). The rites of mourning and the Nazirite vow may have shared more in common than merely thirty days, and this may have led the interpreter to mention the Nazirite vow while commenting on Israel's mourning in Deut. 34.8.

Summary of Evidence

The Halakhic Midrashim, as previously stated, have little to offer respecting the purposes of the present study. There are a few things, however, in which the rabbis take a peculiar interest that may possibly reflect earlier and socially wider concerns; though any degree of certainty in these matters is precluded by the very nature of these sources, as discussed.

In the *Mekhilta de-Rabbi Ishmael* the rabbis have a peculiar interest in the biblical figure Absalom, particularly in respect to his forming a potential model for the Nazirite of lifelong duration. (1) The debates in the *Mekhilta* display concerns already present in the Mishnah, and like the Mishnah, they may reflect a wider perception that Absalom was a Nazirite, and therefore a model after which some making the Nazirite vow could pattern their behavior.

In *Sifre* to Num., a number of practical matters were mentioned that may or may not have been genuine concerns for those making Nazirite vows. (2) Some, like the rabbis, may have questioned whether they could drink wine for religious purposes, or (3) trade in wine, or even use it for medicinal purposes given the Law's explicit and static requirement that they abstain from it. (4) The notion that "wine and strong drink" in Num. 6.3 is to be interpreted as either

---

[227] Ibid., 460.

synonymous, or the former as referring to diluted wine and the latter to undiluted wine, seems to imply that the law may have been confusing to some, and may indicate why other sources simply describe the proscription as including merely *wine*.[228] (5) Though odd given the Law's requirements regarding the growth and depositing of the hair, it may also have been the case that a bald person wanted to become a Nazirite as the rabbis envisage. (6) It may also have been the case, again as the rabbis anticipate, that some began drinking wine as soon as their avowed days were complete (i.e., before they made their actual trek to Jerusalem to offer their sacrifices), justifying it on the grounds that their time under the vow (and its general requirements) was essentially over.

Finally, taking *Sifre* to Deut. into consideration, (7) the significance of the thirty-day period for observing the vow may lay in the traits the Nazirite vow shared in common with the Jewish rite of mourning. The notion that Joseph was made a Nazirite by his brothers in the negative sense of being *separated* or *alienated*, combined with the fact that the interpreter of *Sifre* to Deut. 34.8 based the thirty-day period for observing the Nazirite vow on the rationale that Israel mourned for Moses in the steppes of Moab for thirty days, seems to indicate that the thirty-day customary period for observing the Nazirite vow, together with other traits, had much in common with the Jewish rite of mourning.

1.11 *Genesis Rabbah*

Like *Sifre* to Deut. 33.16, the later Amoraic commentary on Genesis, *Genesis Rabbah*, offers a religious technical interpretation of the reference to Joseph in Genesis 49.26 as being the "*nezir* of his brothers." *Genesis Rabbah* is an exegetical commentary on the book of Genesis compiled and redacted sometime after the turn of the fifth century AD.[229] The work is the earliest of the so-called Exegetical Midrashim on the Pentateuch attributed to the Amoraim, the

---

[228] Josephus and Philo, for instance, generalize the proscription: Philo when referring to Samuel, and Josephus when explaining to his readers that Nazirites are those who "abstain from wine" (see testimonies 1.5.4 and 1.6.1–2).

[229] Stemberger, 279.

epithet *Rabbah*[230] having been passed on to succeeding and similar type compilations (e.g., *Leviticus Rabbah*, *Lamentations Rabbah*, et al.).

Problems facing the use of Amoraic material as evidence for Second Temple Judaism involve not only the late date of the material but also the type of exegesis typically employed. In contrast to the Halakhic Midrashim, Bible interpretation in Amoraic sources tend to involve the use of free or expansive interpretations of a biblical text, phrase, or even a single word within a text. Moreover, various interpretations attributed to different individuals are often grouped together under a single verse, or portion of a verse, and as a collection of interpretations, such commentaries, like *Genesis Rabbah*, may reveal only the thoughts of various Amoraim and not the ideas prevalent among Jews in the period under investigation. In favor of taking these sources more seriously, however, as Vermès has demonstrated, Bible interpretations evidenced in Amoraic sources may in some cases represent later developments of interpretive traditions stemming from a much earlier period.[231] It is possible that this is the case regarding interpretations of the biblical figure Joseph, even though otherwise unattested in earlier and surviving, non-rabbinic sources.

Genesis Rabbah to Genesis 49.26d

AND ON THE CROWN OF THE HEAD OF HIM THAT WAS THE NAZIRITE (NEZIR) OF HIS BRETHREN, for his brothers repulsed him [רחקו אותו] and made him a Nazirite. R. Isaac of Magdala interpreted: You are the crown of your brethren [כלילהון דאחך]. R. Levi said: He was literally a Nazirite. For R. Levi said: During the whole of the twenty-two years that he did not see them he tasted no wine, and they too tasted no wine until they saw him. Thus it says, *And they drank and were merry with him* (Gen. 43.34): with him they drank, but away from him they did not drink.[232]

Of the three interpretations of the cited portion of Gen. 49.26, two exegetes construe the term *nazir* in the construct נזיר אחיו in the reli-

---

[230] Reason for the epithet *rabbah* is speculative. Two possibilities are that it served to distinguish the present commentary from another smaller and contemporary commentary on Genesis, or that it served to distinguish the more elaborate volume of an original two part series; see Stemberger, 277.

[231] G. Vermès, *Scripture and Tradition in Judaism: Haggadic Studies* (StPB 4; Leiden: Brill, 1961).

[232] This is a modified version of H. Freedman's English translation in Freedman and M. Simon, eds., *The Midrash Rabbah* (vol. 2; London: Soncino Press, 1951), 970.

gious technical sense, thus suggesting Joseph was in some sense an actual Nazirite. R. Isaac of Magdala, on the other hand, represents an alternative point of view by rendering the term as *crown*: "You are the *crown* of your brethren (כלילהון דאחך)." The latter view appears to involve an interpretive play on the Aramaic *crown* (כליל) and the Hebrew root of *nazir*, נזר, which may also mean *crown* in certain contexts. Rationales for the former interpretations are more clear: (a) Joseph was a Nazirite because his brothers physically repulsed him (רחקו אותו) and thereby made like a Nazirite, an interpretation witnessed in *Sifre* to Deut. 33.16; and (b) Joseph was a Nazirite as evidenced by his abstention from wine during his years in Egypt, an interpretation induced from Gen. 43.34: "and they drank and were merry with him."

Like *Sifre* to Deut. 33.16, both interpretations of *nazir* in the religious technical sense involve the negative aspect of "one separated" rather than the more positive sense of the term as "one distinguished." Joseph was a Nazirite because he was rejected and repulsed by his brothers (an allusion to his being sold into slavery in Gen. 37.18–28), and because he abstained from drinking wine while separated from his kin (not unlike one mourning over the death of a kin). When seen in juxtaposition to the interpretation of R. Isaac of Magdala, an interpretation that does exude the more positive aspect of the term, this becomes very apparent. The positive rendering by R. Isaac incorporates a different interpretation of *nazir* altogether (i.e., Joseph was the *crown* of his brethren).

Summary of Evidence

That the biblical figure Joseph was a Nazirite is a notion witnessed not only in *Sifre* to Deut. but also (1) here in *Genesis Rabbah* to Gen. 49.26. (2) This rationale is based on the negative aspect of Joseph's separation from his brothers, and this, as was mentioned with respect to *Sifre* to Deut. 33.16, seems to be inspired by the separation from normative social behavior practiced by Nazirites. The idea that Joseph abstained from wine while separated from his brothers, thereby suggesting he was a Nazirite, also rings similar to mourning behavior. This seems to suggest, again, that (3) the Nazirite vow may have shared traits with the Jewish rite of mourning.

1.12   *The Targumim*

Another constituent of the body of literature preserved by the rabbis and composed between the Mishnaic and Medieval periods is the rabbinic Targum tradition:[233] literature comprising translations of the Hebrew Bible into Aramaic.[234] Aramaic translations of the Bible are evidenced as early as the second century BC in manuscripts discovered among the Dead Sea Scrolls (the so-named *Targum of Leviticus* [4Q156] and *Targum of Job* [4Q157; 11Q10]);[235] however, there is a substantial difference between the Qumran Targumim and those shaped and transmitted under the auspices of the rabbinate. Whereas the DSS MSS comprise translations in a very strict sense of the genre, rabbinic Targumim contain a mixture of both translation and (often very expansive) interpretation of the biblical text.

Of the Targumim that survive, some are complete, and some survive only in fragments, and together they comprise translations of every book of the Hebrew Bible with the exception of Ezra, Nehemiah, and Daniel. The MSS include several virtually complete translations of the Pentateuch, such as *Onqelos*, *Neofiti I*, and *Pseudo-Jonathan*, as well as a nearly complete translation of the prophetic books in a compilation known as *Targum Jonathan*. Concerning the Writings, or Hagiographa, no single compilation exists, but all of the biblical books, with the exception of Daniel, survive in Aramaic.

The use of a Targum text in the Jewish synagogue service is presupposed in the Mishnah.[236] The nature of the transmission history of the extant MSS, however, renders any dating of these works conjectural. Concerning those relevant to the study at hand, *Targum Onqelos* likely originated in Palestine in the first to second centuries AD and was subsequently redacted in Babylonia between the fourth and fifth centuries together with *Targum Jonathan* to the Prophets, both of which became the official Targumim of the Babylonian Talmud. *Targum Neofiti I* was likely redacted no later than the third to fourth centuries AD, and *Pseudo-Jonathan* as late as the seventh to

---

[233] On the description of the Targum literature as a "tradition," see Bowker, 15.

[234] For an introduction to the Targumim, especially as they relate to other classical Jewish literature, see Bowker, 3ff.

[235] L. H. Schiffman and J. C. VanderKam, eds. *Encyclopedia of the Dead Sea Scrolls* (New York: Oxford University Press, 2000), s. v. "Targumim," by U. Gleßmer.

[236] *m. Meg.* 4.4.

eight centuries, though both of these works certainly contain much earlier material. The *Fragmentary Targumim* were probably redacted at some point after *Neofiti I*, but prior to *Pseudo-Jonathan*.[237]

In keeping with the nature of the later rabbinic perspectives on Nazirites, the evidence available from the Targum tradition, though significant, is nonetheless sparse. Rather than treating relevant texts individually, therefore, citing each in full, I will simply discuss significant elements within each Targum, citing portions of passages and key terminology where appropriate.

1.12.1 *Targum Onqelos*

Targum Onqelos (*Tg. Onq.*) contains a very literal and carefully edited translation of the Hebrew scriptures into Aramaic in that it typically agrees very strongly with MT with generally few expansions on meaning (as is witnessed, comparatively, in the other Targumim to the Pentateuch). In the blessing of Joseph in Gen. 49.26 and its parallel in Deut. 33.16, Joseph is described as "the man distinguished among his brothers" (נבראַ פּרישׁא דאחוהי): the Aramaic compound נברא פּרישׁא being used to construe the Hebrew נזיר.[238] It is possible that פּרישׁא ("distinguished, separated") is meant to convey an underlying nuance of נזיר in its religious technical sense, as was witnessed in *Sifre* to Deut. 33.16 and *Genesis Rabbah* to Gen. 49.26. However, it is equally possible that the adjective is meant to convey only the generic sense of נזיר (i.e., "the man set apart"). Likewise, *Tg. Onq.* to Num. 6.1–21 closely follows MT with only a few exceptions. Minor alterations include the idiosyncratic substitution of "with" (עם) for the Hebrew dative "to" (אל) in v. 1 ("And the Lord spoke *with* Moses saying, 'Speak *with* the children of Israel . . .'"), as well as the expression "before the Lord" (קדם יוי) in place of the Hebrew dative

---

[237] For a discussion of dates and places of origin of the various Targumim, see D. N. Freedman, ed. *ABD* (New York: Doubleday, 1992), s. v. "Targum, Targumim," by P. Alexander.

[238] According to M. Löwenstein, *Tg. Onq.* renders MT קדקד with נבראַ; however, I believe Aberbach and Grossfeld are correct in seeing MT קדקד and ראשׁ as mere poetical parallels of which *Tg. Onq.* rendered with only a single reference: לרישׁא דיוסף. MT קדקד was, therefore, not translated by *Tg. Onq.*; see M. Aberbach and B. Grossfeld, *Targum Onqelos on Genesis 49: Translation and Analytical Commentary* (Aramaic Studies 1; Missoula, Mont.: Published by Scholars Press for the Society of Biblical Literature, 1976), 62.

"to the Lord" (ליהוה).[239] "Wine and strong drink" (יין ושכר) in v. 2 is interpreted as "new wine and old wine" (מחמר חדת ועתיק), and "peace offering" (שלמים) is consistently rendered as the "sanctified sacrifice" (נכסת קודשיא). More substantially, there are a few instances where *Tg. Onq.* appears to bring the reading of MT into line with current rabbinic interpretation. The prohibition against grape seeds and grape skins in v. 4 of *Tg. Onq.* (מפורצנין ועד עיצורין), for instance, is in keeping with the interpretation of the Hebrew, "from the seeds to the skins" (מחרצנים ועד זג) discussed in *m. Naz.* 6.2 and *b. Naz.* 39a.[240] Likewise in v. 18, which directs the Nazirite to place the shaven hair on the fire under the peace-offering at the conclusion of the vow, *Tg. Onq.* includes the mention of a "cauldron" (דודא): a utensil absent in MT to v. 18 but described in *m. Naz.* 6.8, *m. Midd.* 2.5, and *m. Kel.* 6.2.

1.12.2   *Targum Neofiti I*

In contrast to *Tg. Onq.*, *Targum Neofiti I* (*Tg. Neof.*) contains an expansive version of the blessing of Joseph in Gen. 49.26 and interprets נזיר as חסידא ("pious man"): "Let all these blessings come; let them become a crown of dignity on the head of Joseph, and on the brow of the pious man (נברא חסידא) who was master and ruler over the land of Egypt . . ." Deut. 33.16, on the other hand, contains a shortened version of the blessing and drops any clear rendering of נזיר altogether. Numbers 6.1–21 in *Tg. Neof.* closely parallels *Tg. Onq.* with the exception of a few minor details: (1) the days of the Nazirite's vow are described in v. 6 as those taken "for the name of the Lord" (לשמא דיי), and (2) the נזר, "hair, crown" of the Nazirite in vv. 7, 12, and 19 is rendered consistently with the Aramaic, "crown" (כליל). Also (3), the procedure for purification in the case of accidental corpse uncleanness is introduced with the explanatory clause, "And should a dead man who is near him have died suddenly *without his knowing it* (דלא ידע), he renders the hair of his consecrated head unclean" (v. 9).

---

[239] Verses 2, 5, 6, 8, 12, 14, 17, 20, 21.
[240] Grossfeld, *The Targum Onqelos to Leviticus and the Targum Onqelos to Numbers* (ArBib 8; Wilmington, Del.: M. Glazier, 1988), 91 n. 3.

1.12.3 *Targum Pseudo-Jonathan*

Like *Tg. Neof.*, *Targum Pseudo-Jonathan* (*Tg. Ps.-J.*) is expansive in its version of the blessing of Joseph in both Gen. 49.26 and Deut. 33.16. By contrast, however, there is no clear indication of how *Tg. Ps.-J.* renders the term נזיר in either passage. With respect to Num. 6.1–21, *Tg. Ps.-J.* parallels both *Tg. Onq.* and *Tg. Neof.* with the effect that the reading of MT is brought further into line with current rabbinic interpretation. A phrase found in *b. Naz.* 2b, for example, is interpolated into v. 2, "Speak to the Israelites and say to them: If a man or a woman, *seeing a faithless woman in her moral corruption*, abstains from wine . . ." Similarly, the act of making the Nazirite vow is consistently described as "for the name of the Lord" (לשמא דה 'ה),[241] a motivation stressed in *Sifre* to Num. 6.2. The shaving of the head at the completion of the vow in v. 18 is also commanded to take place "outside, after the slaughtering of the sanctified sacrifice" in accordance with the order of procedure preferred in the Mishnah and, possibly, in accordance with the description of the act described in *m. Midd.* 2.5 as taking place in the Court of Women. Like *Tg. Onq.*, v. 18 also contains a reference to the "cauldron" (דודא) in which the sanctified sacrifice is to be boiled.

1.12.4 Fragmentary Targumim *(P, V)*

Of the portions of the translations surviving only in fragments and labeled by scholars as the *Fragmentary Targumim, Fragmentary Targum* P (*Frg. Tg.* P) to Gen. 49.26 makes reference to Joseph as the "pious man" as does *Tg. Neof.* (a likely rendering of MT נזיר). Deuteronomy 33.16, however, is much less clear. By contrast, and like *Tg. Ps.-J.*, *Fragmentary Targum* V (*Frg. Tg.* V) contains no clear rendering of נזיר in either Gen. 49.26 or Deut. 33.16. With respect to Num. 6.1–21, in both *Frg. Tg.* P and V only portions have survived. *Fragmentary Targum* P contains only an insignificant reference to the razor forbidden to the Nazirite in v. 5, and *Frg. Tg.* V contains only v. 3, which like other Targumim, renders "wine and strong drink" as "new wine and old wine" (חדת ועתיק).

---

[241] Verses 2, 5, and 6.

1.12.5   *Targum Jonathan*

Within *Targum Jonathan* (*Tg. J.*) to the Prophets, there exists a variety of interpretations of נזיר where, as evidenced in the sources examined hitherto, the term has traditionally been understood in its religious
technical sense. With respect to the quintessential Nazirite Samson
in Judg. 13.5, 7; 16.17, *Tg. J.* sticks closely to MT and consistently
describes Samson as the "Nazirite of the Lord" (נזירא דייי). In I Sam.
1.11, however, like the midrash of R. Jose in *m. Naz.* 9.5, מורה, most
often rendered "razor," is translated in the vow of Hannah using
the construct מרות אנש ("fear of man"): "And I will hand him over,
who will be serving before the Lord all the days of his life. And the
fear of man (מרות אנש) will not be upon him." With respect to the
timing of Samuel's dedication in chapter 1 of I Sam. (cf. esp. vv.
21–8), like the LXX and 4QSamᵃ, *Tg. J.* identifies the point of dedication with the annual festival period, although which particular festival remains unnamed: the Hebrew ימים ימימה, lit. "from days to
days," and זבח הימים, "sacrifice of days" in MT I Sam. 1.3 and v. 21
are construed as, "from festival to festival" (מועד למועד)[242] and "sacrifice
of the festival" (דיבח מועדא).[243] Finally, in *Tg. J.* to Amos 2.12, where
MT reads, "You made the Nazirites drink wine, and you commanded
the prophets, saying, 'You shall not prophesy,'" the Hebrew נזרים
(pl. of נזיר) is interestingly rendered with the Aramaic מלפין ("teachers"):[244] "You lead your teachers (מלפיכון) astray with wine, ..."[245]

Summary of Evidence

What the Targumim offer the present study is for the most part
insignificant, yet there are a few elements revealed in the literature
that do prove insightful. (1) Given the variety of interpretations of
Joseph as the "*nezir* of his brothers," a *nazir* (Nazirite) seems to be
thought of as both a pious individual, as well as, possibly, one separated from social norms. (2) From a rabbinic perspective, the ideal
motivation for making the Nazirite vow was personal piety, or "for

---

[242] I Sam. 1.3.

[243] I Sam. 1.21.

[244] Jastrow, *Dictionary*, 790.

[245] The translation is certainly peculiar, but providing a suggestion as to why
Tg. J. translates נזרים with מלפין would be capricious given the sparse context.

the sake of the Name," as well as for the purpose of avoiding moral corruption. (3) The command to avoid "wine and strong drink" is thought to refer merely to wine, albeit wine in differing degrees of potency. Finally, (4) though some disassociated the biblical figure Samuel from the role of a Nazirite, his dedication to serve in the temple was thought to have occurred at the festival period.

1.13   *The Jerusalem Talmud*

In contrast to the later rabbinic sources examined thus far, Talmudic literature (the Jerusalem Talmud [ca. AD 375] and the Babylonian Talmud [ca. AD 500]) proves generally inconsequential to the purposes of the present study in that it is not only chronologically late in origin, but its genre precludes its general relevance. The Talmuds comprise Amoraic commentaries on the Mishnah, and where information contained in these sources has proven insightful, I have already made note of it, particularly where relevant to the discussion of the Mishnah and other earlier rabbinic sources.

There is, however, one portion of material from within Talmudic literature unparalleled in earlier sources that is often cited by scholars as evidence for Nazirites in the period under investigation: an haggadic passage in tractate *Nazir* of the Jerusalem Talmud (*y. Naz.*) relating a story of 300 Nazirites who supposedly visited Jerusalem during the time of Alexander Jannaeus (ca. 103–76 BC) and R. Simeon b. Shetah.[246] Although I believe the above grounds justify automatic suspicion of the reliability of the account, I think it important to recount the text in full and more thoroughly explain why I believe, in contrast to the view of some scholars, that the account bears no direct relevance to the present study.

The Jerusalem Talmud Nazir 5.4

> Three-hundred Nazirites came up [to Jerusalem] in the days of R. Simeon b. Shetah. For one-hundred fifty of them he found grounds for absolution, and for one-hundred fifty of them he did not find grounds for absolution. He came to Yannai the king. He said to him, "There are here three-hundred Nazirites who require nine-hundred offerings. You give half from your [property], and I shall give half from mine." He sent him four-hundred-fifty [sacrifices].

---

[246] A parallel is found in the Babylonian Talmud (*b. Ber.* 47b), but this account omits the episode of the Nazirites.

An evil rumor came to him, "He gave nothing of his own." Yannai the king heard and was angered. Simeon b. Shetah was frightened and fled.

After [some] days, important men came up from the kingdom of Persia to Yannai the king. When they were sitting and eating, they said to him, "We recall that there was here a certain old man who said before us words of wisdom. Let him teach us something." They said to him, "Send and bring him." He sent and gave him his word, and he came. He seated him[self] between the king and the queen. He said to him, "Why did you deceive me?" He said to him, "I did not deceive you. You [gave] of your money and I [gave] of my light [Torah], as it is written [Qoh. 7.12], *'For wisdom is a defense even as money is a defense.'"* He said to him, "Why did you flee?" He said to him, "I heard that my lord was angry against me, and I wanted to carry out this Scripture, 'Hide yourself for a little moment, until the anger be past'" (Is. 26.20). And he [Yannai] cited concerning him [the following Scripture]: *"The advantage of knowledge of wisdom will give life to those that possess it" (Qoh. 7.12)*. He [Yannai] said to him, "Why did you sit down between the king and queen?" He [Simeon] said to him, "In the Book of Ben Sira it is written [Ben Sira 11.1], *'Esteem her, so she shall exalt you and seat you between princes.'"*

He [Yannai] said, "Give him the cup so that he may say the blessing." He [Simeon] took the cup and said, "Let us bless the food that Yannai and his companions have eaten." He said to him, "Are you stubborn even to such an extent?" He said to him, "What shall we say, 'For the food that we have not eaten'?" He said, "Give him something to eat." They gave him food, and he ate and said, "Let us bless the food that we have eaten."

R. Jeremiah said, "It concerned the first [blessing]." R. Ba said, "It concerned the second [blessing]." The opinions assigned to R. Jeremiah are at variance with one another. There he raised this question, and here it was self evident to him [that one who eats vegetables only may say the grace for those who have eaten bread]. The case in which it was a question to him accords with Rabban Simeon b. Gamaliel. For it has been taught: "If one reclined and dipped vegetables with a group, even though he did not even eat with them so much as an olive's bulk of grain, they invoke him in the call to say grace," they words of sages. R. Jacob bar Aha in the mane of R. Yohanan, "Under no conditions do they include him in the call to say grace, unless he should eat with them at least as much as an olive's bulk of grain. For it has been taught: If two ate a piece of bread and one ate vegetables, they say a common call to say grace. The passage accords with the view of Rabban Simeon b. Gamaliel.[247]

---

[247] This translation and passage reference (as well as the reference to *y. Ber.* 7.2) are borrowed from Neusner, *The Talmud of the Land of Israel: A Preliminary Translation and Explanation* (vol. 24; CSJH; Chicago: The University of Chicago Press, 1985), 123–5.

The context in which the account is found is a commentary on *m. Naz.* 5.4, which relates the story of Nahum the Mede and his decision to release a group of Nazirites from their vows when they appeared in Jerusalem to discharge them, only to find that the temple had been destroyed (see testimony 1.8.11). The similarities between the two stories, the large groups of Nazirites appearing in Jerusalem on a single occasion and the decision to release Nazirites from their vows, are the only reasons the current story finds its placement in the present context.[248] The story's placement is thus haphazard and contributes nothing illuminating to the surrounding discussion. The story, in fact, appears to be a later interpolation of a parallel found in *y. Ber.* 7.2, where the story bears a much more logical relationship to its contextual surrounding.[249] The argument between the rabbis over whether one may recite the blessing of wine and bread over a meal consisting merely of vegetables, an argument partially included in the version in *y. Naz.* 5.4 (which I have provided), has absolutely nothing to do with Nazirite halakhah but everything to do with halakhah affecting blessings (*Berakhot*). Accepting *y. Ber.* 7.2 as the original setting of the story will then help to illumine the suspicious nature of the account in terms of historicity.

In terms of historical recollection, rather than an historical case recalling actual events unfolding in the lives of R. Simeon b. Shetah and King Alexander Jannaeus, the story appears to be a parable intended merely to illustrate a point in a related argument; namely and as mentioned, the decision of whether one may recite the blessing of bread and wine over a meal consisting of only vegetables (*y. Ber.* 7.2). The story is tailor made to fit such a context, in that it involves supposed vegetarian dignitaries from Persia (in the likeness of prominent Jewish vegetarians in the book of Daniel?).[250] Secondly, the response of R. Simeon b. Shetah to the queries of the king read more like a rabbinic midrash in their variety of citations from prophetic and hagiographic literature than they do historical facts. Furthermore,

---

[248] Cf. Neusner, *Talmud*, 126, who states that the present passage finds its place in *y. Naz.* 5.4 "only because of its opening theme, the advent of the Nazirites in Jerusalem."

[249] Ibid.

[250] Cf. H. W. Guggenheimer who, viewing the account as historical, holds that these are Jewish dignitaries who brought with them "the yearly subsidy" from Parthia, *The Jerusalem Talmud* (vol. 1; SJ 18; Berlin: Walter de Gruyter, 2000), 528.

the way the story is introduced is markedly disparate from the way historical cases are typically introduced in other rabbinic sources. In the Mishnah and Tosefta historical cases typically begin with the phrase "it once happened" (מעשה ב . . .). Here, the story is introduced with "it was taught . . ." (תני), a phrase typically used to introduce a traditional Tannaitic teaching or halakhah (in this case probably a well-known tale). Also, the sheer length of the story stands in contrast to the brevity typical of similar cases present in the Mishnah and Tosefta. I believe, therefore, in light of these characteristics that the events surrounding the 300 Nazirites in Jerusalem find their significance not in that they are historical, but that they form the general didactic catalyst for the rest of the story in which they are found.

Essentially then, I believe the story of the 300 Nazirites who entered Jerusalem at the time of Alexander Jannaeus and R. Simeon b. Shetah told in *y. Naz.* 5.4 is a later interpolation of the parallel found in *y. Ber.* 7.2. As such, it is used rather haphazardly and is consequentially unimportant within its present context in tractate *Nazir*. Although possible, I find it unlikely that the story represents an actual historical case, but rather likely that the tale represents a parable intended merely to convey a particular point in an argument: in this case an argument having nothing to do with Nazirite matters at all, but only matters affecting blessings. The description of Nazirites given in passing in the story, however, is tacitly assumed to reflect Nazirite behavior in the period under examination, and this, despite the story's fictional qualities, should be taken seriously.

Summary of Evidence

Although I find no evidence in this passage for Nazirites in the late Second Temple period, I do believe it at least enriches the present study in three ways. First, the rabbis of the Amoraic period envisage the possibility that Nazirites in our period could appear in Jerusalem in large numbers on a single occasion. Secondly, the rabbis also believe the required offerings for Nazirites, even a significant number of them, could be paid for out of charity by another individual or pair of individuals. Finally, it is assumed in the story that a rabbi has the power to absolve people from their vows.

CHAPTER TWO

POSSIBLE AND TANGENTIAL
EVIDENCE FOR NAZIRITES

Possible and tangential evidence for Nazirites consists of what appear to be indirect references to the Nazirate in several narrative sources of the period composed in Greek. These sources consist namely of the Synoptic Gospels and Acts, a comment regarding James the Just in a writing by the early church father Hegesippus, and a reference describing the behavior of certain Jews found in a work by the Graeco-Roman biographer Plutarch. I label these sources as "possible" and "tangential" in that, whereas in the case of the former imagery reflecting the Nazirate is employed sparsely to the effect it is unclear whether the Nazirate or some other similar rite is being described, in the case of the latter imagery is borrowed principally for the purpose of attributing to a certain individual only Nazirite-*like* qualities. A certain amount of conjecture, therefore, is required in establishing what it is in these sources that can be viewed as evidence for Nazirites in this period. Naturally, the place of these sources within the scope of my overall argument is, therefore, secondary. However, I intend to demonstrate in the following examination of sources that much of the information contained in them is indeed relevant, and in some cases, highly invaluable.

2.1   *Mark*

Mark 14.25; 15.23

14.25 Truly I say to you, I shall never again drink of the fruit of the vine [γενήματος τῆς ἀμπέλου] until that day when I drink it new in the kingdom of God.

15.23 And they tried to give Him wine mixed with myrrh [ἐσμυρνισμένον οἶνον]; but He did not take it [ὃς δὲ οὐκ ἔλαβεν].[1]

---

[1] All citations from the New Testament are taken from the NAS unless otherwise indicated.

In the Synoptic tradition Jesus makes a vow in the final Paschal meal to never drink again of the fruit of the vine (γενήματος τῆς ἀμπέλου) until the day he drinks it new in the kingdom of God (Mk. 14.25//Mt. 26.29//Lk. 22.18). It is possible, as argued by Wojcie-chowski[2] and more recently Bockmuehl,[3] that such a promise repre-sents a Nazirite vow.[4] Given the context in which the promise is made and the findings of the present study thus far, the possibility of a Nazirite interpretation of the Paschal promise is quite substantial.

First, in the Gospel of Mark, the evangelist is explicit regarding Jesus' refusal of the "wine mixed with myrrh" (ἐσμυρνισμένον οἶνον) offered by soldiers at the point of crucifixion (15.23). Matthew also contains the tradition, adding that Jesus first tasted the mixture (of wine "mixed with gall," οἶνον μετὰ χολῆς μεμιγμένον) but then refused it (Mt. 27.34). Subsequent Gospel tradition is less clear. Luke con-tains the offering of vinegar (ὄξος), yet is silent about Jesus' rejec-tion of the substance (Lk. 23.36), and according to John, Jesus both announces his thirst and actually accepts an offer of vinegar before expiration (Jn. 19.28–30). Bockmuehl suggests there may be a grow-ing influence of LXX Ps. 68.22 [= 69.21], "they gave me vinegar to drink" (ἐπότισάν με ὄξος) on the Gospel tradition, and this may explain the growing disparities.[5] What is clear, however, is that in the earliest tradition, Mark, there is a definite emphasis on Jesus' refusal of the wine concoction when offered, and narrative proxim-ity between these events allows for the two episodes: the promise of abstinence in 14.25 and the subsequent refusal to drink in 15.23, to be interpreted relationally.

Secondly, again within Mark, there appears to be an influence of LXX[B] Judg. on the Jesus tradition. As was suggested in discussion of testimony 1.2.2 of the present study, Samson is uniquely labeled a "holy one," ἅγιος (13.7; 16.17), where in MT he is simply desig-nated a נזיר, "Nazirite." An influence of the text is noted particu-

---

[2] M. Wojciechowski, "Le naziréat et la Passion (Mc 14,25a; 15,23)," *Biblica* 65 (1984): 94–5.

[3] Bockmuehl, 571–2.

[4] W. D. Davies and Dale C. Allison also support this position, *A Critical and Exegetical Commentary on the Gospel According to Saint Matthew* (vol. 1; ICC; Edinburgh: T&T Clark, 1988), 276.

[5] Bockmuehl, 572.

larly in the declaration of the demoniac in Mk. 1.24, "What do we have to do with You, Jesus of Nazareth (Ναζαρηνέ)? . . . I know who you are—the Holy One of God (ὁ ἅγιος τοῦ θεοῦ)!" Long noted by scholars as the first episode in the Markan Messianic Secret, an association between Jesus and the powerfully anointed Samson is likely given the close proximity of the event with the baptism story in Mk. 1.9–11.[6] Moreover, there is an apparent Markan play-on-words in the saying between Nazareth (Ναζαρηνέ), Nazirite (ναζιρ), and holy one (ἅγιος) based on LXX[B] Judg. 13.5, 7.[7] That Jesus was a Nazirite during his earthly ministry is unlikely, for even in Mark, Jesus is accused of eating and drinking (probably wine) with publicans and sinners (Mk. 2.16).[8] However, Nazirite imagery appears to be present within the early Jesus tradition and this may well have made its way into the passion.

Third, regarding the details of the narrative, Jesus' description of wine as "fruit of the vine" has no precise parallel in the LXX[9] but does have such a parallel within later rabbinic idiom (פרי הגפן), as Bockmuehl notes.[10] The promise may reflect an early rendition of such an idiom and might also be compared to the proscription against all produce of the vine in Num. 6.4 (ὅσα γίνεται ἐξ ἀμπέλου—LXX; אשר יעשה מגפן—MT). A possible parallel of the saying is found in *m. Naz.* 2.3 where self-declaration of abstention from a cup full of wine is declared an adequate formula for a Nazirite vow.[11]

But following the halakhic principle conveyed in the possible parallel found in *m. Naz.* 2.3, namely that context determines the intent

---

[6] Cf. Judg. 14.6 and 15.14, "the Spirit of the Lord fell on him."

[7] Davies and Allison, 276.

[8] I do wonder if there may be an indication in this title for Jesus, at least within *Mark*, that the evangelist, and perhaps others, actually did think of Jesus as a Nazirite like Samson. The parallels between the two figures are quite striking. Although "holy," both partook of controversial activity in relation to such a status (e.g., associating with questionable individuals and drinking alcohol; see Mk. 2.16; cf. Q 7.33 where Jesus is accused of being a drunkard [οἰνοπότης]). Both, too, were known to perform miraculous feats. Perhaps the identification of Jesus with Samson, a "holy one of God," was a means of making sense of Jesus' apparent power—at least for Mark, demonstrated as it was, by the Spirit. Such a notion is made particularly clear in Mark, where such power encounters in the ministry of Jesus play a central role.

[9] Cf. Wojciechowski, 95, who makes reference to LXX Is. 32.12, LXX Hab. 3.17, and LXX Judg. 13.14 (A). In all of these, "fruit of the vine" only designates the general product of the vine, not merely wine, as it does here in Mk. 14.25.

[10] Bockmuehl, 572.

[11] Ibid., 571.

of a vow (see testimony 1.8.2), is there evidence in the context of
the promise of Jesus in 14.25 that might support the suggestion he
intended to make a *Nazirite* vow? I believe an affirmative answer will
be found when comparing the context of the promise with what is
known about Nazirites and the Nazirite vow in the evidence delineated in Chapter 1 of the present study.

In discussion of testimony 1.6.1, I suggested that the parallels
between the Nazirite vow and the Jewish rite of mourning known
as the שלשים, "thirty days," were notable—so notable that the two
rites might have shared an amalgamation of behavioral traditions
and, likewise, might easily have been confused. Furthermore, I suggested in discussing testimony 1.11 that the identification of Joseph
as a Nazirite by the rabbis was inspired by Joseph's separation from
his brothers; a separation forced upon him when he was sold into
slavery in Egypt. According to one rabbinic opinion, Joseph abstained
from wine *during* his separation, possibly implying (not unlike one in
a state of mourning) that he took upon himself the behavior of a
Nazirite the moment the pains of separation were felt. It was only
when reunited with his brothers that Joseph again "drank and was
merry" with them.

Given its setting within the general passion narrative and, more
specifically, within the immediate setting of the Last Supper, Jesus
makes his promise to abstain from wine in a context of mourning.
Funerary grief is emphasized throughout the passion, progressing
from Gethsemane to Jesus' final cry of expiration on the cross. Given
Jesus' expectation of death, as expressed in the very words of the
promise, it is precisely at the Paschal meal where his grieving begins.
Furthermore, Jesus promises to abstain from wine specifically during his separation from his disciples. He promises never to drink of
the fruit of the vine, "*until that day* when I drink it new in the kingdom of God" (cf. Mt. 26.29 "until that day I drink it new *with you*
in My Father's kingdom").[12]

I believe the context in which the rabbis envisage Joseph as a
Nazirite is impressively similar to the context in which Jesus makes
his vow to abstain from wine. Both are set within occasions of per-

---

[12] I wonder if there might be some significance in Jesus' specifying the duration
of his vow as "until that *day*," given an expressed number of "days" is the anticipated measurement of time for a Nazirite vow in Num. 6.1–21 (cf. the comments
of the rabbis in *m. Naz.* 1.3–7).

sonal grief due to separation from brethren: Joseph from his brothers while in Egypt, and Jesus from his disciples by means of his imminent crucifixion and death. Moreover, like Joseph who "drank and was merry" with his brothers when reunited with them, Jesus implies in his vow that he will drink again of the fruit of the vine when reunited with his disciples in the kingdom of God (I follow Matthew's understanding of the promise here). Given these contextual similarities and in accordance with the principle communicated by the rabbis in *m. Naz.* 2.3, namely that context determines one's intent to make a Nazirite vow, particularly where it is not explicit, the context in which Jesus uttered his promise to abstain from wine seems to indicate his intent to behave as a Nazirite. This, together with other evidence from the period that suggests the Nazirite vow and acts of ritual mourning shared many behavioral traditions including abstention from wine, in the words of Bockmuehl, the promise of Jesus in Mk. 14.25, in its first-century setting, has "unmistakable Nazirite connotations."[13]

Summary of Evidence

In light of the conclusion drawn about Mk. 14.25, 15.23 and parallels, (1) the Passover promise provides yet another indication that the Nazirite vow and ritual acts of mourning shared much in common, in this case the act of separating from wine and declaring oneself a Nazirite (even implicitly) the moment the pains of grief were felt. (2) If the conclusion drawn about Jesus' promise is true, then there is evidence from early Markan Jesus tradition that suggests Jesus himself made a Nazirite vow.

2.2 Matthew

Matthew 2.23 (22–3)

[22]But when he heard that Archelaus was reigning over Judea in place of his father Herod, he was afraid to go there. And being warned by God in a dream, he departed for the regions of Galilee, [23]and he came and resided in a city called Nazareth [λεγομένην Ναζαρέτ], that what was spoken of through the prophets might be fulfilled, "He shall be called a Nazarene [Ναζωραῖος κληθήσεται]."

---

[13] Bockmuehl, 571.

In the conclusion to Matthew's infancy narrative, Joseph's decision
to take up residence in Nazareth after his return to the land from
Egypt is claimed a fulfillment of the words of the prophets that Jesus
would be called a Nazarene (Ναζωραῖος). What the precise derivation of Ναζωραῖος is and what prophecy or prophecies Matthew has
in mind are not entirely clear. In regards to the former, the term
is phonologically odd given its apparent relationship to the town
Nazareth (Ναζαρέτ/Ναζαρὲθ/Ναζαρὰ); and with respect to the latter, the citation "He shall be called a Nazarene" (Ναζωραῖος κληθήσεται)
is found nowhere in Old Testament literature. Scholars have long
debated these issues, but in the words of Davies and Allison, "Mt.
2.23 almost certainly has to do with a play on the word *nazir*."[14]

Etymologically, Ναζωραῖος is problematic. As a place name, the
spelling is at odds with known words for Nazareth in the New
Testament. In ten occurrences, Nazareth appears as either Ναζαρέτ
or Ναζαρὲθ (Mk. 1.9; Mt. 2.23, 21.11; Lk. 1.26, 2.4, 39, 51; Jn.
1.45, 46; Acts 10.38), and twice it appears as Ναζαρὰ (Mt. 4.13; Lk.
4.16). The ω in Ναζωραῖος fails to correspond well with the second
α in either of the three variations of the name; neither is the τ or θ
in Ναζαρέτ or Ναζαρὲθ represented.[15] A better place name would
be the alternate gentilic adjective utilized for Jesus in the New Testament, and particularly within Matthew's source Mark, Ναζαρηνός
(Mk. 1.24; 10.47; 14.67; 16.6; Lk. 4.34; 24.19). As is, Ναζωραῖος bears a
closer resemblance to the designations of known religious groups of
the period, such as the Pharisees (Φαρισαῖοι) and Sadducees (Σαδδυκαῖοι), and some have posited that that the term may be a derivative of some pre-Christian religious group (cf. Acts 24.5).[16] Seeking
such a derivation is as unnecessary as it is unlikely, however. On
philological grounds, Albright, Moore, and Schaeder have argued
that the term may be understood as a derivative of Nazareth given
the idiosyncrasies of Galilean Aramaic.[17] What is certain, however,

---

[14] Davies and Allison, 276.
[15] Ibid., 281; and Brown, 212.
[16] J. S. Kennard, Jr., "Nazorean and Nazareth," *JBL* 66 (1947): 79–81. Kennard
states his agreement with Bultmann and Loisy that *Nazorean* is likely a religious designation for the followers of John the Baptist. Although he recognizes the phonological similarities between Nazorean and נזיר and applies this to John, he fails to
address any Old Testament prophecies that might have been the basis of Matthew's
citation and, as a result, fails to follow any possible allusive connection between
נזיר, Jesus, and Jesus' followers.
[17] R. E. Brown, *The Birth of the Messiah: A Commentary on the Infancy Narratives in
Matthew and Luke* (1st ed.; ABRL; Garden City, N.Y.: Doubleday, 1977), 210.

is that Matthew understood the term in this way given its use in the text's immediate context, as well as its appearance in what Stendahl considers the more general context of Matthew's "Christological geography"[18] in chapter two.

Accepting the term as a place name, Matthew's derivation of the prophetic citation "He shall be called a Nazarene" is all the more difficult due to the absence of any reference to the town Nazareth in the Old Testament. The closest ideological parallel within Old Testament prophecy is Is. 4.3, "He shall be called holy." Phonologically, however, other parallels may also be found in similarities between the words Ναζωραῖος/נזיר (*Nazirite*) in Judg. 13.5,7; 16.17 and/or Ναζωραῖος/נצר (the Messianic *branch*) in Is. 11.1, both of which are contained in prophetic literature.[19] Because of the absence of any corresponding place name within the prophets, it is possible, granting these philological similarities, that Matthew's citation involves some kind of word play based on allusions to at least two of these references, and quite possibly all three.

In Is. 11.1 the prophet makes mention of the future Messianic branch (נצר) that will bloom forth from the root of Jesse. In Is. 7.14 the birth of the child Immanuel is promised, and Matthew has cited the passage as a prophetic reference to Jesus already in Mt. 1.21. It is possible that Matthew had the words of the prophet still in mind (in this case Is. 11.1) in his citation in 2.23. That Jesus was known as the Messianic root (ῥίζα) is evidenced in early Christian literature (Rom. 15.12; Rev. 5.5).[20] Matthew may have played on the consonantal similarities between Nazareth (Ναζαρά) and "branch" as it appears in Hebrew, נצר. Such a correspondence between the two words has its difficulties, however. The Hebrew consonant צ is usually represented by the Greek σ rather than ζ, though the converse is not impossible.[21] Given that the reference is only an allusion, however, precise phonological equivalence is probably unnecessary.

A closer parallel, though perhaps not to the exclusion of the other, is found in the term נזיר as it appears in reference to Samson. The

---

[18] I adapt this from the citation of Stendahl in J. A. Sanders, "ΝΑΖΩΡΑΙΟΣ in Matt 2.23," *JBL* 84 (1965), 169; For a strictly religious view of Ναζωραῖος, see Kennard (n. 15), and D. B. Taylor, "Jesus—of Nazareth?" *ExpTim* 92 (1981): 336–7.

[19] Other phonological parallels are possible, and for these I refer the reader to the various commentaries. Only the two most prominent are discussed here.

[20] Davies and Allison, 277.

[21] Ibid., 278; and Brown, 212.

parallels between the Matthean infancy narrative and the birth narrative of Samson are many, and it is indubitable that Judges lies
behind Matthew's account.[22] First, based on the similarities in content and literary structure, the Samson narrative likely formed a literary model for Matthew. A miraculous birth is announced and
confirmed by an angel on behalf of both figures (Judg. 13.1–14//Mt.
1.18–24). For both, the role of the child is that of a deliverer: Samson
of Israel from the hands of the Philistines and Jesus his people from
their sins (Judg. 13.5//Mt. 1.21). There is also a similarity in literary construction where neither narrative includes any detail of the
anointed's adolescent years. Both narratives get going with the child's
sudden appearance as a mature adult (Judg. 13.24–14.1//Mt.
2.23–3.13). Secondly, as noted in testimonies 1.2.2 and 2.1, the
Septuagint version of Judges contains a reference to Samson as a
holy one, ἅγιος, where MT reads נזיר (cf. LXX[B] Judg. 13.7; 16.17).
There is a precedent in Mark, Matthew's source, for a play on the
words "Nazareth" (Ναζαρήνε) and "holy one" (ἅγιος) based on this
version; and such a wordplay likely influenced Matthew in 2.23.
Combining this with Is. 4.3, "He shall be called holy (קדשׁ—MT;
ἅγιος—LXX)," it is possible that Matthew substituted ναζιρ/ναζιραῖος
freely for ἅγιος, resulting in the playful citation, "He shall be called
a Ναζωραῖος." Again, there is a lack of precise phonological equivalence between the two terms ναζ(ι)ραῖος and Ναζ(ω)ραῖος; however,
such precision may be unnecessary due to the playful nature of the
word association.

The possibility that all three terms: Nazareth, Nazirite, and the
Messianic branch (Hebrew—נצר) are present in the mind of the
evangelist is interestingly supported, as Davies and Allison have
pointed out, by the single passage of Is. 4.2–3.[23] Granting that Is.
4.3 forms the principal citation of Mt. 2.23, in the previous verse
(v. 2) reference is made to the future "branch (נצר) of the Lord"
that will blossom and bear fruit.

That Jesus was thought of as a Nazirite, as has already been mentioned, lacks any detailed substantiation in the Gospel tradition, and
here in Mt. 2.23, Jesus' association with Naziriteship is purely allusive. In utilizing a play on the words "Nazirite," "Nazareth," and

---

[22] For comparisons between the Matthean infancy narrative and Judg. 13, see
J. A. Sanders, 170–1.
[23] Davies and Allison, 278.

the words of the prophet Isaiah, "He shall be called holy," Matthew merely applies the imagery of the Nazirite as a holy person to Jesus, known in pre-Matthean tradition as the "Holy One of God."

Summary of Evidence

For the purposes of the present study, I believe Mt. 2.23 provides evidence for the popularity of the Samson narrative within late Second Temple Jewish thought. Because Matthew creates a play-on-words in 2.23, had Matthew's audience not been familiar with the LXX[B] version of the Samson story, they would have failed to understand such a word play. As was shown in the discussion of testimony 1.8.1, the rabbis of the Mishnah assumed that people could make Nazirite vows based on what they knew of Samson from the biblical narrative. By evidence of the apparent common knowledge of the Greek version of the story, manifest in Matthew's Gospel, making Nazirite vows based on the knowledge that Samson was ἅγιος, a "holy one," would have undoubtedly had an impact on the way people perceived themselves when making such a vow: they would have perceived themselves, like Samson, as being holy.

2.3   Luke

Luke 1.15

[15]For he will be great in the sight of the Lord, and he will drink no wine or liquor [οἶνον καὶ σίκερα οὐ μὴ πίῃ]; and he will be filled with the Holy Spirit, while yet in his mother's womb [καὶ πνεύματος ἁγίου πλησθήσεται ἔτι ἐκ κοιλίας μητρὸς αὐτοῦ].

There is a single passage in the Gospel tradition that appears to suggest John the Baptist was a Nazirite. In the narrative of John's birth, found only in the Gospel of Luke, John is assigned a special diet respecting his future role as prophet and preacher of repentance. In announcing to the priest Zacharias that his barren wife Elizabeth will conceive and give birth to a son, the angel Gabriel announces that the child "will drink no wine or liquor."

Many have seen in this dietary commission evidence that John observed the sanctifying regime of the Nazirite vow.[24] Others, however,

---

[24] See for a classic example F. B. Meyer, *John the Baptist* (London: Lakeland, 1975), 25, 32–4.

taking a slightly more critical approach, have seen in this logion only
evidence of later Lukan embellishment; the historical John, based on
the testimony of earlier Gospel tradition, was no Nazirite but merely
an ascetic.[25] Of the two suggestions neither seems entirely correct,[26]
for it is not exactly clear whether Luke actually intends to portray
John as a Nazirite.

First, in terms of earlier Gospel testimony, none name John as a
Nazirite. Mark and Q, two of the earliest Gospel sources interested
in John, and consequently two of Luke's main sources, make no such
claim. Both do, however, appear to be interested in John's diet. Mark
mentions the Baptist's appearance in the desert and describes him
as one clad in camel's hair and a leather belt (Mk. 1.6). For his
diet, he tells us John ate only locusts and wild honey. In a Jesus
saying recorded in Q (7.33), a comment is made respecting John's
diet stating, "John the Baptist has come eating no bread and drinking no wine; and you say, 'He has a demon!'" Luke may have
inferred from such texts that John was under a Nazirite vow, but
this is unlikely. Luke ignores Mark's description completely, and
based on his use of Q (3.7–9; 3.16ff.), he seems more interested in
the preaching of John than any ascetic tendencies he might have had.

Secondly, Luke does draw on Nazirite imagery for his depiction
of John in the infancy narrative, but his use of such imagery is limited. The angelic logion in 1.15 rings similar to the requirement for
the Nazirite vow in Num. 6.3; "wine and strong drink" (οἶνον καὶ
σίκερα) is lexically identical with the LXX. Moreover, the birth narrative of John as a whole is modeled largely on the birth stories of
Samuel and Samson in the Bible,[27] both of whom represent Nazirites.
For Samuel, this is especially made clear in the LXX where the
mandate to abstain from wine and strong drink is present in the

---

[25] C. H. Kraeling, *John the Baptist* (New York: Charles Scribner's Sons, 1951),
13; and C. H. H. Scobie, *John the Baptist* (London: SCM, 1964), 137.

[26] Recently, J. E. Taylor has presented a slightly more medial position stating
that *some* may have thought John was a Nazirite based on his wilderness diet. With
respect to Luke's narrative, "What we may be permitted to conjecture is that the
nativity account found in Luke suggests that people saw him as either a *nazir* or
someone resembling a *nazir*," *The Immerser: John the Baptist within Second Temple Judaism*
(Studying the Historical Jesus; London: SPCK, 1997), 34.

[27] For discussions on Lk. 1.15 and parallels with these Old Testament narratives,
see Brown, 273–5; and R. C. Tannehill, *Luke* (ANTC; Nashville: Abingdon Press,
1996), 45–6.

vow of Hannah (contra MT, see testimony 1.2.3). It is indubitable that Luke's narrative reflects Hannah's vow; the priest Zachariah and Hannah (mother of the prophet Samuel) both receive angelic help in answer to a "request" made from a plight of barrenness (Lk. 1.7,13; I Sam. 1.2–11). Furthermore, it is likely that the third angelic logion, "and he will be filled with the Holy Spirit from the womb," is a Lukan adaptation of the angelic saying repeated by Samson's mother in LXX[B] Judg. 13.7, "for the child will be a holy one of God (ἅγιος θεοῦ) from the womb."[28] For Luke, the phrase "filled" tends to mean "fell upon," or "came upon" (see Lk. 4.14, 18; Acts 1.8; 2.16–18), and the saying here in Lk. 1.15 possibly reflects the role of the Spirit in the life of Samson in a type of word play between "holy one of God" (ἅγιος Θεοῦ) and "holy spirit" (πνεύματος ἅγιον). Based upon the narrative imagery drawn from such figures, it does seem Luke means to portray John in their likeness.

But that Luke intends to depict John as a Nazirite based on this use of imagery is doubtful. With respect to what Luke knows about Nazirites, John doesn't seem to fit the mold. In Acts 18.18, Paul is depicted as under a vow, as are four others in Acts 21.23–27a (see discussion of testimonies 2.4.1 and 2.4.2 to follow). In both instances, the vow involves not abstinence from alcohol but the cutting of the hair. Similarly, though Luke is undoubtedly aware of the regulations for the vow in Num. 6.1–21, the biblical cases upon which his infancy narrative is based both mention, predominantly in the case of Samson, the proscription against the use of a razor upon the head. The only proscription given John in Lk. 1.15 is drinking wine and strong drink. Because of this, Luke's portrayal of John as a Nazirite seems only limited or incomplete. Had Luke really thought of John as a Nazirite and intended to portray him as such, it seems a better wording for the angel's command would have been, "and no razor shall come upon his head."[29]

What appears to be going on in Lk. 1.15 then, is the creation of an association between John and the three elements of prophecy, abstention from alcohol, and holiness, all three of which are found in the Nazirite figures Samuel and Samson. Luke borrows these

---

[28] Brown also notes the similarity between these two passages, particularly with respect to the role of prophecy, 275.

[29] Cf. the statement applied to James the Just in Hegesippus (see testimony 2.5, following).

motifs and places them on John, not to convey the notion that John was a Nazirite, but simply that he was a prophet. A similar treatment was witnessed in Josephus' characterization of Samson and Samuel in testimonies 1.6.3 and 1.6.4. Though Josephus understands the figures to be Nazirites, he portrays them for his readers merely as prophets. Luke's primary interest in depicting John as a prophet is demonstrated in the style of his narrative. Comparing the statements in the Old Testament where the Spirit of the Lord is said to come upon a prophet and enable him to speak the word of the Lord, Luke's notion of being filled with the Holy Spirit in 1.15 is an unequivocal expression of this same principle.[30] As stated earlier, Luke is also interested to a large extent in John's preaching, certainly far more than any ascetic tendencies he might have had. Such an interest in preaching is befitting of his depiction of John as a prophet, or herald of the Word of God (cf. Lk. 3.2). With respect to alcohol abstention, this seems to be a concept borrowed from Samson and Samuel in addition to the prophecy motif,[31] and possibly reflects an understanding current in Jewish and certainly Christian circles at the time, that alcohol abstention was virtuous and befitting an aspiration to personal holiness. A similar view was evidenced in Philo's treatment of Samuel in his treatise *De ebrietate* discussed in testimony 1.5.4. Such a view may also be witnessed in the writings of Paul. In a command issued to the Ephesian believers in the context of a discussion on purity of lifestyle, Paul orders, "Do not be drunk with wine, . . . but be filled with the Spirit, . . . (Eph. 5.18)." As with Luke in the infancy narrative, the role of the Holy Spirit appears to conflict with intoxication. Such a motif, borrowed from the figures Samson and Samuel, is here applied to the prophet and preacher of repentance, John the Baptist.

Summary of Evidence

If anything at all respecting Nazirites in this period can be drawn from Luke's reference to John the Baptist as one who abstained from wine and strong drink, it is (1) that Nazirites were well known as

---

[30] Brown, 274–5.

[31] That Samson and Samuel were regarded as prophets may be taken from the placement of the narratives within the so-named biblical division; cf. Brown, n. 40; cf. Josephus' designation of both Samson and Samuel as "prophets" (see testimonies 1.6.3 and 1.6.4).

holy individuals, based especially as this text is on the popular Greek version of the Samson story. (2) Secondly, whereas in the actual story of Samson it was the growth of hair that led the translator to associate holiness with the Nazirite (see testimony 1.2.2), in Lk. 1.15 it was the single act of abstaining from wine—the only ostensible Nazirite motif borrowed by Luke—that formed an expression of the Nazirite's holy status.

2.4   *Acts*

2.4.1   *Acts 18.18 (18–22)*

> [18]And Paul, having remained many days longer, took leave of the brethren and put out to sea for Syria, and with him were Priscilla and Aquila. In Cenchrea he had his hair cut [κειράμενος ἐν Κεγχρεαῖς τὴν κεφαλήν], for he was keeping a vow [εἶχεν γὰρ εὐχήν]. [19]And they came to Ephesus, and he left them there. Now he himself entered the synagogue and reasoned with the Jews. [20]And when they asked him to stay for a long time, he did not consent, [21]but taking leave of them and saying, "I will return to you again if God wills," he set sail from Ephesus. [22]And when he had landed in Caesarea, he went up [ἀναβὰς] and greeted the church, and went down to Antioch.

In Acts 18.18 Luke makes reference to the apostle Paul having his hair cut while on missionary route to Syria from Achaia. Paul had his hair cut, Luke relates, because "he was keeping a vow" (εἶχεν γὰρ εὐχήν).[32] Why Paul made a vow,[33] and when he made it, is never stated by Luke. More significantly, what *type* of vow Paul was maintaining is not exactly clear given authorial brevity. Scholars typically, and in my view correctly, see the vow in v. 18 to be a reference to the Nazirite vow, yet many simultaneously assert Luke's allusion

---

[32] Although reference to Aquila precedes the action of vowing and cutting the hair in v. 18, it is most likely that Paul is the subject of this behavior, as Paul is Luke's principal character throughout vv. 18–22; cf. C. K. Barrett who states that the subject of the vow is uncertain, *A Critical and Exegetical Commentary on the Acts of the Apostles* (vol. 2; ICC; Edinburgh: T&T Clark, 1998), 877.

[33] There is a consensus among scholars that Paul's vow here is Luke's own way of representing Paul as a pious Jew, see E. Haenchen, *The Acts of the Apostles* (trans. by B. Noble et al.; Oxford: Basil Blackwell, 1971), 546; and H. Conzelmann, *Acts of the Apostles: A Commentary on the Acts of the Apostles* (trans. by J. Limburg et al.; ed. by E. J. Epp with C. R. Matthews; Hermeneia; Philadelphia: Fortress Press, 1987), 155; cf. Barrett, however, who argues against this, 877.

involves serious difficulties; namely, it is doubtful whether the historical Paul would have observed such a legalistic regime as the Nazirite vow. Moreover, when compared with other and contemporary sources, Luke's delineation of Paul's behavior conflicts with known prescriptions for Nazirites in the period Acts was composed. In examining the passage, I shall deal with the latter of these issues first.

The problems allegedly facing Luke's representation of the vow— if it is to be identified with the Nazirate—are that sources such as Josephus and the writings of the early rabbis provide evidence to suggest that by the time of the late Second Temple period, Nazirites typically discharged their vows in the Jerusalem temple following the biblical legislation of Num. 6.1–21 (especially vv. 13–8). Furthermore, according to the more lenient ruling of the School of Shammai in the Mishnah (a decision relevant to the time Paul supposedly made his vow), Nazirites entering Palestine from abroad had to re-observe their vows for at least thirty days before discharging them in the temple.[34] Luke, however, records Paul cutting his hair in Cenchrea, an eastern seaport of Corinth (κειράμενος ἐν Κεγχρεαῖς τὴν κεφαλήν), rather than in Jerusalem. Moreover, he says nothing of Paul re-observing his vow for thirty days when entering the land in v. 22.

Because of these disparities, Barrett[35] and Tomes[36] reason that the vow may be an allusion to a Greek rather than Jewish custom: one sharing similar traits with the Nazirate *sans* the legal idiosyncrasies associated with the cutting of the hair. Haenchen[37] and, likewise, Conzelmann[38] argue to the contrary: the vow in v. 18 can be none other than the Nazirite vow. Luke, however, "possessed no exact idea"[39] of the rite. Stolle[40] and Dunn,[41] also agreeing with the Nazirite interpretation, see no problem with Luke's description, provided the timing of Paul's haircut in 18.18 is reckoned with a much later visit

---

[34] *m. Naz.* 3.6.

[35] Barrett, 877.

[36] R. Tomes, "Why Did Paul Get His Hair Cut? (Acts 18.18; 21.23–24)," in *Luke's Literary Achievement: Collected Essays* (ed. C. M. Tuckett; JSNTSup 116; Sheffield, Eng.: Sheffield Academic Press, 1995), 189, 197.

[37] Haenchen, 543 n. 2.

[38] Conzelmann, 155.

[39] Haenchen, 543 n. 2; see also Conzelmann's comment on Acts 21.23ff., p. 180.

[40] V. Stolle, *Der Zeuge als Angeklagter: Untersuchungen zum Paulisbild des Lukas* (BWANT 6:2; Stuttgart: W. Kohlhammer, 1973), 76–7.

[41] J. D. G. Dunn, *The Acts of the Apostles* (Epworth Commentaries; Peterborough: Epworth Press, 1996), 246.

to Jerusalem recorded in Acts 21.23ff. There, reason Stolle and Dunn, Paul completed his own vow when purifying himself in the temple with four other Nazirites: his prior haircut marking either an initial stage in the completion of Paul's vow[42] or "Paul's final haircut before the vow took effect."[43] Billerbeck, viewing v. 18 as an allusion to the Nazirate as well, alternatively posits that in spite of other sources, Luke's narrative is evidence that Nazirite hair was allowed to be cut outside Palestine: "Apg 18.18 zeigt jedenfalls, daß, die Praxis dahin ging, das Scheren des Haares auch im Auslande vollziehen zu lassen."[44] In addition, within the Western Text (D) reading of 18.21, "I must by all means keep the feast in Jerusalem," Paul expressed an intention to visit the city,[45] an intention he seems to have fulfilled in v. 22. It would have been then, suggests Billerbeck, that Paul offered his cut hair and requisite sacrifices at the temple, though the ruling of the School of Shammai in the Mishnah remains a difficulty (for Luke seems to think Paul's visit to Jerusalem, rather than thirty days, was only brief).[46]

It is my contention that scholars have generally missed the mark regarding Luke's account. In keeping with the majority, and as mentioned previously, I believe Luke is representing the Nazirite vow in v. 18; but unlike many, I also believe Luke's narrative is perfectly cogent as it stands. Scholars, in my opinion, have neglected, and at times wrongly assessed certain sources for Nazirites in this period, and as a result, have simply failed to notice how Luke's narrative is congruent to the available evidence for Nazirites, both in regard to the timing of Paul's haircut and known rules for the Nazirate.

First, that the case does involve a Nazirite vow as opposed to a similar Greek custom (Barrett and Tomes) is most likely considering Luke's knowledge of the Jewish rite in Acts 21.23ff. It makes little sense for Luke to describe a Jewish custom on the one hand (21.23ff.) and a Greek custom on the other (18.18), particularly where both rites involve the same character, Paul. It is true that Luke mentions only the cutting of the hair and nothing of the additional characteristics discussed of Nazirites in previous testimonies, such as abstinence

---

[42] Stolle, 76–7.
[43] Dunn, 246.
[44] Str-B 2:749.
[45] Ibid., 747.
[46] Ibid.

from wine or a disheveled appearance on Paul's part. Such details
are incidental to Luke's account, however, and there are other sources
that speak of Nazirites simply by referring to their shaven hair.[47]
That Paul's haircut marks the end of an avowed period (contra
Dunn) is indicated by the grammar of v. 18: εἶχεν γὰρ εὐχήν suggests the cutting of the hair was part of the vow itself.[48] There is
one other possibility, that Paul's haircut marks the interruption of a
vow due to defilement from a corpse (cf. Num. 6.9–12). However,
Luke's account lacks any information that would merit this suggestion.

Secondly, Billerbeck is correct in pointing to the Western Text
reading of Acts 18.21 as possibly reflecting the original circumstances
surrounding Paul's visit to Syria. Paul in D states that he must reach
Jerusalem in order to observe an approaching feast (εἰπών, Δεῖμε
πάντως τὴν ἑορτὴν τὴν ἐρχομένην ποιῆσαι εἰς Ἱεροσόλυμα).[49] In v. 22
Luke comments that Paul "went up" (ἀναβὰς) to greet the Church
after landing in Caesarea. ἀναβὰς is a term frequently used by Luke
in Acts to describe treks to Jerusalem,[50] and ἐκκλησία, therefore,
likely refers to the Jerusalem church. This would allow (Billerbeck)
for the full termination of Paul's vow to take place (though Luke is
silent about these details). Interestingly, evidence in Josephus and
Philo suggests Jews often coincided the making and discharging of
Nazirite vows with pilgrimages to the holy city because of a festival,
particularly Pentecost. Although the festival in D is unnamed, it may
have been Pentecost. Alternatively, coinciding a pilgrimage to Jerusalem
because of a festival (any festival) with the termination of a vow may
have been a convenient way for Paul to avoid making multiple trips.

---

[47] Cf. Josephus, *A. J.* 19.294 and *m. Naz.* 2.5–6 where Nazirites are described
simply as those being "shaved."

[48] Conzelmann, 155; Tomes, 191.

[49] D, H, L, P, Ψ, 049, 056, 0120, 0142, 88, et al.; see W. A. Strange, *The Problem
of the Text of Acts* (SNTSMS 71; Cambridge, Eng.: Cambridge University Press,
1992), 41–8. Strange sees the Western reading as later interpolation providing commentary on Luke's narrative. The reading provides an explanation as to the motivation behind Paul's departure for Palestine; see also B. Metzger, *A Textual Commentary
on the Greek New Testament* (2nd ed.; Stuttgart: Deutsche Bibelgesellschaft, 1994), 412.
Metzger attributes the reading to the "Western reviser" and holds it improbable
that such detail, if original, would have been omitted by a wide variety of MSS
and versions; cf. J. M. Ross who supports the originality of the Western reading,
"The Extra Words in Acts 18.21," *NovT* 34 (1992): 247–9.

[50] Acts 11.2; 15.2; 21.12, 15; 24.11; 25.19; see also Luke's use of the term in
Lk. 18.31 and 19.28; and F. Horn, "Paulus, das Nasiräat und die Nasiräer," *NovT*
39/2 (1997): 120–1.

Third, although with the D reading Luke's account is certainly plausible, Paul cutting his hair outside Jerusalem and failing to re-observe his vow for thirty days upon entering the land from overseas allegedly remain problematic for Luke. I suggested in discussing testimonies 1.6.2 and 1.8, however, that evidence in both Josephus and the Mishnah suggests Nazirites did not always follow the "letter of the Law" when observing their vows, particularly with respect to the treatment of the hair. According to *A. J.* 4.72, Nazirites cut their hair and offered it to the administering priests at the temple rather than burn it on the fire as explicitly required by the Law in Num. 6.18. Likewise, although the law requires that upon completion of the vow the hair is to be shaved "at the doorway of the tent of meeting" (Num. 6.13), deliberation in the Mishnah presupposes some votaries cut their hair in the vicinity of the city, outside the temple precincts.[51] Such evidence suggests many were *bending* known rules for the Nazirate and quite comfortably doing so. Luke, I propose, is a witness to this type of behavior in v. 18 with respect to Paul's haircut in Cenchreae.

With regard to the decision of the School of Shammai that pilgrim Nazirites re-observe their vows for thirty days when entering the land from abroad, I asserted in discussion of testimony 1.8 that rabbinic decisions involving the Nazirite vow in the Mishnah do not represent a compendium of rules commonly observed by Jews but rather components of a pedagogical tool designed for the promotion of *ideal* behavior. Although the decision of the School of Shammai does involve a case where rabbinic advice was apparently sought and given in this period (the case of Queen Helena), evidence in the Mishnah suggests such occasions were rare and that the rabbis held little influence over individuals when making their vows. The very case of Queen Helena, moreover, is internally problematic, and the decision of the School of Shammai is contradicted by other decisions respecting those entering the land to discharge their vows.[52] As I suggested in the summary of evidence for testimony 1.8, Mishnaic evidence overall suggests Nazirite vows were made and observed with great flexibility and personal freedom of expression, not merely with regard to the treatment of the hair but also with respect to the

---

[51] *m. Naz.* 6.8; see I. H. Marshall, *Acts of the Apostles* (TNTC; Leicester: Inter-Varsity Press, 1992), 300.

[52] See *m. Naz.* 5.4 and 7.4.

temporal aspect of vow observation. *Some* may have re-observed vows when entering the land from abroad, but most did not. Luke in Acts 18.18–22, I also propose, gives us an example of the latter rather than the former.[53]

Finally, with regard to whether or not Luke is here representing an event in the life of the historical Paul, I find no reason why Paul would have objected to a Nazirite vow. For as many arguments as there are against this suggestion,[54] there are those that support it.[55] Marshall posits that this was Paul's way of identifying with "those under the law," as expressed in Paul's poly-cultural missionary method found in I Cor. 9.19–23.[56] This is certainly possible, though there is some evidence in the Pauline corpus to suggest Paul remained a devout Jew while among Jew and Gentile alike.[57] Whether Paul truly observed the custom is a secondary matter, for it is Luke that is of primary concern. Evidence for the Nazirite vow is in *Acts*, and it is what Luke thinks of the custom that is of greatest relevance to the present study.

Summary of Evidence

Luke's brief account of Paul's vow in Acts 18.18, in my opinion, provides further evidence that (1) the Nazirite vow was observed in the Diaspora. Furthermore, (2) like Josephus and the Mishnah, Luke

---

[53] The case of Bernice in *B. J.* 2.313–4 might be cited in support of the decision of the School of Shammai. Bernice, Josephus relates, was in Jerusalem discharging a vow to God—one customarily observed for thirty days after which sacrifices had to be offered (i.e., the Nazirite vow). I asserted regarding the testimony of Bernice (see testimony 1.6.1), however, that although Josephus states that the vow was customarily observed for thirty days, it is not clear whether Bernice was observing the entire thirty-day period while visiting Jerusalem. Josephus seems rather to suggest that she was there primarily because of the requisite sacrifices, as he says she was there "discharging a vow" (though an overlap of observed days while in the city is certainly plausible).

[54] Haenchen, 546, states that neither Luke nor his readers were aware that making such a vow was "diametrically opposed to the Pauline doctrine of grace"; see also Conzelmann, 155, who simply asserts that "one is not dealing with the historical Paul here at all"; see also J. A. Fitzmyer who posits Luke's portrait of Paul may be derived from "Luke's own hand," thereby affecting the Lukan "Paulinism" of Acts, *The Acts of the Apostles* (AB 31; New York: Doubleday, 1998), 633.

[55] See for example F. F. Bruce, *Commentary on the Book of Acts* (The New London Commentary on the New Testament; London: Marshall, Morgan & Scott, 1956), 377–8; and Marshall, 300; see also Dunn, 246–7.

[56] Marshall, 300.

[57] II Cor. 11.24; see also Phil. 3.4.

provides evidence that legislation for the vow, particularly respecting the treatment of the hair, was observed liberally, or with a certain degree of flexibility. In addition, granting the D reading of Acts 18.21 the status of a true reading, Luke's narrative provides (3) an actual case example of an individual coinciding pilgrimage to Jerusalem with a festival because of the termination of his Nazirite vow. Finally, (4) it is possible that one of the foremost figures in early Christianity, the apostle Paul, observed the Nazirite vow at least for a time.

2.4.2 *Acts 21.23–7a (17–27a)*

[17]And when he had come to Jerusalem, the brethren received us gladly. [18]And now the following day Paul went in with us to James, and all the elders were present. [19]And after he had greeted them, he began to relate one by one the things which God had done among the Gentiles through his ministry. [20]And when they heard it they began glorifying God; and they said to him, "You see, brother, how many thousands there are among the Jews who have believed, and they are all zealous for the Law; [21]and they have been told about you, that you are teaching all the Jews who are among the Gentiles to forsake Moses, telling them not to circumcise their children nor to walk according to the customs. [22]What, then, is to be done? They will certainly hear that you have come. [23]Therefore do this that we tell you. We have four men who are under a vow [εὐχὴν ἔχοντες ἔφ᾽ ἑαυτῶν]; [24]take them and purify yourself along with them [ἀγνίσθητι σὺν αὐτοῖς], and pay their expenses in order that may shave their heads [ξυρήσονται τὴν κεφαλήν]; and all will know that there is nothing to the things which they have been told about you, but that you yourself also walk orderly, keeping the Law [στοικεῖς καὶ φυλάσσων τὸν νόμον]; [25]But concerning the Gentiles who have believed, we wrote, having decided that they should abstain from meat sacrificed to idols and from blood and from what is strangled and from fornication." [26]Then Paul took the men, and the next day, purifying himself along with them [σὺν αὐτοῖς ἀγνισθείς], went into the temple, giving notice of the completion of the days of purification, until the sacrifice was offered for each one of them [ἕως οὗ προσνέχθη ὑπὲρ ἑνὸς ἑχάστου αὐτῶν ἡ προσφορά]. [27]And when the seven days were almost over, . . .

In Acts 21.23–7a Luke again makes reference to a vow, this time in the context of describing Paul's visit to Jerusalem and subsequent arrest following his third and final missionary journey. After landing in Caesarea from Asia Minor, Luke relates that Paul made a personal report of his missionary successes to James and the elders of the Jerusalem church only to face mixed reactions due to rumors of his alleged antinomianism while on excursion. According to the report of James, the many thousands of Torah-zealous believers in Jerusalem had all been informed that Paul taught fellow Jews in the Diaspora to forsake the Law of Moses and to refrain from circumcising their children. In an effort to curb the allegations, James advised Paul to purify himself with four bystanders who were under a vow and pay for their heads to be shaved. Such action, James reasoned, would demonstrate Paul's own willingness to embrace the Law, and thereby satisfy those in Jerusalem that the rumors circulating against him were false.

Though a consensus among scholars reasons that the vow described in Acts 21.23ff. is an allusion to the Nazirite vow, Luke's description of the rite in this passage, as in Acts 18.18, has been a source of much confusion. It is not entirely clear, for example, what type of ceremony, or ceremonies, Luke refers to when describing Paul and the four men *purifying themselves* in vv. 24, 26ff. Is this Luke's own designation for the Nazirite vow (i.e., a purification process) and is he here implying that Paul joined with the men in a Nazirate of his own for a mere seven days? Or is he referring to a separate, pre-ceremonial cleansing, perhaps one required of all pilgrims before participating in a temple ritual such as the discharging of a Nazirite vow? Perhaps, alternatively, this is simply an allusion to the ritual required for impure Nazirites (cf. Num. 6.9–12). Furthermore, Luke makes it explicit (through the mouth of James) in vv. 23–4 that Paul's association with, and payment in behalf of the four men is a means for Paul to publicly demonstrate his devotion to the Law. According to a recent article by Neusner, when compared with evidence from rabbinic sources, Luke's use of the Nazirate in this manner is odd or misinformed.[58]

With respect to Luke's description of the Nazirate, Billerbeck reasons the four men under a vow in vv. 23ff. are defiled Nazirites (i.e., those contaminated by a corpse in accordance with Num. 6.9–12).[59] Paul himself, on the other hand, is levitically impure due to his travels abroad.[60] By purifying himself *with the four men* in vv. 24, 26–7a, Paul simply joined in the same rite as the four so that he could pay

---

[58] Neusner, "Vow-Taking, The Nazirites, and the Law: Does James' Advice to Paul Accord with Halakah [sic]?" in *James the Just and Christian Origins* (eds. B. Chilton and C. A. Evans; NovTSup 98; Leiden: Brill, 1999), 59–82.

[59] Str-B 2:758–9.

[60] Ibid., 757–8.

for the shaving of their heads (i.e., sacrificial obligations) once the days of purification were concluded (v. 26–7a). Paul shared in the rite of the four men, in other words, without sharing their same defilement.[61]

For Haenchen, on the other hand, Luke has simply confused his sources, namely the itinerary of Paul's travels and LXX Num. 6.4 (sic—read 5).[62] Luke read LXX Num. 6.4 (πάσας τὰς ἡμέρας τῆς εὐχῆς τοῦ ἁγνισμοῦ and ἕως ἂν πληρωθῶσιν αἱ ἡμέραι) and could not distinguish between a seven-day rite of purification for Levitical impurity (cf. LXX Num. 19.12—the use of ἁγνίζω), which Paul underwent because of his return from abroad, and the Nazirate itself.[63] He confused the two sources, thinking Paul underwent a seven-day Nazirate with the four men who were at the terminal point of their vows.[64] In disagreement with Billerbeck, Haenchen sees the notion that all four Nazirites were simultaneously in a state of defilement at precisely the same time Paul entered Jerusalem as "scarcely conceivable."[65] To account for their numbers, Haenchen suggests (and this is in agreement with Billerbeck) that the four men were poor Nazirites who could not afford their sacrificial requirements, which given the number and nature of required items would have been very costly.[66] When Paul arrived in Jerusalem, the expenses of the four men could have been paid for by the charitable contribution Paul brought from the Gentile churches, although Luke is strangely silent about this detail (cf. Acts 24.17).[67]

Stolle, in contrast to both Billerbeck and Haenchen, argues that although Paul concluded a Nazirite vow in 18.18 with the cutting of his hair, his concurrent intention to visit Jerusalem was only expressed much later in 20.16 (ignoring the D reading of 18.21 and the possible visit to Jerusalem referred to in 18.22).[68] The visit occurred in 21.17ff. and it was here (21.23ff.) that Paul proposed to offer up the sacrifices required to end his vow.[69] Stolle denies it was necessary for Paul to undergo a purification rite as an ordinary pilgrim,

---

[61] Ibid.
[62] Haenchen, 610 n. 3, and 611.
[63] Ibid.
[64] Ibid., 611.
[65] Ibid., 610 n. 3.
[66] Ibid. 610–11; These are "four destitute Nazirites."
[67] Ibid., 612–4.
[68] Stolle, 76–7.
[69] Ibid.

yet he does accept the notion that Paul, along with the other four
Nazirites (being travelers themselves), would have required levitical
purification for participation in the aggregation[70] ceremony necessary
to complete their vows.[71] Furthermore, the paying of the sacrificial
requirements, including Paul's own vow, would not have occurred
for another thirty days following the rabbinic tradition in the Mishnah[72]
(although Luke says nothing of this scenario).

More recent scholars tend to follow in the steps of either Billerbeck,
Haenchen or Stolle in their interpretations of Acts 21.23–7a. F. F.
Bruce perhaps best represents the position of Billerbeck. He sees little problem with the Lukan account and holds that the four men
in 21.23ff. were impure Nazirites in accordance with Num. 6.9–12.[73]
Bruce says nothing of Paul's need for purification, however, and simply states that Paul was advised to adjoin in purification with the
four in order to pay for their heads to be shaved.[74] Similarly, J. A.
Fitzmyer reasons that the four men in 21.23ff. were impure Nazirites;
Paul's own act of purification involved the same rite but for different
reasons (as Billerbeck proposes).

Those following Haenchen with regard to Luke's seeming lack of
knowledge and confusion of sources are Conzelmann, Barrett, Tomes,
and Marshall. Conzelmann states that the account "raises difficulties
if we look closely at Jewish prescriptions about vows."[75] With regards
to v. 24 Conzelmann asserts "Luke has misunderstood a report" and
subsequently follows Haenchen's argument completely.[76] Barrett and
Tomes both reason Luke simply had insufficient knowledge of the
Nazirate.[77]

Dunn presents a similar argument to that of Stolle, in the sense
that the vow in Acts 18.18 is connected with Paul's temple ritual in
Acts 21.23ff. As such, when James and the Jerusalem elders advised

---

[70] I take this term from S. M. Olyan, "What Do Shaving Rites Accomplish and
What Do They Signal in Biblical Ritual Contexts?" *JBL* 117/4 (1998): 614–5.
"Aggregation" here refers to the incorporation of the Nazirite back into a normal
existence within society.
[71] Stolle, 66–7; see also Marshall who discusses Stolle's theory, 345.
[72] Stolle, 77–8.
[73] Bruce, 430–1.
[74] Ibid.; Bruce is interested primarily in the issue of the historical Paul.
[75] Conzelmann, 180.
[76] Ibid.
[77] Barrett, 1011; Tomes, 196.

Paul to purify himself with the four men, all five were at the completion of their vows but required (again, similar to Stolle) a levitical cleansing before they could participate in the final ritual.[78]

With respect to Luke's narrative use of Nazirites and the Nazirite vow, Neusner has challenged the Lukan scenario in vv. 23–4 by comparing Luke's account with the Nazirate as understood among the rabbis in rabbinic sources. Neusner asserts that the rabbis in sum held an altogether negative view of vow taking, and Nazirites in particular as "weak" and "arrogant."[79] At least from the perspective of rabbinic literature, by telling Paul to observe the Nazirite vow for the purpose of demonstrating his allegiance to the Mosaic Law, James has given Paul "poor advice."[80]

Of the various explanations offered by scholars, I believe Billerbeck has again offered a theory that best matches Luke's original intention. Furthermore, in regard to Luke's narrative use of the custom, I find Neusner's rationale unsatisfactory. Neusner has approached the issue from the perspective of the *whole* of rabbinic literature and drawn a single conclusion regarding the rabbinic conception of Nazirites. This approach is certainly questionable, not only in terms of practical application to the period in which Luke wrote, but also in terms of methodology. Can solidarity of rabbinic consensus actually be deduced from such a vast body of literature? I think not. In addition, I believe Neusner's assessment of the rabbinic opinion on Nazirites and Nazirite vow making is wrong, particularly as evidenced in the earliest stratum of rabbinic literature (that which is most relevant to the period at hand).

First, I believe scholars are correct in seeing the vows in 21.23ff. to be an allusion to the Nazirite vow. Though Luke never employs the religious technical term ναζιραῖοι (Nazirites) in reference to the four men discussed in vv. 23ff., as seen in previous testimony (e.g., LXX Num. 6.1–21 and Josephus' *B. J.* 2.313–14), Nazirites may be described in a source without that source utilizing the religious technical term in the process, especially for a Greek-speaking readership that may have been unfamiliar with the custom. References to the four men having a vow on themselves (εὐχὴν ἔχοντες ἔφ' ἑαυτῶν [v. 23)]),

---

[78] Ibid., 287.
[79] Neusner, "Vow-Taking," 76–9.
[80] Ibid., 81.

and that such vows involved both the shaving of the head (ξυρήσονται τὴν κεφαλήν [v. 24]) and the offering of sacrifices (ἕως οὗ προσηνέχθη ὑπὲρ ἑνὸς ἑχάστου αὐτῶν ἡ προσφορά [v. 26]) unmistakably refer to Naziriteship. As with the case of Acts 18.18, Luke says nothing of the abstinence from wine on the part of the individuals, nor does he describe their physical appearance (see testimony 1.8). However, as asserted in the previous testimony, while such characteristics would have been true, not all sources describe Nazirites in such detail.

Secondly, Haenchen is correct in recognizing an influence of LXX Num. 6.1–21 on Luke. That Luke could have confused a seven-day rite of purification taken by Paul for levitical cleansing (cf. LXX Num. 19.12) with the reference to the Nazarate in LXX Num 6.5 as "the fullness of the days of purification" is a viable argument given the evidence suggested in discussion of testimony 1.2.1. LXX Num. 6.2, 3, 5 and 21 definitely refer to the Nazirite vow as a vow of purity. But it seems highly unlikely that Luke's eyes would have either stopped short of Num. 6.9–12 when reading the LXX, or that he necessarily would have followed the precise lexicography of his source. LXX Num. 6.9–12, like MT, speaks of a seven-day purification rite that involved the shaving of the head and the offering of sacrifices once seven days were completed. This is exactly what Luke has described in the passage at hand. Verse 24 speaks of the shaving of the head for the four men, v. 26 of a purification process involving sacrifices, and v. 27a makes it clear that it was at the end of a seven-day period that sacrifices were to be offered. It is true that the LXX translator used καθαρίζω in v. 9 to describe the seven-day purification ceremony rather than ἁγνίζω, which Luke uses in vv. 26–27a, but liberty with semantically related terminology must be allowed for. I see no reason why Luke, given that he used the LXX as a source for his account, would have been confused simply by lexicography. Billerbeck's thesis, therefore, with regard to the four men, seems to make the best sense of Luke's account.

Third, Luke remains silent with regard to Paul's need for purification. Most who have followed Billerbeck's argument have understood the Lukan account as a description of a levitical purification performed by Paul because of uncleanness due to Paul's sojourning beyond Palestine. Following Second Temple customs with regard to purity, since he had just arrived to Jerusalem from abroad, he would have needed purification with the sprinkling of water on the third and seventh days in order to attend the ceremonies of the four in the temple and to pay for their sacrificial costs. The rites of both parties, Paul on the one hand and the defiled Nazirites on the other, could, therefore, have easily taken place together. Although this makes sense of the Lukan account, we know little about these supposed purification rites.[81] I believe, although it must be admitted Luke says nothing of this in 21.23ff., that Paul was unclean for the very same reason as the four men under a Nazirite vow; namely, because he had contact with a corpse. Interestingly, just before Paul's voyage to Jerusalem Luke records (in 20.9–10) that Paul raised a certain Eutychus from the dead while in Troas. The man was "picked up dead" after falling from the third story of a building in which Paul was publicly speaking. Luke describes the manner in which Paul healed the man as through the medium of physical contact, "But Paul went down and fell upon him and embracing him, he said, 'Do not be troubled for his life is in him.'"[82] It is doubtful Luke's detailed description involving Paul's physical contact with the dead Eutychus would not have left an impression on him. In light of Num. 19.12, Paul would then have needed to attend a rite of purification in the temple. When would Paul have visited Jerusalem to partake of such a rite? What better time than when he visited James and the Jerusalem church soon after the event in 21.17ff.?

Fourth, is it inconceivable, as Haenchen suggests, that all five defiled individuals appeared in Jerusalem at precisely the same time? Taking evidence from previous testimonies into consideration, not at all. As I suggested with respect to Acts 18.18, Pentecost was a time when Nazirites would often appear in Jerusalem, arguably en masse. According to Acts 20.16,[83] Paul expressed a desire to appear in the city by Pentecost; there is no indication in Luke's narrative to suggest

---

[81] For a treatment on the issues of purity in this period, including those relative to festivals, see G. Alon, *Jews, Judaism and the Classical World*: *Studies in Jewish History in the Times of the Second Temple and Talmud* (Jerusalem: Magnes Press, 1977), 190–234. Scriptural references to purification during a festival include Jn. 11.55, 18.28, 2 Chr. 10.13ff., and Num. 9.6ff., but all speak of Passover. Philo in *Spec.* 3.205 states that as a general practice even Jews who were clean had to purify themselves for seven days before entering the temple. The notion that the purification rite spoken of by Luke might refer simply to a common practice respecting all five needing to enter the temple seems implausible, as the "fullness of the days of purification" in v. 26 must be a reference to the same process Paul is said to have undergone with the men. Luke seems to think (via the ἕως clause) that for the four men this process included the giving of sacrifices. Only Num. 6.9–12 describes this type of purification rite.

[82] Cf. the similar manner in which Elijah healed the widow's son in I Ki. 17.17–24.

[83] Acts 20.16 states, "For Paul had decided to sail past Ephesus in order that he might not have to spend time in Asia; for he was hurrying to be in Jerusalem, if possible, on the day of Pentecost."

Paul did not make it by the desired date. That a group of four
Nazirites appeared in Jerusalem during such festivities is in accord
with evidence of the period. Moreover, with regard to their defilement
due to a corpse, again, as witnessed in the available evidence, such
was a genuine concern for Nazirites in this period and there is no
reason to suppose Luke's account stands totally on its own in this
matter. One might consider the biblical institution of Second Passover
(Num. 9.6ff.). Because defilement due to a corpse was a genuine
concern for festival pilgrims, a second Passover was instituted to take
place a month following the primary observance. That Nazirites
could face such a dilemma during a festive occasion seems very tenable. Alternatively, it might have been the case that all five individuals simply waited until an opportune time to attend to their
purification needs. Such is even anticipated in the Num. 6.1–21 legislation. The Law states that although the Nazirite must shave his/her
head on the seventh day after being defiled, the seven-day period of
purification culminated "in whatever day he shall become clean" (καὶ
ξυρήσεται τὴν κεφαλὴν αὐτοῦ ᾗ ἄν ἡμέρᾳ καθαρισθῇ—LXX; ביום טהרתו—
MT).[84] This seems to imply that a person's seven days of observing
the rite would begin whenever s/he was fit to do so; and this was
likely when an individual could made it up to the temple to begin
the process. Although in Num. 6.9 this applies specifically to the
Nazirite, there is no reason, given that the purification process itself
was a general rule (cf. Num. 19.12), that the timing principle with
regard to such purification was not always understood. What better
time to take care of such a rite than during a pilgrim festival? Again
in Luke's account, this is when all five appeared impure in Jerusalem.

Fifth, v. 24 is explicit that Luke understood Paul's association with
the four Nazirites and agreement to pay for their sacrificial costs as
a means of Paul portraying himself as a pious, Law-abiding Jew.
James declares that by purifying himself along with the four and
paying so that they might shave their heads, all would know that
Paul walked "orderly, keeping the law" (στοικεῖς καὶ φυλάσσων τὸν
νόμον). By purifying himself in the temple, Paul would certainly have
been observing the regulations of the law respecting his own impurity, and by associating himself with four Nazirites, popular and

---

[84] Num. 6.9.

noticeable as they were at such a time in Jerusalem, James' plot in
the narrative is actually quite clever. Nazirites would have been a
popular sight in the temple during Pentecost and easily noticed
because of their appearance (see testimonies 1.6.1 and 1.8). By being
present with such figures, Paul's action of purifying himself and paying for the four men to have haircuts and sacrifices offered to renew
their vows would likely have been easily witnessed. Moreover, with
specific regard to the motivation for making the Nazirite vow, in
sources examined in Chapter 1 of the present study, it was shown to
have been a custom not only performed as a means of petitioning
God for some desired need, but as a means of expressing worship
in the giving of oneself as a form of dedicated offering. Philo[85] testifies
to this as well as the early rabbis,[86] contrary to Neusner's opinion.[87]
That Paul's actions would have assured onlookers that he was a Jew
well observant of Mosaic custom seems highly plausible. That James'
advice to Paul was *good* advice, therefore, seems most tenable given what
we know about Nazirites and Nazirite vow making in this period.[88]

Lastly, many have suggested that Paul's act of paying for the Nazirites
to have their heads shaved would also have been considered a pious
deed and this is certainly correct given the case of Agrippa in *A. J.*
19.294. That the Nazirites in either case are poor, however, is unstated
in the case of Agrippa or Acts 21.23ff. Sacrifices for defiled Nazirites
would not have been as costly as the sacrifices for Nazirites completing their vows, and it is tempting to see Luke's account as a reference to the latter. However, Paul's payment for the sacrifices of
Nazirites who needed to start their vows over again seems a better
portrayal of his piety.

In summation, like Acts 18.18, Luke's information regarding Nazirite
behavior in 21.23–7a is historically plausible as it stands, and there
is no basis for the rationale that Luke misconstrued his facts. The
reference to the purification process of all five individuals, all due

---

[85] See testimony 1.5.1.
[86] See testimonies 1.9.2–3.
[87] See ns. 79–80.
[88] It is precisely this scenario in Luke's narrative that leads to Paul's arrest and
eventual deportation to Rome. Luke informs his readers that ". . . the Jews from
Asia, who had seen him in the temple, . . . seized him," Acts 21.27. Moreover,
according to Luke, Paul's accusers needed an additional charge in order to arouse
the temple bystanders against Paul; they accused him (falsely, Luke states) of bringing a Greek, Trophimus the Ephesian, into the temple with him, Acts 21.28–9.

to corpse contamination and all taking place simultaneously, is easily conceivable given what is known about Nazirites in the period Luke composed his account. Moreover, there is no need to suppose that Luke considered Paul as having taken a mere seven-day Nazirate, nor that he completed a vow taken some time previously, nor that Luke confused his sources. In addition, Luke's narrative use of the Nazirite custom is sound. There is no reason to suppose Luke's use of Nazirites in Acts 21.23–4, namely as a means of portraying Paul as a pious, Law-minded Jew, stands out as odd either when comparing Luke's account with early rabbinic or other sources of the period. Not only would Nazirites have been thought of as pious individuals (in some cases), but by purifying himself along with four impure Nazirites and covering their costs to restart their avowed periods, Paul would have had a high chance of being seen participating and promoting Mosaic cult ritual and associating himself with Law-minded Jews.

Summary of Evidence

Granting, again, that Luke's account is plausible both in terms of its historical details and its narrative use of the Nazirate, what may be gleaned from Acts 21.23–7a as evidence for Nazirites in this period is (1) that Nazirites were known to appear in Jerusalem during the feast of Pentecost. (2) Furthermore, the passage provides testimony that having to start a vow over again because of corpse uncleanness was a legitimate concern for those observing the Nazirite vow, and (3) that the vow was thought of as an act of supererogation.

2.5   Hegesippus (according to Eusebius, Historia ecclesiastica 2.23.5 [4–7])

⁴The charge of the Church passed to James the brother of the Lord, together with the Apostles. He was called the "Just" [ὁ ὀνομασθεὶς δίκαιος] by all men from the Lord's time to ours, since many are called James, [ἐπεὶ πολλοὶ Ἰάκωβοι ἐκαλοῦντο] but he was holy from his mother's womb. ⁵He drank no wine or strong drink, nor did he eat flesh; no razor came upon his head; he did not anoint himself with oil, and he did not go to the baths. ⁶He alone was allowed to enter into the sanctuary, for he did not wear wool but linen, and he used to enter alone into the temple and be found kneeling and praying for forgiveness for the people, so that his knees grew hard like a camel's because of his constant worship of God, kneeling and asking

for the forgiveness for the people. [7]So from his excessive righteousness he was called the Just [διὰ γέτοι τὴν ὑπερβολὴν τῆς δικαιοσύνης αὐτοῦ ἐκαλεῖτο Δίκαιος] and Oblias, that is in Greek, "Rampart of the people and righteousness," as the prophets declare concerning him.[89]

Eusebius' citation of Hegesippus on the supposed Naziriteship of James the Just, the brother of Jesus and leader of the Jerusalem church to ca. AD 62, is historically problematic for a number of reasons. Hegesippus is not only the earliest and sole source of information regarding the details of James' lifestyle and dietary habits, including those that depict him as observing Nazirite behavior, but also his account is so highly legendary that its historical veracity is exceedingly implausible.

Hegesippus, a Christian writer of the second century AD (d. 175–189),[90] may have been a Jew by birth, though this is uncertain. He lived in Rome for a number of years and wrote a series of treatises on the acts of the Church (Πέντε ὑπομνήματα ἐκκλησιαστικῶν πραξέων), all of which have survived only in fragments and almost exclusively in Eusebius' *Historia ecclesiastica*. The treatises contain some history of the early church and, as exemplified by the portion of text cited above, were utilized by Eusebius particularly as a source of information regarding the church in Jerusalem.

Among the parallel accounts of James' martyrdom, within which this passage in Eusebius is set, Josephus in *A. J.* 20.200 tells us nothing regarding James' character and the supposed account by Clement in *Hypotyposes*, which Eusebius claims is in complete agreement with Hegesippus, is no longer independently extant.[91] Whether or not Clement's account contained any depiction of James observing Nazirite behavior cannot be known.

The legendary quality of Hegesippus' report is noticeable in his reference to James being allowed to enter into the temple sanctuary—something historically unlikely for someone with no known claim to the high priesthood. Jerome seems to have been the first to notice this difficulty in the tradition with the specific notation that James had Davidic, and therefore non-Levitical genealogy.[92] Other indications

---

[89] Eusebius, *Hist. eccl.*, 2.23.4–7.
[90] See the commentary by K. Lake in *Eusebius*, vol. 1, p. xlvi.
[91] Lake, p. xlv.
[92] Cited in Smith, ed. *A Dictionary of the Bible* (vol. 2; London: John Murray, 1863), s. v. "Nazarite [sic]," by S. Clark, 472.

of legendary motifs surrounding the historical James in Hegesippus are numerous;[93] however, the most relevant to the portion of text at hand include the following: (1) Hegesippus is the first known source to refer to James by the surname "Just," despite his insistence that he was called such (ὁ ὀνομασθεὶς δίκαιος) from the Lord's time until his own;[94] and (2) his account appears to be an early martyr legend embellished by motifs based on biblical prophecy. None of the works in the New Testament canon, or in any known source prior to Hegesippus, make any reference to James as the "Just."[95] It is certainly conceivable that a tradition did exist prior to Hegesippus, but the fact that he bases such a designation on biblical prophecy, a frequent feature in Hegesippus' overall account of James' martyrdom, may betray an embellishment originating from his own hand. The very structure of the text seems to reveal that the details of James' behavior patterns, including those involving Naziriteship, consist of a block of material most likely composed of later legendary interpolation.[96] The entire section delineating James as an ascetic, priest-like figure occurs directly between the comments in line five (LCL), ". . . for many are called James (ἐπεὶ πολλοὶ Ἰάκωβοι ἐκαλοῦντο) . . .," and line seven, ". . . Because of his excessive righteousness he was called 'Just' (διὰ γέτοι τὴν ὑπερβολὴν τῆς δικαιοσύνης αὐτοῦ ἐκαλεῖτο Δίκαιος) . . ." The central purpose of the description, indicated by its placement between these two statements, is to provide the grounds upon which James' surname "the Just" had been given. As can be seen from the wording in line seven, the lengthy list of character traits, of which being a Nazirite is one, is wholly unnecessary and was probably inserted at a later stage.[97]

In reference to the textual depiction of James as a Nazirite, there appears to be transmission of a developed martyr legend that sought

---

[93] See M. Dibelius, *James: A Commentary on the Epistle of James* (rev. by H. Greeven; trans. by M. A. Williams; ed. by H. Koester; Hermeneia; Philadelphia: Fortress Press, 1976), 16–7.

[94] R. P. Martin, *James* (WBC 48; Waco, Tex.: Word Books, 1988), 1.

[95] Ibid., p. li.

[96] Zuckschwerdt, "Das Naziräat des Herrenbruders Jakobus nach Hegesipp," *ZNW* 68 (1977): 276.

[97] Zuckschwerdt maintains that the purpose of the interpolation is to portray James as not only righteous, but holy, reflecting a tradition based on the LXX[B] portrayal of Samson in Judg. 13.7; 16.17. The flow of sections five through seven is interrupted, "unterbricht," by a change to a holiness theme.

to place James in line with the biblical hero figures Samson and Samuel.[98] The references to James disallowing any razor to pass over his head, his abstinence from wine and strong drink, together with his priest-like intercession in the temple, reflect an influence of the LXX of I Samuel.[99] In addition, the only known biblical texts that contains a phrase equivalent to "holy from his mother's womb" are LXX[B] Judg. 13.7; 16.17 where Samson, a Nazirite from birth, is declared "a holy one of God from the womb."[100]

For historical purposes, it appears that the account of Hegesippus on the Naziriteship of James the Just is entirely legendary. The tradition, noted as one of the earliest Christian martyr legends,[101] appears to be based on a heterogeneous mixture of ascetic and priestly, biblical and post-biblical motifs, seeking to venerate James as the ideal holy hero after his death in ca. AD 62. The legend does seem to provide, however, traces of early Christian thought about Nazirites. Based on the influence of the LXX, like the early Gospel tradition, the motif of Nazirite holiness is particularly apparent. With respect to Samuel, his dedication to serve at the temple and his wearing linen (as would a priest) is particularly notable.

Summary of Evidence

I believe the text of Hegesippus is too problematic to provide any historical certainties respecting the behavior of James, surnamed the Just. However, I do believe the legend possibly reflects contemporary thoughts about Nazirites, given the Nazirite imagery used to depict James. (1) Based on its adaptation of the holiness motif, the legend suggests, like the Gospel tradition, that Nazirites may have been seen predominantly as holy individuals. (2) Based on the influence of the biblical portrayal of Samuel, Nazirites may have been thought of as individuals exhibiting a priest-like dedication, particularly in light of Samuel's own dedication at the temple and wearing of linen.

---

[98] Ibid.

[99] See testimony 1.2.3.

[100] See testimony 1.2.2; see also the similar use of the Judg. text by Luke when describing John the Baptist, as discussed in testimony 2.3.

[101] Dibelius, 16–7.

2.6　*Plutarch*

A work by the classical writer Plutarch (ca. AD 40's–120's) contains one possible allusion to the Nazirate; namely, his multi-volume composition, *Quaestiones convivales*. As the title implies, *Quaestiones convivales* (*Quaest. conv.*) consists of a series of dialogues, or questions and answers, on a variety of convivial matters, such as banqueting customs and other loosely related topics, to matters of science, philosophy, philology, mythology, and religion, to name only a few.[102] In the fourth book of the series, Plutarch addresses questions relating to Jewish religion, including (and specifically relating to the topic at hand) abstention from the use of wine in religious services.

Quaestiones convivales 4.6.2 (134–7)

> To show that what I have said is the practice of the Jews we may find no slight confirmation in the fact that among many penalties employed among them the one most disliked is the exclusion of a convicted offender from the use of wine for such a period as the sentencing judge may prescribe. Those thus punished . . .[103]

The brief reference to Jews abstaining from wine for a designated period is thought by Stern to be a "vague allusion to the institution of Naziriteship."[104] Similarly, Teodorsson cites the law of Num. 6.1–21 as a possible explanation for the behavior being described. Where Plutarch derived such information on the Jews is uncertain. He relies on a number of sources, primarily classical;[105] however, he was a resident of Boetia, Greece, where early records of a Jewish community exist, and he was an extensive traveler.[106] Taking into consideration the references in the dialogue of *Quaest. conv.* to Jewish customs practiced in the temple, it is also possible that apart from potential synagogue contact, he may have attained information from a Semitic source prior to the destruction of the Second Temple.

---

[102] Sven-Tage Teodorsson, *A Commentary on Plutarch's Table Talks* (vol. 1; Studia Graeca et Latina Gothoburgensia 51; Göteborg, Sweden: Acta Universitatis Gothoburgensis, 1989), see his Abstract.

[103] M. Stern, ed., *Greek and Latin Authors on Jews and Judaism* (vol. 1; Fontes ad res Judaicas Spectantes; Jerusalem: Israel Academy of Sciences and Humanities, 1976), 558.

[104] Ibid., 562.

[105] Teodorsson, see his Abstract.

[106] Ibid.; see also M. Grant, *Greek and Roman Historians: Information and Misinformation* (London: Routledge, 1995), 18–9.

The purpose of the brief segment is to supply a proof for an argument in the preceding narrative that a shared identity exists between Dionysus and the Jewish God *Adonis*. Furthermore, it stems from a series of discussions detailing similarities between Jewish and Dionysiac cult ritual. Among such similarities is supposedly abstention from the use of mead in religious services. It is at this point that the illustration of offenders being forced to abstain from wine as punishment by a sentencing judge appears. Unfortunately, due to a lacuna in the extant text, further details describing these individuals are lost.

Whatever Jewish custom this is a reference to, it is certainly, as Stern suggests, vague. That it is a reference to the institution of Naziriteship may be the case, considering not only the mention of abstinence from wine but also the fact that such abstinence took place for a designated period of time. There are no known Jewish practices of this period pertaining to punishment of offenders by restrictions on wine that correspond to the one described, and so this may be a confused representation of the abstention from wine taken on for a self-avowed period observed by Nazirites, regulated perhaps, by some Jewish official (priest or *archisynagogos*). On the other hand, there is no mention of a vow being involved, and Jewish abstinence from wine for a variety of reasons was as common among Jews (cf. testimony 1.8—"Korban") as it was among non-Jews. Among possible rituals, this could also be a confused reference, as described in discussion of testimonies 1.6.1, 1.10.4 and 2.1, to a Jewish rite of mourning. An individual undergoing a period of mourning may have appeared to an outsider as one suffering from some form of inflicted punishment.

Summary of Evidence

For historical purposes, Plutarch's description of Jewish individuals abstaining from wine in *Quaest. conv.* is indeed vague, too vague in fact to supply any certain information on how the institution of Naziriteship may have been perceived by an outside Greek populace. The opacity of the account, coupled with the fact that this is the only source of information remotely resembling the institution of the Nazirate from among Greek and Latin authors writing in the early Roman imperial period, seems only to indicate (if anything) that (1) Nazirite practice was either unpopular in the Diaspora or (2) indistinguishable from similar Greek custom(s) to the degree that, as opposed to such Jewish customs as *kashrut* or Sabbath observance, it failed to merit special attention.

CHAPTER THREE

MAKING SENSE OF THE EVIDENCE

Taking the results of the previous examinations into consideration, it is now possible to offer an explanation of how the various bits and pieces of evidence come together to reveal a particular portrait of who Nazirites were in this period, and more specifically, what role they held within the social lives of Jews. The method by which I will conduct this task will be first to discuss the various thoughts about Nazirites as found in sources; and secondly, to describe how Nazirites generally behaved according to those sources. Such an approach, I believe, best fits the overall character of the available evidence in that some, such as that gleaned from Bible interpretation and Bible translation material for example, consist largely of perceptions or beliefs about Nazirites while other, such as that found among works of contemporary history or sources produced by the early rabbis, comprise information typically relating Nazirite demeanor. Finally, based on these two elaborations, I shall discuss what this particular evidence suggests was the role of the Nazirite within Judaism.

3.1 *Thoughts about Nazirites*

3.1.1 In terms of the general knowledge of Hebrew cult ritual among Jews, sources reveal that not all in this period knew who a "Nazirite" was, though conceivably by the turn of the first century AD most did. In discussion of testimony 1.2.1, I posited that in the formative years of the LXX, Greek-speaking Jews familiar only with the Mosaic legislation were aware of those who made the "special purity vow" but were generally uninformed of their respective Hebrew nomenclature.[1] It is likely, however, that by the turn of the era the term "Nazirite," in the religious technical sense, became well known among Jews in Hebrew, Aramaic, and Greek. This is particularly likely

---

[1] See 1.2.1.

given the introduction and use of the transliteration ναζιρ/ναζιραῖος in later Jewish sources in Greek,[2] as well as the growth in popularity of the Greek version of the Samson story manifest in early Gospel tradition.[3]

3.1.2   Sources also reveal that Nazirites were thought of fundamentally as those who made, or who were placed under (such as a child by vow of a parent), a special type of vow or verbal promise. Again as suggested in discussion of testimony 1.2.1, within the LXX (Num. 6.1–21) the specific "vow of the Nazirite" was translated as the "special purity vow"; given the widespread influence of the LXX among Jews (both in Egypt as well as in Palestine), though some were possibly ignorant of the religious technical term "Nazirite," Jews did at least perceive the vow as a special, or exceptional, form of votive behavior. Evidence of this notion was witnessed in the writings of Philo of Alexandria, where in *Spec.* 1.247–8 Philo referred to the custom as "the Great Vow" (εὐχὴ μεγάλη) and stated this is what the vow was called.[4] Although Philo's description appears in context of a brief commentary on the biblical law of Num. in the LXX, in discussing testimony 1.5.1 I maintained that his comment might have been an allusion to common reference to the practice among fellow Jews. A perception consistent with this idea was also witnessed among the later rabbis in the Mishnah and Tosefta where halakhah respecting the Nazirate, though sharing the same order as halakhah respecting the general practice of vow making (*m. Ned./t. Ned.*), was accorded its own designated treatment (*m. Naz./t. Naz.*).[5]

3.1.3   Nazirites are furthermore perceived, according to sources such as Philo, Josephus, and the Tosefta, as a type of dedicated self-offering.[6] Philo and Josephus, both in the context of discussing temple offerings, state that those who made the vow dedicated their very person.[7] More explicitly, according to Philo, those who made the vow did so as a means of making their selves as a type of first-fruit offering

---

[2] See 1.2.2, 5; and 1.4; see also 1.6.2, 5.
[3] See 2.1–3; and 2.5.
[4] See 1.5.1.
[5] See 1.8; and 1.9.
[6] See 1.5.1, 3; and 1.6.2; see also 1.9.3.
[7] See 1.5.1, 3; and 1.6.2.

(*Spec.* 1.248). Likewise, according to the testimony of R. Judah in the Tosefta, the pious men of old used to make free-will offerings of *Nazirite* vows (*t. Ned.* 1.2). This association between the Nazirate and the giving of offerings, particularly first-fruits, will be explained in more detail following, suffice to mention that there appears to be an influence exerted on this conception by the biblical story of Samuel. In discussion of testimonies 1.1, 1.2.3, 1.3, 1.5.4, 1.6.4, and 1.8, I posited that Samuel was considered a Nazirite by many in this period (a designation unclear in the version of Samuel in MT). Furthermore, in discussion of testimonies 1.1 and 1.2.3, I suggested that the annual festival on which his mother in the biblical legend dedicated Samuel appears to be identified with the annual festival of First-Fruits, or Pentecost. Samuel himself, as a Nazirite, therefore, seems to have been considered by some as a type of first-fruit offering, and so, likewise, did some consider those who made the Nazirite vow.

3.1.4   In terms of general character, Nazirites are apprehended foremost in sources as *holy* individuals. The theme of Nazirite holiness was communicated particularly within the LXX. I suggested in discussion of testimony 1.2.2 that the reviser of LXX[B] Judg. defined the Nazirite as a "holy one" (ἅγιος) when introducing the religious technical term in Judg. 13.5,7, and 16.17. Similarly in LXX Amos 2.11–2, Nazirites were regarded as those who were "sanctified" (ἡγιασμενοι), or "made holy."[8] Jews were apparently very familiar with this characterization of the Nazirite, at least within Palestine of the first century AD, given its thematic association with such figures as Jesus, John the Baptist, and the early church leader James.[9] Nuances, however, were also witnessed in Philo, the Tosefta, and the rabbinic Targum tradition, where in *Spec.* 1.248ff. Philo compared the Nazirite (because of his/her abstention from wine) to the administering priest in the temple,[10] and within the Tosefta and Targumim to Genesis (*Tg. Neof.*; *Frg. Tg.* P) where the rabbis appear to have associated "nazir" with the Aramaic word for "pious."[11]

---

[8] See 1.2.4.
[9] See 2.1–3, 5.
[10] See 1.5.1.
[11] See 1.12.2, 4.

3.1.5   Sources also reveal that in addition to being holy, those who made the vow were perceived as being *pure*. Purity language was used poetically in LXX Lam. 4.7–8 to describe Nazirites,[12] and as mentioned, in LXX Num. 6.1–21 the vow of the Nazirite was translated specifically as a *purity* vow.[13] Though the notion may seem another nuance of holiness, purity, rather than being strictly synonymous with holiness, appears to be thought of in sources as its cause or affecting agent. As I posited in discussion of testimony 1.2.1, the act of purifying oneself from wine, cutting the hair, and contacting a corpse in the law of Num. 6.2–8 was considered an act of taking on a state of purification greater than that normally required of Jews (cf. the laws of *kashrut*) and was reflective of the additional purity requirements expected of the serving priest, especially the High Priest. Rather than the consequence of sacred status, as in the case of the administering priest, for the Nazirite it was the act of purifying oneself from proscribed behavior that resulted in sacrosanctity, or was the means by which the Nazirite achieved his/her required holy stature (Num. 6.4). There is good reason to believe based on this evidence, that among purity trends common among Jews in this period, making the Nazirite vow was considered one of them.

3.1.6   Nazirites also appear in certain sources as those in a state of grief. This seems to have been the case in later rabbinic sources where the biblical patriarch Joseph was considered a Nazirite. In discussion of testimonies 1.10.4 and 1.11, I suggested that Joseph's Nazirite status was perceived particularly as in relation to his forced separation from his brothers while in Egypt. I posited in discussion of *Genesis Rabbah* to Gen. 49.26 that Joseph's choice to abstain from wine was reminiscent of mourning behavior: he abstained as a Nazirite from what appears to have been personal grief due to separation from his family. I further posited that a similar notion was witnessed in the passion narrative in Mark's Gospel, where Jesus made a Nazirite vow during the final Paschal meal.[14] Much like the rabbinic perception of Joseph, Jesus' choice to abstain from wine was done so in the context of personal grief, or mourning, in the face of his imminent death and departure from his beloved disciples.

---

[12] See 1.2.5.
[13] See 1.2.1.
[14] See 2.1.

3.2   *Nazirite Behavior*

3.2.1   Though references to Nazirites in the sources often fail to distinguish gender, evidence in Josephus, the Mishnah, and the Tosefta suggest that women, as well as men, commonly observed the rite. As I proposed in discussion of testimony 1.6.1, the most detailed description of the vow, particularly among works of the historical genre, involved a case of a female Nazirite (*B. J.* 2.313–4). Furthermore, in testimonies 1.8 and 1.9 the rabbis of the Mishnah and Tosefta envisaged women freely taking up the Nazirate, with the possible exception of those under the authority of a husband (who had permission to annul it). The vision of the rabbis suggests that for married women, and perhaps women in general, the vow was likely more difficult to observe than for men; rabbinic discourse assumes the possibility that a husband could annul his wife's vow merely on the condition of his displeasure in her unkempt or shorn appearance. Such aesthetic effects may have had a generally greater social impact on women than upon men. Women, nevertheless, were known to have observed the custom, three of whom were specifically named in sources: Bernice, sister of King Agrippa II (*B. J.* 2.313–4); Queen Helena of Adiabene (*m. Naz.* 3.6) and Miriam of Tadmor (*m. Naz.* 6.11).

3.2.2   There were no cases describing slaves becoming Nazirites, though the rabbis in the Mishnah, again, envisaged this as a possibility.[15] According to the Mishnah, the slave who wished to become a Nazirite faced a similar circumstance as a wife who wished to do the same; namely, both could have had their vows annulled by the authority of another, in this case the word of a master. Likewise, like a child aged a minor, those owning slaves may have forced their servants to undergo the Nazirate though, again, we have no actual case history of such behavior in the surviving sources.

3.2.3   Children becoming Nazirites was exemplified only once in sources of this period, though the rabbis in the Mishnah anticipated this behavior as being quite common place.[16] The case of R. Hananiah

---

[15] See 1.8.20; see also W. H. D. Rouse who notes the discovery of inscriptions dated to the Roman era at Panamara in Caria which refer to hair-offerings made by slaves, *Greek Votive Offerings* (Cambridge, Eng.: Cambridge University Press, 1902), 243.

[16] See 1.8.9; and 1.9.2.

b. Hananiah in the Tosefta involved a parent placing his child under
a Nazirite vow; a circumstance in the testimony considered applicable only until the child was of the age of maturity (I asserted to
be the age of 12–13).[17] Prior testimony in the Mishnah, on the other
hand, expected that this behavior could have been common among
Jews,[18] ruling that only a father could place his son under a vow
and providing decisions affecting potential problem scenarios where
a son rebelled from his vow (possibly by cutting or chopping his
hair in defiance) or where relatives protest on the son's behalf. Such
scenarios, I suggested, may have been accurate of behavior typical
in the period under discussion.[19]

Why parents may have placed a child under a vow may have
been to pattern behavior after Hannah in the biblical story of Samuel
(I Sam. 1.11ff.). Like Hannah, a parent may have done so to fulfill
a vow made in the circumstance of bareness, or possibly for any
number of reasons. Given the popularity of the Samuel story and
the idealistic nature of rabbinic decisions in the Mishnah, it may
have been the case that mothers as well as fathers placed their children under the vow on occasion (as did Samuel's mother Hannah),
and it is possible that girls were placed under the vow as well as
boys, though we have no cases of girls being placed under the vow
in available sources.

3.2.4   The widespread practice of the vow is evident in a variety
of testimonies. According to I Macc. 3.49, Josephus (*A. J.* 19.294),
Acts 21.23–7a., and the Mishnah (*m. Naz.* 5.4), Nazirites often appeared
in Jerusalem in groups. Moreover, in his account of the Jewish war,
Josephus described the vow as customarily observed in a time of illness or other malady (*B. J.* 2.313–4). Given the vicissitudes of pesti-
lence together with its non-respective nature, a priori the custom
was both popular and widespread. The aforesaid cases involving
women Nazirites also provide evidence suggesting that Nazirites were
known among the socially elite, as well as among common Jewry.
Bernice, sister of King Agrippa II, on whose account Josephus
described the vow in *B. J.* 2.313–4, was a figure among the ruling

---

[17] See 1.9.2.
[18] See 1.8.9.
[19] See 1.8, esp. "Assessment of Tractate *Mishnah Nazir.*"

aristocracy. Furthermore, so was Helena, Queen of Adiabene, named a Nazirite in the Mishnah (*m. Naz.* 3.6). Other prominent figures in this period who are described making the vow include the apostle Paul (Acts 18.18) and, possibly, as I posited in discussion of testimony 2.1, Jesus of Nazareth (Mk. 14.25; 15.23).

3.2.5 Scholars, as mentioned in the Introduction, have often proposed that Nazirites were also known among the poor and destitute. This is in light of the substantial monetary means needed to complete a vow (i.e., the multiple sacrificial goods required) and the number of references to groups of Nazirites loitering in the temple precincts and on whose behalf donations of offerings were sometimes given (such as exemplified in the case of Agrippa I in *A. J.* 19.294 and Paul in Acts 21.23ff.). That Nazirites were among the wealthy is evident in the cases of royalty mentioned previously, as well as the case of the first century AD tomb owned by a Nazirite described in testimony 1.7. I noted in discussion of testimonies 1.6.5 and 2.4.2, however, that Nazirites are never described as poor either in *A. J.* 19.294 or Acts 21.23ff. Though I believe poor Jews, as well as the wealthy could have made and brought to completion their vows, evidence for this is found only implicitly in the Mishnah and Tosefta where a specific surplus of funds used to purchase Nazirite offerings is envisaged by the rabbis as existing in the temple treasury.[20] The poor, ipso facto, possibly made recourse to these funds, if the rabbis' vision is historically accurate. That the wealthy made contributions of offerings for Nazirites is certain, perhaps for specific individuals or even groups.[21] In *A. J.* 19.294 and Acts 21.23ff., this is precisely what occurs. That these groups of Nazirites were poor, however, again, is never stated, and there is a better rationale for the simultaneous appearance of Nazirites at the temple, which I will later discuss.

3.2.6 In the Halakhic Midrashim it is humorous that the issue of the Nazirite with no hair is discussed. In testimony 1.10, I maintained that in many instances the evidence within the Halakhic Midrashim is late and expansive on the material already presented in both the Mishnah and Tosefta. I believe such a scenario is possible, though

---

[20] See 1.8.25; and 1.9.4.
[21] Ibid.

admittedly there is no available case example of a bald person making the Nazirite vow in either the Mishnah, the Tosefta or the Halakhic Midrashim. Given that the hair could not be grown or shaven at the completion of the vow, a bald individual could have allowed a razor to pass over his/her head when the vow was completed, as the rabbis deemed appropriate. It is more likely, however, that a bald Nazirite might have simply accentuated the behavior s/he could have performed. As will be discussed, there were other means of demonstrating that the vow was being observed than merely growing long hair or allowing it to go unkempt. Alternatively, by mingling with other Nazirites in the temple when required offerings were due, some Nazirites of whom would have already had their heads shaved, being bald might actually have escaped notice.

3.2.7   In testimony 2.4.2 I discussed the opinion of Neusner that the rabbis in rabbinic sources held an altogether negative opinion of vow making and of Nazirites, in particular, as "weak" and "arrogant." I find Neusner's[22] opinion ill founded, especially in regard to early rabbinic evidence for Nazirites.[23] The case of R. Hananiah b. Hananiah in the Tosefta (*t. Nidd.* 5.15), mentioned previously, not only exemplifies a case in which a child was placed under the regime of the Nazirite vow by the will of a parent, but is a case testifying to the practice of the custom among those in early rabbinic circles; namely, two: R. Hananiah b. Hananiah and his father (likely Hananiah, the prefect of the temple and contemporary of R. Simeon b. Gamaliel). The significance of this case is also manifest, as I mentioned in discussion of testimony 1.9, in the fact R. Hananiah b. Hananiah was represented as a Nazirite of lifelong duration, of his own choice, and moreover was testified by eyewitnesses to have been a prominent teacher in rabbinic circles, possibly even at Yavneh.

3.2.8   Sources tend to indicate that those who made the vow were careful to adhere at least to the general rules of the Nazirate; however, specific requirements were often generalized. Nazirites are often portrayed discharging their vows in the Jerusalem temple when their avowed days were completed (e.g., I Macc. 3.49). Likewise in discussion

---

[22] See ns. 79–80 above.
[23] See 1.9.2; and 1.9.3.

of testimony 2.4.2, I proposed that the four men under a vow in Acts 21.23ff. were impure Nazirites, and such evidence suggests that some were careful to keep the stipulations of the Law at the cost of both time and money. Furthermore, in the Mishnah Queen Helena is envisaged as concerned about compliance to the degree that she sought advice from the rabbis; and rabbinic decisions in the Mishnah and Tosefta both visualize the possibility that some who observed the vow could question whether or not they had violated known rules in certain circumstances, such as eating food or bread soaked in wine, or traversing in an area close to a cemetery. Where the rules for the Nazirate are spelled out in detail, however, such as the require-ments that the votary abstain from "wine and strong drink," from "vinegar of wine or vinegar of strong drink," grape juice, all fruit of the vine, etc. (Num. 6.3–4), evidence suggests that these details were often ignored by observers. Josephus, for example, described Nazirites as merely "those who abstain from wine and who grow long hair" (*A. J.* 4.72), omitting the details of the various rules respect-ing wine and the hair. Likewise, there was debate among the early rabbis over the precise meaning of "wine" as opposed to "strong drink" (*Sifre* to Num. 6.3–4), and what is meant by the command to avoid grape produce "from the seeds to the skin" (*m. Naz.* 6.2). Rather than be concerned with such details of the Law as written in the sacred scrolls, as I proposed in discussion of testimony 1.8, most in this period likely followed the behavior modeled by peers, or the behavior exhibited by Nazirites known from the Bible, such as Samson and Samuel. As a result, though familiar with the basic requirements of the Law, many simply adhered to the most general requirements of abstaining from wine, having contact with a corpse, cutting the hair, and giving appropriate offerings when their vows were completed—offerings, I suggested in discussion of testimonies 1.8 and 1.9, were possibly even pre-packaged in the market place and/or the temple precincts.[24]

3.2.9   In addition to generalizing known rules for the Nazirate, sources indicate that it was often the case that some explicit rules were bent by vow makers. In Num. 6.13–21, for example, the Law is explicit that a votary cut his/her hair "at the doorway of the tent

---

[24] See 1.8.24–5.

of meeting" (Num. 6.13) and afterward cast the shaven hair onto
the fire "under the peace-offering" (Num. 6.18). In discussion of testimony 1.8 and 2.4.1, I suggested that some cut their hair in the
vicinity of the city of Jerusalem as evidenced in the Mishnah,[25] or
even outside the land of Palestine en route to Jerusalem as in the
case of Paul in Acts 18.18. Furthermore, as I indicated in discussion
of testimony 1.6.2, Josephus described Nazirites as those who cut
their hair and offered it to the administering priest as a form of first-
fruit offering, rather than burn it on the fire. Though a seemingly
odd gift, there is evidence of this activity in the Mishnah where the
rabbis describe the possibility of Nazirite hair being woven into a
sack.[26] Such behavior is in stark contrast to the requirements of the
Law in Num.

3.2.10   Where the law for the vow is not explicit, such as when it
fails to give any prescribed formula for how one should be uttered
(Num. 6.2), how long a vow should be in terms of the number of
days (Num. 6.4, 5, 6, 8), what one can give in addition to the
required sacrifices (Num. 6.21), or how one is to act given the behavior of Nazirites known from the biblical past, sources suggest that
great flexibility and personal freedom of expression were the norm.
In discussion of testimony 1.8, I posited that people likely used all
manner of words for expressing a Nazirite vow (cf. *m. Naz.* 1.1). In
some instances, it might even have been confusing whether one was
actually making the vow or merely stating intent to abstain from
wine for a time or from another form of behavior typical of Nazirites.
Context in such cases, as demonstrated in testimony 2.1, was likely
the determining factor. In testimonies 1.6.1 and 1.8–10, it was shown
that according to Josephus and early rabbinic sources, the length for
the Nazirate in this period was a standard, or customary, thirty days.
Why the length was thirty days is undisclosed in sources; though,
by description of the rite as given by Josephus and the comparisons
made between mourning behavior and the Nazirate in early rabbinic
works, it is likely that the origin of the thirty days lay in an amalgamation of behavior shared with the Jewish rite of mourning known
as the *Shloshim*, or "thirty days." Though such a period was described

---

[25] See 1.8.15.
[26] See 1.8.23.

as customary, it was by no means universal. Against the assertion of Gray,[27] the rabbis envisaged people making the Nazirite vow for any length of "days;" some even for the duration of a lifetime (their behavior being modeled in some instances on the pattern of the biblical Nazirite Samson [and possibly Samuel or even Absalom]). The rabbis anticipated Samson's behavior exemplified in the Bible as being problematic and permitted certain exemptions for those who patterned their behavior after him.[28] Suffice to mention that because this story was well known among Jews in this period, there was likely room for all manner of behavior respecting Nazirite law—behavior appearing to some as controversial. Likewise, in terms of giving in addition to the prescribed offerings, evidence in testimonies 1.8–9 suggests people were sometimes paying for the offerings required of other Nazirites in addition to their own. Supererogatory giving might also have included, though there were no cases depicting such, any manner and number of gifts.

3.2.11   Another manner in which votaries may have expressed their observance of the rite was in their manner of attire. I noted in discussion of testimonies 1.6.1 and 1.8, that Nazirites may have accentuated their appearance in effort to demonstrate in some public fashion that they were under the vow. Given that thirty days was the customary period for observing the rite, the length of hair, the only physically ostensible aspect of the vow prior to its completion, would not have grown sufficiently; and as a result a Nazirite would likely have been indistinguishable from any other individual in society. According to Josephus in *B. J.* 2.313–4, however, Bernice traversed barefoot while under the vow. In addition, as I posited in discussion of testimony 1.8, those observing the vow may not have combed their hair but likely allowed it to grow wild and unkempt.[29] Given the similarities between such behavior and the behavior exhibited by those in a state of mourning, it appears Nazirites opted for a disheveled look, though any manner of outward accentuate may have been possible.

---

[27] See the Introduction, p. 11.
[28] See 1.8.1.
[29] See 1.8.1; and 1.8.13.

3.2.12   In the Introduction I mentioned the theory of Smith,[30] also
shared by Gray,[31] that the Nazirate in this period functioned primarily
as a type of "hair-offering" similar in practice to the hair-vows common among Greeks (as exemplified by the legendary vow of Achilles).
This stands in contrast to the common notion that the rite was rather
a form of pious *self*-dedication, the hair forming merely an outward
sign that the vow was undertaken and which, once the vow was completed, was burned on the fire in accordance with the Law in Num.
6.18. Evidence from sources describing Greek votive practices involving the offering of the hair, however, as well the evidence for the
Nazirate as found in Jewish sources, such as Philo, Josephus, and
the Mishnah, suggests that both of these views are likely correct.

According to ancient Greek literary sources and epigraphic remains,
the practice of vowing one's hair to the gods was a widespread phenomenon within Greek culture of this period.[32] Sources suggest it
was a common form of river worship, but was also performed in the
worship of the greater Greek deities and even heroes.[33] Hair was
offered to various gods and goddesses for a variety of reasons: as a
request for good health, the birth of a child, a happy marriage, deliverance from some perceived danger or for virtually any number of
rationales. When a vow was fulfilled, the hair was often shaved and
cast into a river or hung up in (or deposited in stele which were
then stood up in) temple precincts.[34] According to Pausanius (ca. AD
160), a statue of young man cutting his hair stood near the river
Cephisus in Attica,[35] and shorn hair from women covered the image
of Health at Titane.[36] When describing the hair ritual performed by
Theseus, Plutarch mentions it was an old and common custom among
youths at Delphi to offer their hair as "first-fruits" to Apollo.[37]

Philo and Josephus, as mentioned previously, both describe the
Nazirate as a means of first-fruit dedication. For Philo, it was the
Nazirite's *self* that was offered; but for Josephus it was the *hair* that

---

[30] See the Introduction, pp. 7–10.
[31] Ibid.
[32] Rouse, 240–2; and J. Hastings, ed. *The Encyclopedia of Religion and Ethics* (2nd
ed.; New York: Charles Scribner's Sons, 1922), s. v. "Vows (Greek and Roman),"
by A. C. Pearson; see also Ibid., s. v. "Votive Offering (Greek)," by Rouse.
[33] Rouse, *Greek Votive Offerings*, 240–2.
[34] Ibid., 243.
[35] Pausanius, *Descr.* 1.37.3.
[36] Ibid., 2.11.6.
[37] Plutarch, *Vit.* Thes. 5.

was given (in stark contrast to the Law in Num. 6.18). I suggested in discussion of testimonies 1.6.2 and 1.8.23 that Josephus' odd description was supported by evidence in the Mishnah, where in a remarkably similar literary context (a discussion of animal hair deemed sacred, particularly the wool shorn from sheep), Nazirite hair was envisaged as being woven into a sack. Although Philo, Josephus, and the evidence of the Mishnah may seem at odds, I believe they represent a variety of practices among Jews. Some, in other words, may have used the Nazirate as a means of dedicating *themselves* as a form of first-fruit offering, while others, perhaps under the influence of practice common within the surrounding Greek culture, simply vowed their *hair* to the temple as a type of offering. Those who assigned their locks to the priest, rather than burn it on the fire as required by the Law, may have thought it appropriate in such a context to assign all *sacred* hair, including their own, to the priests. Perhaps on this basis, according Nazirite hair with a sacred status,[38] sacks were woven from it and used (by priests?) possibly as a type of talisman.

3.2.13   Where the Nazirite vow in this period was observed was both within the land of Palestine as well as abroad. According to available testimony, Nazirites were seen primarily when they appeared in Jerusalem to discharge their vows, though often they are depicted entering the land to do so from abroad. As I proposed in discussion of testimony 1.8, rabbinic testimony entertained the possibility that some may have terminated their vows at the Temple of Onias in Egypt.[39] This vision may have been accurate, though evidence substantiating the notion is lacking. One case explicitly depicted Nazirite behavior in the Diaspora, namely the vow of Paul in Acts. 18.18. In discussion of testimony 2.6, I maintained that although the vow was observed by Jews in the Diaspora, it was likely uncommon to the degree that it failed to gain the attention of the surrounding Graeco-Roman culture (as compared to other things Jewish, such as the observance of the Sabbath and dietary laws). Another possibility may have been that the practice simply failed to draw outward attention because it was manifestly indistinguishable from similar Greek practice (as described previously).

---

[38] That the hair of the Nazirite, in addition to his person, is considered sacred by some, see rabbinic discussion in *Sifre* to Num. 6.1–21 in testimony 1.10.3.
[39] See 1.8.26.

3.2.14   When people decided to become Nazirites was presumably
any time they wished. Evidence suggests, however, that many did
so at certain temporal junctures, such as when they found themselves
in some kind of personal distress, whether physical or otherwise, or,
in contrast to the theory of Smith,[40] at a period leading up to or
during a pilgrim festival, especially the feast of Pentecost.

Josephus states explicitly that the vow was observed when suffering
from sickness or other malady.[41] Likewise, Philo appears to suggest
that people made the vow as a form of petition for divine healing.[42]
According to the evidence of Josephus,[43] early rabbinic description
of the vow in the Mishnah,[44] Halakhic Midrashim,[45] and *Genesis
Rabbah*,[46] together with the evidence for the vow in the Gospel of
Mark,[47] one might understand "malady" as a state of personal grief
or period of mourning. Given these were circumstances in which the
vow was made, some may have taken on the vow after the divine end
of the votive bargain was fulfilled (i.e., after the relative crisis had
subsided). Others, however, appear to have begun their vows the
moment the pangs of suffering were felt. Those who were physically
ill may have purified themselves from wine, for example, as soon as
they were aware of their demise. In testimonies 1.10.4, 1.11, and
2.1 both Joseph and Jesus were portrayed as observing the Nazirate,
not after their suffering had been salved, but while in midst of their
suffering.

Discussed previously, sources such as Josephus and Philo make it
clear that there was also an understood association between the making of Nazirite vows in this period and the giving of first-fruits. In
I Macc. 3.49 first-fruits and tithes were mentioned in the context of
the "Nazirites who had completed their days," and in Acts 21.23ff.
there were at least four Nazirites described participating in a purification
ritual with the apostle Paul, all of whom appeared in Jerusalem at
the festival of First-Fruits, or Pentecost. Suggested previously, why
such an association was made may have been due to a mixture of

---

[40] See the Introduction, p. 9.
[41] See 1.6.1.
[42] See 1.5.1.
[43] See 1.6.1.
[44] See 1.8.
[45] See 1.10.4.
[46] See 1.11.
[47] See 2.1.

both Jewish and Greek influences. With respect to the former, mentioned previously, there appears to have been an influence exerted on thoughts about the vow by the story of Samuel in the Bible. Sources such as the LXX (I Sam. 1.11, 21), 4QSam[a] (I Sam. 1.22), and *Targum Jonathan* (I Sam. 1.3, 21) appear to have associated Samuel's dedication as a Nazirite with an annual festival (during which Hannah and her husband appeared before the temple in Shiloh).[48] Furthermore, I asserted in discussion of testimony 1.2.3, that this festival was possibly identified in the LXX as the festival of First-Fruits. Given that Samuel was thought of by many as a Nazirite, making the Nazirite vow during the feast of Pentecost may have been an act imitating Samuel's dedication; an act which may have been considered as a type of religious preparation rite, not unlike perhaps, the rite of Lent practiced among modern Christians during the approach of Easter. Others, however, may have been motivated by a less biblical rationale. Like the youths at Delphi, many may have participated in such a practice simply because dedicating the hair as a first-fruit offering was what people did in the surrounding culture.

It seems also the case that people became Nazirites, or at least fully discharged their vows, during a period surrounding any pilgrim festival. In Acts 18.18, Paul was described as observing the vow leading up to a festival, but which feast was intended is undisclosed by Luke. As I proposed in discussion of testimony 2.4.1, the festival may have been Pentecost, or it may simply have been the case that Paul was observing the rite at such a time out of convenience to coincide his need to appear in Jerusalem due to festival worship with his need to appear in the city for the purpose of fully terminating his vow, thus avoiding making multiple treks. Making a trek to Jerusalem from afar was difficult for anyone in this period, and many likely observed or completed their vows during or while participating in any approaching pilgrim festival, whether Pentecost, Passover, or Booths, as a matter of convenient timing.[49] This, I believe, is the reason why Nazirites often appear in sources in large groups. Though

---

[48] See 1.1, 1.2.3; and 1.12.5.

[49] The rabbis in *Sifre* to Num., for instance, are concerned with the matter of votaries drinking wine in the interim period between the completion of avowed days and the moment requisite sacrifices are actually offered (see *Sifre* to Num. 6.3 discussed in testimony 1.10.3).

a pilgrim festival was not always mentioned in the context of discussing Nazirites in sources, it does afford a more plausible explanation, given the above evidence, than that these groups of Nazirites
were poor or destitute and loitering in the temple precincts for the
purpose of waiting for someone to pay for their required sacrifices.
Even if they were poor, what better time to loiter in temple than
when crowds of people (some of whom were wealthy and eager to
give alms) typically appeared in the vicinity of the temple precincts,
namely during a pilgrim festival?

3.2.15   Finally, sources reveal that people became Nazirites in this
period for a variety of reasons both conditional and, against the
assertion of Cartledge,[50] unconditional, and well intentioned, as well
as on whim. Sources suggest that the most common reason Jews
made the vow was to solicit divine assistance in a time of personal
crisis. Noted previously, I posited in discussion of testimony 1.6.1
that Josephus described the vow as taken in a time of illness. Likewise
in testimonies 1.5.2–3, Philo appeared to suggest that some made the
vow as a means of petitioning God for divine healing. Making the
vow as a request for divine intervention in the case of a barren wife
was also envisaged in the Mishnah.[51] Furthermore, I asserted in discussion of testimonies 1.6.1, 1.10.4, 1.11, and 2.1, that a personal
crisis may have included a state of personal grief, or mourning. In
such circumstances, it may have varied as to which element of the
vow was considered catalytic in soliciting God's help. For some it
may have been the quantity, and perhaps quality, of sacrifices offered
(such as for the author of I Macc.), while for others (e.g., Philo) it
was the consecrated state of the self. In the cases of those who took
the vow while in a state of personal mourning, the primary significance
of the vow lay in the votary's state of consecration, the effect of
which appears to have provided some sort of spiritual comfort. In
discussion of testimony 1.8, I also suggested that the rabbis visual-
ized two types of motivation for making the vow: bound-duty to
fulfill a conditional promise (such as the cases described previously),
or freewill.[52] The latter included a motivation of thanksgiving, such

---

[50] See the Introduction, p. 14.
[51] See 1.8.5.
[52] Ibid.

as at the announcement of childbirth or any other circumstance perceived as the result of divine blessing, as well as (particularly evidenced in the Tosefta) a desire to exhibit personal piety or holiness
(*t. Nid.* 5.15). Another reason people took up the Nazirate, at least
for a temporary period, was, as discussed, in a form of worship in
the events leading up to or taking place during the festival of Pentecost.
Lastly, in contradistinction to these well-intentioned motives, rabbinic
evidence suggests people sometimes made the vow whimsically or
thoughtlessly, such as on the condition of a bet.[53] Such circumstances
might find analogy with one today who jovially announces the prospect
of becoming a monk or nun.[54]

3.3   *The Role of the Nazirite*

In light of the various thoughts about Nazirites in this period and
the manner in which they tended to behave, the role of the Nazirite
in late Second Temple Judaism seems best described as that of a
religious devotee: "devotee" being understood in the sense of one
who gave to God both oneself and, most commonly, of one's possessions. Pragmatically, how one gave oneself and possessions to God
was by living pure from certain behavior normally allowed Jews (such
as drinking wine, cutting the hair, and attending funerals), and by
supporting the temple priesthood, God's earthly agents, with requisite offerings in addition to whatever else one could afford. For some,
like the Greeks, these offerings included the giving of one's hair. For
others, no material offerings were given but rather, as an extreme
form of devotion, offering the self by abstaining from proscribed
behavior was a manner of permanent lifestyle.

Given the variety of motivations for making the vow, Nazirites
were thus "devotees" in a multiplicity of ways. Some were devotees
out of a duty to fulfill a verbal contract made with God, or perhaps
out of a need to draw near to the divine presence in a time of personal grief or mourning. Some were devotees out of thanksgiving to
God for some perceived unsolicited intervention, or even out of a
personal desire to live a pious or holy life, whether temporarily or
for the duration of a lifetime. Nazirites were also known as devotees

---

[53] See 1.8.8, 12.
[54] In Modern Hebrew the term נזיר is used in reference to monks.

in a form of worship during the events leading up to or taking place during the annual festival of Pentecost, an activity illustrating the very nature of the Nazirate. The festival of Pentecost was a time when Jews dedicated a portion of their earthly goods to God, and as a result was when the priesthood received a primary portion of its annual support. Like Hannah who dedicated her son Samuel as a Nazirite during a festival in the Bible, what better time to devote oneself in addition to one's possessions?

CONCLUSION

The significance of the Nazirite custom in late Second Temple Judaism lay, in part, in its egalitarian nature. In comparison to religious groups of the period where devotion to God was expressed through certain commonly held practices and/or beliefs (such as the Pharisees, Sadducees, and early Christians), or where certain restrictions precluded membership (such as with the Essenes, the Qumran Community, or the Therapeutae), according to the portrait revealed by the pertinent evidence, Nazirites were known from all walks of Jewish life, whether man, woman or child, possibly slave as well as free, rich or poor, common as well as the socially elite, the *Am-ha'arets* as well as the *Hakamim*, irrespective of belief beyond the simple desire to express personal devotion to the God of Israel. The beauty of the custom, furthermore, lay in its allowance for flexibility, personal freedom of expression, and even adaptation to outside cultural norms with respect to its prescribed rules. Though the law for the Nazirite (Num. 6.1–21) stipulated certain behavior, beyond the basics of abstaining from wine, cutting their hair, attending funerals, and offering certain gifts at the temple, Nazirites likely did what they wished and gave what they wished, justifying their actions with all manner of rationale.

In terms of the role of the Nazirite, though scholars have offered a variety of perspectives respecting other primary interests, there is no need to justify one characterization of the Nazirite over another. In essence, the differing opinions of scholars are more or less all correct. "Lay-priest," "ascetic," "hair-offerer," etc.,[1] all accurately describe Nazirites given the variety of thought and behavior respecting these figures in sources of this period. "Religious devotee," however, in my opinion best pinpoints the precise role of the Nazirite in the available sources, considering the comprehensive nature and scope of the evidence examined.

---

[1] See the discussion of previous scholarship in the Introduction, pp. 7–15.

BIBLIOGRAPHY

Primary Sources

Aland, B. et al., eds. *The Greek New Testament*. 4th revised edition. Stuttgart: Deutsche Bibelgesellschaft, 1993.

Albeck, Ch., ed. *Shishah sidre Mishnah*. 6 vols. Jerusalem: Mosad Byalik, 1952–8.

——, and J. Theodor, eds. *Midrash Bereshit raba*. Vol. 3. Berlin: M. Poppeloyer, 1927.

Albrecht, K. *'Orla: Text, Übersetzung und Erklärung nebst textkritischen Anhang*. Vol. 1:10 of *Die Mischna: Text, Übersetzung und ausführliche Erklärung*, eds. K. H. Rengstorf, L. Rost, and S. Herrmann. Gießen: Alfred Töpelmann (vormals J. Ricker), 1916.

Beentjes, P. C. *The Book of Ben Sira in Hebrew: A Text Edition of All Extant Hebrew Manuscripts and a Synopsis of All Parallel Hebrew Ben Sira Texts*. Supplements to Vetus Testamentum 68. Leiden: Brill, 1997.

Beer, G. *Pesachim: Text, Übersetzung und Erklärung nebst textkritischen Anhang*. Vol. 2:3 of *Die Mischna: Text, Übersetzung und ausführliche Erklärung*, eds. K. H. Rengstorf, L. Rost, and S. Herrmann. Gießen: Alfred Töpelmann (vormals J. Ricker), 1912.

Boertien, M. *Nazir: Text, Übersetzung und Erklärung nebst textkritischen Anhang*. Vol. 3:4 of *Die Mischna: Text, Übersetzung und ausfürliche Erklärung*, eds. K. H. Rengstorf, L. Rost, and S. Herrmann. Berlin: Walter de Gruyter, 1971.

Bunte, W. *Kelim: Text, Übersetzung und Erklärung nebst textkritischen Anhang*. Vol. 6:1 of *Die Mischna: Text, Übersetzung und ausfürliche Erklärung*, eds. K. H. Rengstorf, L. Rost, and S. Herrmann. Berlin: Walter de Gruyter, 1972.

Cross, F. M. "A New Qumran Biblical Fragment Related to the Original Hebrew Underlying the Septuagint." *Bulletin of the American School of Oriental Research* 132 (1953): 15–26.

Díez Macho, A., ed. *Neophyti 1, Targum Palestinense ms. de la Biblioteca Vaticana*. Seminario Filológico Cardenal Cisneros del Instituto Arias Montano. Textos y Estudios 7–11, 20. Madrid: Consejo Superior de Investigaciones Científicas, 1968–79.

Finkelstein, L., ed. *Sifra deve Rav*. 5 vols. New York: Jewish Theological Seminary of America, 1983–.

——, and S. Horovitz, eds. *Sifre 'al Sefer Devarim*. Corpus Tannaiticum 3:3:2. New York: Jewish Theological Seminary of America, 1969.

Ginsburger, M., ed. *Pseudo-Jonathan (Thargum Jonathan ben Usiel zum Pentateuch)*. Berlin: S. Calvary, 1903.

Guggenheimer, H. W. *The Jerusalem Talmud*. Vol. 1. Studia judaica 18. Berlin: Walter de Gruyter, 2000–.

Holtzmann, O. *Middot: Text, Übersetzung und Erklärung nebst textkritischen Anhang*. Vol. 5:10 of *Die Mischna: Text, Übersetzung und ausführliche Erklärung*, eds. K. H. Rengstorf, L. Rost, and S. Herrmann. Gießen: Alfred Töpelmann (vormals J. Ricker), 1913.

Horovitz, H. S., ed. *Sifre de-be Rav*. 2 vols. Schriften (Gesellschaft zur Förderung der Wissenschaft des Judentums (Germany)). Laiptsig: [G. Fock, 1917]-1939.

Josephus, Flavius. *Flavii Iosephi Opera*. Edited by B. Niese. 7 vols. Berlin: Weidmann, 1887–95.

Kittel, R., ed. *Biblia Hebraica Stuttgartensia*. 2nd edition. Stuttgart: Deutsche Bibelgesellschaft, 1984.

Lauterbach, J. Z., ed. *Mekilta de-Rabbi Ishmael*. Vol. 2. Schiff Library of Jewish Classics. Philadelphia: Jewish Publication Society of America, 1933–5.

Lisowsky, G. and E. Schereschewsky. *Seder VI: Tohorot: Übersetszt und erklärt.* Vol. 6:2 of *Die Tosefta: Text, Überzetsung, Erklärung,* eds. G. Kittel and K. H. Rengstorf. Rabbinische Texte, erste Reihe. Stuttgart: W. Kohlhammer, 1965.

Philo, of Alexandria. *Philonis Alexandrini Opera quæ supersunt.* 7 vols. Edited by L. Cohn and P. Wendland. Berlin: George Reimer, 1896–1906.

Pisano, S. *Additions or Omissions in the Books of Samuel: The Significant Pluses and Minuses in the Massoretic, LXX and Qumran Texts.* Orbis biblicus et orientalis 57. Freiburg, Schweiz: Universitätsverlag, 1984.

Rahlfs, A., ed. *Septuaginta.* Stuttgart: Deutsche Bibelgesellschaft, 1979.

Routh, M. J., ed. *Reliquiæ sacræ.* Vol. 1. Oxford: E Typographeo Academico, 1846.

Sperber, A., ed. *The Bible in Aramaic.* 4 vols. Leiden: Brill, 1959–73.

Stern, M., ed. *Greek and Latin Authors on Jews and Judaism.* Vol. 1. Fontes ad res Judaicas Spectantes. Jerusalem: Israel Academy of Sciences and Humanities, 1976.

Ulrich, E. *The Qumran Text of Samuel and Josephus.* Harvard Semitic Monographs 19. Missoula, Mont.: Published by Scholars Press for Harvard Semitic Museum, 1978.

Zuckermandel, M. S., ed. *Tosefta.* Jerusalem: Bamberger and Warhman, 1937.

Secondary Sources

Aberbach, M., and B. Grossfeld. *Targum Onqelos on Genesis 49: Translation and Analytical Commentary.* Aramaic Studies 1. Missoula, Mont.: Published by Scholars Press for the Society of Biblical Literature, 1976.

Alon, G. *Jews, Judaism and the Classical World: Studies in Jewish History in the Times of the Second Temple and Talmud.* Jerusalem: Magnes Press, 1977.

Avigad, N. "The Burial Vault of a Nazirite Family on Mount Scopus." *Israel Exploration Journal* 21/4 (1971): 185–200.

Barrett, C. K. *A Critical and Exegetical Commentary on the Acts of the Apostles.* Vol. 2. International Critical Commentary. Edinburgh: T&T Clark, 1998.

Barthélemy, D. and O. Rickenbacher. *Konkordanz zum hebräischen Sirach: mit syrisch-hebräischem Index.* Göttingen: Vandenhoeck & Ruprecht, 1973.

Bediako, G. M. *Primal Religion and the Bible: William Robertson Smith and His Heritage.* Journal for the Study of the Old Testament: Supplemental Series 246. Sheffield, Eng.: Sheffield Academic Press, 1997.

Berlinerblau, J. *The Vow and the "Popular Religious Groups" of Ancient Israel: A Philological Sociological Inquiry.* Journal for the Study of the Old Testament: Supplemental Series 210. Sheffield, Eng.: Sheffield Academic Press, 1996.

Blackman, P. *Mishnayoth.* 7 vols. London: Mishna Press, 1951–6.

Bockmuehl, M. "'Let the Dead Bury their Dead' (Matt. 8.22/Luke 9.60): Jesus and the Halakhah." *Journal of Theological Studies* 49/2 (1998): 553–81.

Bodine, W. R. *The Greek Text of Judges: Recensional Developments.* Harvard Semitic Monographs 23. Chico, Calif.: Scholars Press, 1980.

———. "*Kaige* and Other Recensional Developments in the Greek Text of Judges." *Bulletin of the International Organization for Septuagint and Cognate Studies* 13 (1980): 45–57.

Botterweck, G. J. and H. Ringgren, eds. *Theologisches Wörterbuch zum Alten Testament.* Stuttgart: W. Kohlhammer, 1970–. S. v. "נזר" by G. Mayer.

Bowker, J. *The Targums and Rabbinic Literature: An Introduction to Jewish Interpretations of Scripture.* Cambridge, Eng.: Cambridge University Press, 1969.

Brown, R. E. *The Birth of the Messiah: A Commentary on the Infancy Narratives in Matthew and Luke.* 1st edition. Anchor Bible Reference Library. Garden City, N.Y.: Doubleday, 1977.

Bruce, F. F. *Commentary on the Book of Acts.* The New London Commentary on the New Testament. London: Marshall, Morgan & Scott, 1956.

Cartledge, T. "Were Nazirite Vows Unconditional?" *Catholic Biblical Quarterly* 51 (1989): 409–22.

——. *Vows in the Hebrew Bible and the Ancient Near East*. Journal for the Study of the Old Testament: Supplemental Series 147. Sheffield, Eng.: JSOT Press, 1992.

Chepey, S. D. "Samson the 'Holy One': A Suggestion Regarding the Reviser's Use of ἅγιος in Judg. 13,7; 16,17 LXX Vaticanus." *Biblica* 83 (2002): 97–9.

Coggins, R. J. *Sirach*. Guides to Apocrypha and Pseudepigrapha. Sheffield, Eng.: Sheffield Academic Press, 1998.

Conzelmann, H. *Acts of the Apostles: A Commentary on the Acts of the Apostles*. Translated by J. Limburg et al. Edited by E. J. Epp with C. R. Matthews. Hermeneia. Philadelphia: Fortress Press, 1987.

Cross, F. M. "A New Qumran Biblical Fragment Related to the Original Hebrew Underlying the Septuagint." *Bulletin of the American School of Oriental Research* 132 (1953): 15–26.

Danby, H. *The Mishnah*. Oxford: Oxford University Press, 1933.

Davies, W. D., and Dale C. Allison. *A Critical and Exegetical Commentary on the Gospel According to Saint Matthew*. Vol. 1. International Critical Commentary. Edinburgh: T&T Clark, 1988.

Dibelius, M. *James: A Commentary on the Epistle of James*. Revised by H. Greeven. Translated by M. A. Williams. Edited by H. Koester. Hermeneia. Philadelphia: Fortress Press, 1976.

Dorival, G. *La Bible Grecque des Septante: du Judaïsme Hellénistique au Christianisme Ancien*. Initiations au Christianisme Ancien. Paris: Éditions du CERF, 1988.

——. "Remarques sur L'Originalite du Livré Grec des Nombres." In *VIII Congress of the International Organization for Septuagint and Cognate Studies, Paris 1992*, eds. L. Greenspoon and O. Munnich. Society of Biblical Literature Septuagint and Cognate Studies Series 41. Atlanta, Ga.: Scholars Press, 1995.

Dunn, J. D. G. *The Acts of the Apostles*. Epworth Commentaries. Peterborough: Epworth Press, 1996.

Eichrodt, W. *Theology of the Old Testament*. Vol. 1. Translated by J. A. Baker. Old Testament Library. London: SCM, 1961.

Epstein, J. N. "ללשון נזירות" In *Magnes Anniversary Book*, eds. F. I. Baer et al. Jerusalem: Hebrew University Press, 1938.

Eusebius. Translated by K. Lake. Vol. 1. Loeb Classical Library. Cambridge, Mass.: Harvard University Press, 1980.

Feldman, L. H. *Josephus's Interpretation of the Bible*. Hellenistic Culture and Society 27. Berkley: University of California Press, 1998.

Fitzmyer, J. A. *The Acts of the Apostles*. The Anchor Bible 31. New York: Doubleday, 1998.

Freedman, D. N., ed. *The Anchor Bible Dictionary*. New York: Doubleday, 1992. S. v. "Targum, Targumim," by P. Alexander.

Freedman, H., and M. Simon, eds. *The Midrash Rabbah*. Vol. 2. London: Soncino Press, 1951.

Goldstein, J. A. *I Maccabees: A New Translation, with Introduction and Commentary*. The Anchor Bible 41. Garden City, N.Y.: Doubleday, 1976.

Goodenough, E. R. *An Introduction to Philo Judaeus*. 2nd edition. Oxford: Basil Blackwell, 1962.

Goodman, M. *The Roman World, 44 BC–AD 180*. Routledge History of the Ancient World. London: Routledge, 1997.

Grant, M. *Greek and Roman Historians: Information and Misinformation*. London: Routledge, 1995.

Gray, G. B. "The Nazirite." *Journal of Theological Studies* 1 (1900): 201–11.

——. *A Critical and Exegetical Commentary on Numbers*. International Critical Commentary. Edinburgh: T&T Clark, 1903.

Grossfeld, B. *The Targum Onqelos to Leviticus and the Targum Onqelos to Numbers*. The Aramaic Bible 8. Wilmington, Del.: M. Glazier, 1988.

Hadas, M., ed. *Aristeas to Philocrates.* Jewish Apocryphal Literature. New York: Published for the Dropsie College for Hebrew and Cognate Learning by Harper, 1951.

Haenchen, E. *The Acts of the Apostles.* Translated by B. Noble et al. Oxford: Basil Blackwell, 1971.

Hartman, L. "Sirach in Hebrew and in Greek." *Catholic Biblical Quarterly* 23 (1961): 443–51.

Hastings, J., ed. *The Encyclopedia of Religion and Ethics.* 2nd edition. New York: Charles Scribner's Sons, 1922. S. v. "Vows (Greek and Roman)," by A. C. Pearson.

———, ed. *The Encyclopedia of Religion and Ethics.* 2nd edition. New York: Charles Scribner's Sons, 1922. S. v. "Votive Offerings (Greek)," by W. H. D. Rouse.

Hauptman, J. "Mishnah as a Response to 'Tosefta'." In *The Synoptic Problem in Rabbinic Literature,* ed. S. J. D. Cohen. Brown Judaica Studies 326. Providence, R.I.: Brown Judaica Studies, 2000.

Herbert, E. D. "4QSam^a and its Relationship to the LXX: An Exploration in Stemmatological Analysis." In *IX Congress of the International Organization for Septuagint and Cognate Studies, Cambridge, 1995,* ed. B. A. Taylor. Society of Biblical Literature Septuagint and Cognate Studies Series 45. Atlanta, Ga.: Scholars Press, 1997.

Holladay, C. R. *Fragments from Hellenistic Jewish Authors.* Vol. 1. Texts and Translations 20. Chico, Calif.: Scholars Press, 1983.

Horn, F. "Paulus, das Nasiräat und die Nasiräer." *Novum Testamentum* 39/2 (1997): 117–37.

Jastrow, M. "The 'Nazir' Legislation." *Journal of Biblical Literature* 33 (1914): 266–85.

———. *Dictionary of the Targumim, the Talmud Babli and Yerushalmi, and the Midrashic Literature, with an Index of Scriptural Quotations.* New York: Judaica Press, 1996.

Jellicoe, S. *The Septuagint and Modern Study.* Oxford: Clarendon Press, 1968.

Jenni, E. and C. Westermann. eds. *Theologisches Handwörterbuch zum Alten Testament.* Zürich: Theologischer Verlag, 1971–6. S. v. "נזיר," by J. Kühlewein.

Josephus. Translated by H. St. Thackeray et al. 10 vols. Loeb Classical Library. Cambridge, Mass.: Harvard University Press, 1926–65.

Josephus, Flavius. *The Complete Works of Josephus.* Translated by W. Whiston. New Updated edition. Peabody, Mass.: Hendrickson Publishers, 1987.

Kehati, P. *The Mishnah: A New Translation.* Vol. 3:2. Jerusalem: Eliner Library, 1994.

Kennard, J. S., Jr. "Nazorean and Nazareth." *Journal of Biblical Literature* 66 (1947): 79–81.

Koet, B. J. "Why Did Paul Shave His Hair (Acts 18.18)? Nazirate and Temple in the Book of Acts." In *The Centrality of Jerusalem: Historical Perspectives,* eds. M. Poorthuis and Ch. Safrai. Kampen: KoK Pharos, 1996.

Kraeling, C. H. *John the Baptist.* New York: Charles Scribner's Sons, 1951.

Lieberman, S. *Greek in Jewish Palestine: Studies in the Life and Manners of Jewish Palestine in the II–IV Centuries C.E.* 2nd edition. New York: P. Feldheim, 1965.

——— et al. *Tosefet Rishonim.* Vol. 2. Jerusalem: Bamberger and Warhman, 1937–9.

Marcos, N. F. *The Septuagint in Context: Introduction to the Greek Version of the Bible.* Leiden: Brill, 2000.

Marshall, I. H. *Acts of the Apostles.* Tyndale New Testament Commentaries. Leicester, Eng.: Inter-Varsity Press, 1992.

Martin, R. P. *James.* Word Biblical Commentary 48. Waco, Tex.: Word Books, 1988.

McCarter, P. K. *I Samuel: A New Translation.* The Anchor Bible 8. Garden City, N.Y.: Doubleday, 1980.

McLaren, J. S. *Turbulent Times?: Josephus and Scholarship on Judaea in the First Century CE.* Journal for the Study of the Pseudepigrapha Supplemental Series 29. Sheffield, Eng.: Sheffield Academic Press, 1998.

Metzger, B. *A Textual Commentary on the Greek New Testament.* 2nd edition. Stuttgart: Deutsche Bibelgesellschaft, 1994.

Meyer, F. B. *John the Baptist.* London: Lakeland, 1975.

Milgrom, J. *Numbers = [Ba-midbar]: The Traditional Hebrew Text with the New JPS Translation.* The JPS Torah Commentary. Philadelphia: Jewish Publication Society, 1990.

Moore, G. F. "The Sources." Chap. in *Judaism in the First Centuries of the Christian Era: The Age of the Tannaim.* Vol. 1. Cambridge, Eng.: Cambridge University Press, 1958.

Morris, J. "The Jewish Philosopher Philo." In *History of the Jewish People in the Age of Jesus Christ*, vol. 3:2, eds. M. Goodman, F. Millar, and G. Vermès. Edinburgh: T&T Clark, 1987.

Müller, M. *The First Bible of the Church: A Plea for the Septuagint.* Journal for the Study of the Old Testament: Supplemental Series 206. Sheffield, Eng.: Sheffield Academic Press, 1996.

Muraoka, T., ed. *Semantics of Ancient Hebrew.* Abr-Nahrain: Supplement Series 6. Louvain-la-Nueve: Peeters, 1998. S. v. "נזר," by A. Salvesen.

Neusner, J. *Tosefta.* 6 vols. New York: Ktav, 1977–86.

——. *A History of the Mishnaic Law of Women.* Studies in Judaism in Late Antiquity 33:3. Leiden: E. J. Brill, 1980.

——. *The Talmud of the Land of Israel: A Preliminary Translation and Explanation.* Vol. 24. Chicago Studies in the History of Judaism. Chicago: The University of Chicago Press, 1985.

——. *Sifré to Numbers: An American Translation and Explanation.* Vol. 1. Brown Judaica Studies 118. Atlanta, Ga.: Scholars Press, 1986.

——. *Sifré to Deuteronomy: An Analytical Translation.* Vol. 2. Brown Judaica Studies 101. Atlanta, Ga.: Scholars Press, 1987.

——. *Sifra: An Analytical Translation.* Vols. 1–3. Brown Judaica Studies 138–40. Atlanta, Ga.: Scholar Press, 1988.

——. "Vow-Taking, The Nazirites, and the Law: Does James' Advice to Paul Accord with Halakah?" In *James the Just and Christian Origins*, eds. B. Chilton and C. A. Evans. Supplements to Novum Testamentum 98. Leiden: Brill, 1999.

Nicholson, E. W. *The Pentateuch in the Twentieth Century: The Legacy of Julius Wellhausen.* New York: Oxford University Press, 1998.

Olyan, S. M. "What Do Shaving Rites Accomplish and What Do They Signal in Biblical Ritual Contexts?" *Journal of Biblical Literature* 117/4 (1998): 611–22.

Pedersen, J. *Israel: Its Life and Culture.* Vols. 3–4. London: Geoffrey Cumberlege, 1949.

Peters, N. *Das Buch Jesus Sirach oder Ecclesiasticus.* Exegetisches Handbuch zum Alten Testament 25. Münster in Westf.: Aschendorff Verlagsbuchhandlung, 1913. *Philo.* Translated by F. H. Colson and G. H. Whitaker. 11 vols. Loeb Classical Library. Cambridge, Mass.: Harvard University Press, 1949–.

Pretzl, O. "Septuagintaprobleme im Buch der Richter." *Biblica* 7 (1926): 233–69, 353–83.

Rad, G. von. *Old Testament Theology.* Vol. 1. Translated by D. M. G. Stalker. Edinburgh: Oliver and Boyd, 1963.

Rajak, T. *Josephus, the Historian and His Society.* London: Duckworth, 1983.

Rogerson, J. W. *The Bible and Criticism in Victorian Britain: Profiles of F.D. Maurice and William Robertson Smith.* Journal for the Study of the Old Testament: Supplemental Series 201. Sheffield, Eng.: Sheffield Academic Press, 1995.

Ross, J. M. "The Extra Words in Acts 18.21." *Novum Testamentum* 34 (1992): 247–9.

Roth, C., ed. *The Standard Jewish Encyclopedia.* Garden City, N.Y.: Doubleday, 1959. S. v. "Judah Ha-Nasi."

Rouse, W. H. D. *Greek Votive Offerings.* Cambridge, Eng.: Cambridge University Press, 1902.

Salmanowitsch, H. "Das Naziräat nach Bibel und Talmud." Ph. D. diss. Gießen, 1931.

Sanders, E. P. *Judaism: Practice and Belief, 63 BCE–66 CE.* London: SCM, 1992.

Sanders, J. A. "ΝΑΖΩΡΑΙΟΣ in Matt 2.23." *Journal of Biblical Literature* 84 (1965): 169–72.

Schürer, E. *History of the Jewish People in the Age of Jesus Christ.* 3 vols. Revised edition, eds. F. Millar et al. Edinburgh: T&T Clark, 1973–86.

Schwartz, S. "Israel and the Nations Roundabout: I Maccabees and the Hasmonean Expansion." *Journal of Jewish Studies* 42 (1991): 16–38.

Scobie, C. H. H. *John the Baptist.* London: SCM, 1964.

Schiffman, L. H. and VanderKam, J. C., eds. *Encyclopedia of the Dead Sea Scrolls.* New York: Oxford University Press, 2000. S. v. "Targumim," by U. Gleßmer.

Skehan, P. W. *The Wisdom of Ben Sira: A New Translation with Notes.* The Anchor Bible 39. Garden City, N.Y.: Doubleday, 1987.

Smith, W. R., ed. *A Dictionary of the Bible.* Vol. 2. London: John Murray, 1863. S. v. "Nazarite [sic]," by S. Clark.

——. *Religion of the Semites; the Fundamental Institutions.* New York: Meridian Books, 1956.

——. *Lectures on the Religion of the Semites: Second and Third Series.* Edited by J. Day. Journal for the Study of the Old Testament: Supplemental Series 183. Sheffield, Eng.: Sheffield Academic Press, 1995.

Stemberger, G. *Introduction to the Talmud and Midrash.* 2nd edition. Translated and edited by M. Bockmuehl. Edinburgh: T.&T. Clark, 1996.

Stolle, V. *Der Zeuge als Angeklagter: Untersuchungen zum Paulisbild des Lukas.* Beiträge zur Wissenschaft vom Alten und Neuen Testament, 6. Folge, Heft 2 (der ganzen Sammlung Heft 102). Stuttgart: W. Kohlhammer, 1973.

Strack, H. L., and P. Billerbeck. *Kommentar zum Neuen Testament aus Talmud und Midrash.* Vol. 2. München: C. H. Beck, 1924.

Strange, W. A. *The Problem of the Text of Acts.* Society for New Testament Studies Monograph Series 71. Cambridge, Eng.: Cambridge University Press, 1992.

Swete, H. B. *An Introduction to the Old Testament in Greek.* 2nd edition. Cambridge, Eng.: Cambridge University Press, 1914.

Tannehill, R. C. *Luke.* Abingdon New Testament Commentaries. Nashville: Abingdon Press, 1996.

Taylor, D. B. "Jesus—of Nazareth?" *Expository Times* 92 (1981): 336–7.

Taylor, J. E. *The Immerser: John the Baptist within Second Temple Judaism.* Studying the Historical Jesus. London: SPCK, 1997.

Teodorsson, Sven-Tage. *A Commentary on Plutarch's Table Talks.* Vol. 1. Studia Graeca et Latina Gothoburgensia 51. Göteborg, Sweden: Acta Universitatis Gothoburgensis, 1989.

Tomes, R. "Why Did Paul Get His Hair Cut? (Acts 18.18; 21.23–24)." In *Luke's Literary Achievement: Collected Essays,* ed. C. M. Tuckett. Journal for the Study of the New Testament: Supplemental Series 116. Sheffield, Eng.: Sheffield Academic Press, 1995.

Tov, E. "Loan-Words, Homophony, and Transliterations in the Septuagint." *Biblica* 60 (1979): 216–36.

Tsevat, M. "Was Samuel a Nazirite?" In *Sha'arei Talmon: Studies in the Bible, Qumran, and the Ancient Near East Presented to Shemaryahu Talmon,* eds. M. Fishbane and E. Tov. Winona Lake, Ind.: Eisenbrauns, 1992.

Vaux, R. de. *Ancient Israel: Its Life and Institutions.* Translated by J. McHugh. London: Darton, Longman & Todd, 1961.

Vermès, G. *Scripture and Tradition in Judaism: Haggadic Studies.* Studia post-biblica 4. Leiden: Brill, 1961.

Wevers, J. W. "An Apologia for Septuagint Studies." *Bulletin of the International Organization for Septuagint and Cognate Studies* 18 (1985): 16–38.

——. *Notes on the Greek Text of Numbers.* Society of Biblical Literature Septuagint and Cognate Studies Series 46. Atlanta, Ga.: Scholars Press, 1998.

Wojciechowski, M. "Le naziréat et la Passion (Mc 14,25a; 15,23)." *Biblica* 65 (1984): 94–5.

Zuckschwerdt, E. "Nazoraios in Matth. 2,23." *Theologische Zeitschrift* 31/2 (1975): 65–77.

——. "Das Naziräat des Herrenbruders Jakobus nach Hegesipp." *Zeitschrift für die neutestamentliche Wissenschaft und die Kunde der älteren Kirche* 68 (1977): 276–87.

INDEX OF SUBJECTS

INDEX OF NAMES

INDEX OF MODERN AUTHORS